RIVER OF EARTH AND SKY:
Poems for the 21st Century

Selected by Diane Frank

BLUE LIGHT PRESS

BLUE LIGHT PRESS
www.bluelightpress.com
Email: bluelightpress@aol.com

Poems Selected by Diane Frank
Chief Editor, Blue Light Press

Book Design and Art:
Melanie Gendron

Cover Art:
"Nurturing Forest" by Melanie Gendron

FIRST EDITION

Library of Congress Catalog Card Number: 2015945557

ISBN 9781421837406

DEDICATION:

For the poets of the future
to discover what we saw, felt and knew
during these times.

CONTENTS

INTRODUCTION

Apoem is a parallel universe that creates an experience line by line. The universe unfolds in a series of images which change the inner experience of the reader. If the poem goes deep enough, the writer and the reader will be changed in a significant way by the end of the poem.

River of Earth and Sky: Poems for the 21st Century mixes the poetry mahatmas of our generation with the grass roots. In these pages, you will find poets who have won the Pulitzer Prize and the National Book Award, along with lesser known poets who also deserve to be read.

I like to think of poetry as an open dialog with your soul. The poems I have loved for a lifetime speak to body, mind, heart and soul. All of the poems in this book are important to me, and I hope that many of them will also speak deeply to you.

Blessings,

Diane Frank
Chief Editor, Blue Light Press

FIRST POEM FOR YOU

I love to touch your tattoos in complete
darkness, when I can't see them. I'm sure of
where they are, know by heart the neat
lines of lightning pulsing just above
your nipple, can find, as if by instinct, the blue
swirls of water on your shoulder where a serpent
twists, facing a dragon. When I pull you
to me, taking you until we're spent
and quiet on the sheets, I love to kiss
the pictures in your skin. They'll last until
you're seared to ashes; whatever persists
or turns to pain between us, they will still
be there. Such permanence is terrifying.
So I touch them in the dark; but touch them, trying.

THE NUMBERS

How many nights have I lain here like this, feverish with plans,
with fears, with the last sentence someone spoke, still trying to finish
a conversation already over? How many nights were wasted
in not sleeping, how many in sleep — I don't know
how many hungers there are, how much radiance or salt, how many
          times
the world breaks apart, disintegrates to nothing and starts up again
in the course of an ordinary hour. I don't know how God can bear
seeing everything at once: the falling bodies, the monuments and
          burnings,
the lovers pacing the floors of how many locked hearts. I want to close
my eyes and find a quiet field in fog, a few sheep moving toward a
          fence.
I want to count them, I want them to end. I don't want to wonder
how many people are sitting in restaurants about to close down,
which of them will wander the sidewalks all night
while the pies revolve in the refrigerated dark. How many days
are left of my life, how much does it matter if I manage to say
one true thing about it — how often have I tried, how often
failed and fallen into depression? The field is wet, each grass blade
gleaming with its own particularity, even here, so that I can't help
asking again, the white sky filling with footprints, bricks,
with mutterings over rosaries, with hands that pass over flames
before covering the eyes. I'm tired, I want to rest now.
I want to kiss the body of my lover, the one mouth, the simple name
without a shadow. Let me go. How many prayers
are there tonight, how many of us must stay awake and listen?

GENERATIONS

Somewhere a shop of hanging meats,
shop of stink and blood, block and cleaver;

somewhere an immigrant, grandfather, stranger
with my last name. That man

untying his apron in 1910, scrubbing off
the pale fat, going home past brownstones

and churches, past vendors, streetcars, arias,
past the clatter of supper dishes, going home

to his new son, my father —
What is he to me, butcher with sausage fingers,

old Italian leaning over a child somewhere
in New York City, somewhere alive, what is he

that I go back to look for him, years after his death
and my father's death, knowing only

a name, a few scraps my father fed me?
My father who shortened that name, who hacked off

three lovely syllables, who raised American children.
What is the past to me

that I have to go back, pronouncing that word
in the silence of a cemetery, what is this stone

coming apart in my hands like bread, name
I eat and expel? Somewhere the smell of figs

and brine, strung garlic, rosemary and olives;
somewhere that place. Somewhere a boat

rocking, crossing over, entering the harbor. I wait
on the dock, one face in a crowd of faces.

Families disembark and stream toward the city,
and though I walk among them for hours,

hungry, haunting the streets,
I can't tell which of them is mine.

Somewhere a steak is wrapped in thick paper,
somewhere my grandmother is laid in the earth,

and my young father shines shoes on a corner,
turning his back to the old world, forgetting.

I walk the night city, looking up at lit windows,
and there is no table set for me, nowhere

I can go to be filled. This is the city
of grandparents, immigrants, arrivals,

where I've come too late with my name,
an empty plate. This is the place.

"WHAT DO WOMEN WANT?"

I want a red dress.
I want it flimsy and cheap,
I want it too tight, I want to wear it
until someone tears it off me.
I want it sleeveless and backless,
this dress, so no one has to guess
what's underneath. I want to walk down
the street past Thrifty's and the hardware store
with all those keys glittering in the window,
past Mr. and Mrs. Wong selling day-old
donuts in their café, past the Guerra brothers
slinging pigs from the truck and onto the dolly,
hoisting the slick snouts over their shoulders.
I want to walk like I'm the only
woman on earth and I can have my pick.
I want that red dress bad.
I want it to confirm
your worst fears about me,
to show you how little I care about you
or anything except what
I want. When I find it, I'll pull that garment
from its hanger like I'm choosing a body
to carry me into this world, through
the birth-cries and the love-cries too,
and I'll wear it like bones, like skin,
it'll be the goddamned
dress they bury me in.

HOW TO KISS FIRE

Dozens of flame skimmers
spark orange and red
at the edge of water and land.
The devil's knitting needles,
these dragonflies, stitch the pond to sky.

All magic transpires in this elemental mix.
When water or earth touches air or fire,
intersections birth thunderstorms,
forest fires, water spouts.

Whoever makes a friend of fire
will not drown in the shallow end.
Wade out past the hips
where the flame skimmers weigh
a soul with simple calculations:

How heavy are your arms, your heart, your feet?
What have you held? What have you lost?

WHEN I LEFT MY COUNTRY,

there were 53 words for lost
and only 1 for found.
I built a city of postcards.
I hid the word home under my tongue
and slept in no one's room.
I split the miles between us,
searching for middle ground.

The desert teaches one to want
so little and yet we want it even more.
In the shimmer, hope plays tricks,
leaves me rubbing sand in my eyes.
Maybe I see you. Maybe I don't.
I draw a map of what together looks like
with its plain white door.
When I knock, who will open?

BEYOND THE CLOVER MEADOW

The grey horse from the other forest
knows that a storm
can steal breath from a sleeping mouth.
She leans into the bark of the dogwood,
her back against the wet wind.

Learn how to lean into the forest,
bury your face into the fallen
leaves until you are the color
of loss, until you can only
be seen as the reflection
on a beetle's shiny back.

In the forest the angels carry
ladders of light from cloud to cloud.
One day they will break the grey
between squalls and you will climb.
You will climb, and you will sleep.

I Never Heard My Grandmother Sing

> An *alphabet's molecules,*
> *tasting of honey, iron and salt.* — Jane Hirschfield

A letter, a leaf
    her thoughts spiral to childhood's
    barefoot trudge to school
    pausing at the creek to wash sleep's salt
    before the '30s dusted the land, left grit in the teeth.

A word, a stone
    war bride hides fear, hangs cloth
    on lines ranged like battlefronts
    throat rusted shut to the honey,
    the vinegar of her baby's birth, death.

A phrase, a river
    molecules of grief compounded
    into an alphabet that presses like lead
    on her chest, her heart
    an ocean choking the notes of her song.

EVEN THE ROCKS CRY OUT

Good Friday Earthquake, Alaska 1964

Sky reddens, slips into place.
A stillness enters the air. No breath.
Sparrows and chickadees stop chattering.
Kelso's growl wilts to a whimper
as he paces the carpet. The eggs, colors drying,
begin to quiver, dishes picking up
the beat — muted clickety-clacks swelling.

The bed shakes me awake,
sleep splintered by shivering walls,
shaking floor. Kelso's barks echo
along the raining roof,
paintings and photographs unhitching.
Baskets shimmy across the countertop,
tumble in pastel kaleidoscopes.

Outside, pines tremble and the river widens,
water rushing the rocks. Starlings take flight
into paling blue. In the woods, leaves whisper,
branches groan and crack.
A fox darts from sheltering trees,
and across the field, a rooster crows.
Only the dogwoods remain silent.

A Hint of Joy

Here's the joyful face you've been wanting to see. –Rumi

Last night you sighed my name, called to me
in sleep. Your fingers on my cheek whispered
me awake. Bad dreams again. I feather-touched
your shoulders until your breaths deepened,
warmed my neck. When daylight edged the window,
you were gone — cracked sleep only a puddle
of night clothes on the floor.

I will wait for you to come home,
watch waves measure the shore as day fades,
a string of light on the horizon.
The lyrics of salt air and foam taste of summer —
                    fruit ripening and bursting.

What Comes of Waiting

The moth-hour has come,
nutshells fleck the yard
and steam swirls from the asphalt
after late rain — a veil
between mountaintop and valley.
Ghost-like wings pearl the darkness,
wind spiraling over barberry and jessamine.

Love and death come on nights like this —
a coolness crackling the air,
sizzle of hope, dread in the owl's sigh.
The spit of rain as it holds back
the moth-flickering moment
before drifting away.

GRIEF

Between grief and nothing, I will take grief. –William Faulkner

I.
Grief is discovering the world is flat after all,
that people really do fall off.

II.
Grief is a red-winged blackbird
that startles when it lands
in empty, outstretched hands —
delicate, feathery thing
that keeps coming back
in familiar patterns
like seasons, dreams.

Hold it tenderly when it lights,
despite its sharp claws,
and it will sing you
to another world,
then bring you home.

NEVER BECOME NOTHING

Like a note of music,
you are about to become nothing. –Robert Bly

I asked Miles Davis
how he feels
when the notes he blows
become nothing.

He turned his back on me,
he was over by the piano,
but said in a loud enough kind of way,
"Notes I sound never become nothing."

He shook spit from his trumpet's valve,
watched it fall to the red carpet
where long cords from amps and mics snaked
around. He kicked at them, pissed.

Then, with his head tilted way down,
he lifted his horn to his lips, his embouchure,
and blew out one single note
low and slow and breathy.

"You got ears, girl?" the note
teased. "You listening?"

MESSAGE

I would like to put it on paper for you
not on the paper really, but threaded through the words —
metamorphosis, transcendence, transmigration.
Yet I fall so short.
Can't seem to change, and into what?
Certainly can't cross over
How can we meet?

You're on that side;
I'm on this.
And here I am with another.
Once, I called him by your name.

Sometimes in dreams when you're coming home
I don't know what to do with his being here.
In the dreams houses by water, wings,
boats that are beds.

You rode waves as if you had wings.
He makes houses into sailing ships:
the kitchen a galley with high shelving,
what used to be our bedroom
now a pilot house.
I write and look out
at the same trees you saw
in skies which still fold spring into fall.
This is our home:
yours, mine;
now mine, his.

The first time I said love to him
after the glider ride and my undeniable
greed for his kiss,
he said I don't know what love is.

I used to be so sure —
should I have waited
until my ashes were taken to be scattered
with yours?
Could we swim together then?

I think of running,
the simple intricate physics that moves me forward
the breath heart pumping transforming
body to spirit energy light.
Is that the secret to solving love?
Just keep putting one foot in front of the other
and trust?

When I think I've found the way
after a morning that lifts the new two of us
into the blue of day,
I remember the slow blessing of the Hopis,
their small rafts over silk water
making the ground sacred for movement.
They had no word for past or present.
This is the fourth world, another chance to get it right.

Einstein said that gravity cannot be held responsible
for people falling
in love.
I chose to jump.

From bright skies
I fall into memories of the hemlock you planned to take
when it was too painful, maybe too hopeless,
but you didn't, wanting to hold on
to me I suppose, to our daughter,
to the yellow primrose along the coast
trembling in the small breezes of evening,
to light glancing off ocean silver green,

to the light that explodes inside
when you're making love.

Something about those wings,
falling through light
while feeling warm and climbing light again and soaring
down on Daedalus wings doomed
and still soaring and laughing
is what I wanted to try to tell you.

GLIDING

They are thigh to thigh in the narrow seat,
dipping, turning
on insubstantial air.
The pilot wonders if they'd like to do a loop.
He wants to answer yes, but he asks her first.
She's afraid, so he tells the pilot no.

They are in love. Or she is in love.
It's too soon.
He's too young.
She is in love with his arm
around her shoulders.
It's been so long.

Or in love with the curly crowd of blond hairs
glistening on his brown forearm,
muscled from hammer and saw,
with the smile in his voice on the phone.
But up here, floating
with the raptors, who can tell?

They don't talk, sitting so close,
looking down at vineyards,
barns, canopied oaks
spread out like illustrations in a children's book.
The glider rattles.
But she doesn't hear.

She's thinking she wouldn't mind
if he kissed her.
But it's too soon
after her husband's death.
He was too young to die,
and she's old enough to know better.
Isn't she?
She's probably just
a little giddy
up here,
so far above the earth.

CIRCLE OF STICKS

He arranged his quiver of surfboards around the room
with the window open
for the cats
who sometimes marked the boards as theirs.
My husband's desk, with piles of papers in rubber bands,
was dwarfed by the circle of sticks:
that's what surfers called them sometimes —
graceful ellipses, six feet or so, coated on top with layers of wax
gritty and gray with sand from beaches like Año,
Pacifica, Ocean Beach, Salmon Creek,
Ten Mile, and the river mouth at Jenner.

He'd slide into me kneeling and grinning,
one browned arm out like a wing,
the other hand guiding the board
on its way down the wave face that glinted in the sun.

On the nose of the board
two dolphins forming a yin-yang,
his sea brothers, his guardian spirits.
We didn't know the legends:
all the dolphins who have rescued drowning humans.

We didn't know his dolphins wouldn't save him
from the cancer swimming in his lymphatic system
but when he surfed they were with him
and surfing, he said, was his religion.

After he died, I gave the first of John's boards away,
the clear one, white with brown stringer and rails,
to Will the plumber.
He'd seen the boards in the crawl space
when he worked on the furnace.
Will said he'd like one to hang in his barn in Omaha.
At first it seemed a good idea

but as he walked down the driveway
the board under his arm
I wondered why I'd ever let it go.

I gave the tan one with dolphins on the deck,
to our daughter, Kristy,
and another like it,
but sky blue, to Pete, John's English knee-boarding mate.
That was right, I knew.
I gave John's old-style longboard to Jason,
now gone, like John, from cancer too,
the two of them riding waves
only in snapshots.

Some of the pictures still surprise me
when I sift through the basket:

there, coming in at Lighthouse, five or six feet,
and a little one at Sunset Beach,
turquoise water, disarmingly soft pink clouds,
as if nothing could ever go wrong.

Last year I gave Leo the blue and black board,
a college graduation present.
He's surfed in all the places we knew, and more.
He wrote to me he was fixing the dings,
so he could take it out at Pleasure Point,
bring it to Bali;
and I kept giving the boards away,
the last one at a yard sale to a father and his eager teenage son,
Until the quiver's arrows had been scattered,
as John's ashes were, at Año,
swirling now
in all the oceans of the world.

Transparent

Every night this winter
owls came with questions
to the bare branches.
In the dark,
I could feel their interrogation,
asking me, if I still could remember
those I loved.

I would wake the next morning,
after dreaming about buildings collapsing,
the illogic of the dreamworld
carrying over into the day.

The world was not transparent
but jumbled
like the color spectrum,
red signifying howl,
purple speaking wine,
black and brick red
speaking tenements
where the poor dream their dreams.
The same slim hungering moon
hangs over each of us in the dark.

DOLPHIN REPORT

Look inside the center of my heart.
You'll find a newspaper clipping of yourself
in your white First Communion veil
or a snapshot of your grandson at his Bar Mitzvah,
smiling in front of the chopped liver swan.
I am in love from the moment I am born
until the moment I die.
Why else would I leap thirty feet in the air,
whistling and clicking,
spinning seven times
before I touch down in the dark sea
where I am born, tail-first
and nudged to the surface to breathe;
before I even taste the rich milk of my mother
I fall in love with everything above and below sea level.
With the currents pressing fast on my soft, new skin,
with the sun sending shafts through the top of the ocean,
with the woman on the boat in the yellow scarf
shouting, pointing,
holding a drink and a camera in one hand.
When I am in love I swim like a fish,
fly like a bird,
and breathe like a man.

Listen to the center of my heart.
You'll hear that quiet song you used to sing over and over
in a thin, high voice
when your mother thought you were asleep.
The awkward, tinny piano of your first recital.
You'll hear the joke about the sailor
that will still make you laugh
five minutes before
you close your eyes for the last time in this body.

It patterns my face in a fixed grin
and lets me glide and play on the waves from your ships,
falling backward
into joy crackling like early electricity.
But that same love
makes me need to guide those ships
every night for twenty years
through the sharp coral reefs of Australia.
The same love that lets me hold you to the surface
when you're drowning
makes me cling to an abandoned dinghy
like a giant rag doll.
It makes me haunt one beach for ten years
waiting for a dead boy to ride on my back.
That which lifts me up also weighs me down,
but you already understand this.
I live only to breathe in unison.

So I learn to speak without vocal chords
and recognize geometric shapes in waterproof books.
Small things like this make you so happy.
But look inside the center of my heart.
You'll find a hologram
of the part of you you've been wanting to worship
for a long, long time.

I Could Have Danced All Night If I Hadn't Spontaneously Combusted

When it was still there in August,
my landlady threatened to call the fire department.
The pine needles were already so thick and dry
and sharp on the carpet,
even with socks on,
you couldn't walk without drawing blood.
But I was in love
and it was bigger than anything they'd ever shown on television.
My Christmas tree had become a Magnificent Obsession.
It was more than the red, black, fuschia, and turquoise lace
draped around it,
or the *Rudraksha*, crystal, and angelskin coral.
It was more than the gracefully curved plastic corkscrew drinking
straw
and the brass pennywhistle all the way from Ireland
balanced skillfully in the nether branches.
It was more than the paper boats made of theatre programs
or the ecumenical touches —
luminous postcards of St. Anne and the Virgin,
Krishna neatly shellacked on a maple leaf,
the copper ornament that spelled *Shalom* in English and Hebrew.
It was more than every piece of cheap, miraculous jewelry
I ever used to turn *myself* into a Christmas tree.
It was more than the fact that they never let me have one
when I was a kid
because I was Jewish.
It was more even than the most spectacular neon star
you ever saw
wearing a long striped hawk feather
at exactly the same jaunty angle
Maurice Chevalier wore his perfect straw hat.
(The package said
"DO NOT MAKE THIS STAR STEADY BURNING"

but I did it anyway and burnt out all the miniature bulbs,
wanting, as always, too much at once.)
But God, it was more than all that.

There was something that made me keep that tree
through Valentine's Day
and hang little pastel hearts all over it.
There was something, on Easter,
that made me hang all those hollow eggs
I decorated myself with Day-Glo paint and macaroni.
I had to stop letting people over — they didn't understand.
My Christmas tree and I celebrated the Fourth of July together.
I wore a red, white, and blue jumpsuit.
The tree wore at least 100 tiny American flags.

You see, when they said my Christmas tree had become
a fire hazard,
I knew they didn't mean somebody would strike a match nearby.
It was a fire hazard
because someday it would spontaneously combust
from the intense heat of its own unbearable beauty.
And I was waiting,
ready to see at least one of us go out
in a supremely self-sufficient blaze of glory.

It was right there on page 433 in the Book of Lists
between the brain radiation levels of 60 celebrated persons
and a collection of 10 people who had Stigmata.
There it was in glorious black and white:
"Eight Cases of Spontaneous Combustion."
And while I realized I might never develop holy wounds
on my hands and feet,
and the only person who knew how to measure brain radiation
died in 1952,
deep inside I knew that some day,
with the flawless timing of a fine Swiss watch,
I had as good a chance as anybody to spontaneously combust.

Just like Euphemia Johnson, age 68,
who spontaneously blazed one rainy day in England
while drinking her afternoon tea.

Or Mr. and Mrs. Patrick Rooney
who crossed over together one Christmas Eve
during the second chorus of "Silent Night"
when Mrs. Rooney suddenly turned into a pillar of fire
and Mr. Rooney died from the smoke in the air.
That one went deep.
Now I know when people say
"Do you love me?"
they really mean
"If I spontaneously combusted, would you inhale the smoke?"

But best by far,
Miss Phyllis Newcombe,
age 22,
who probably spent 3 or 4 months
perfecting a pink organdy gown
with pearl buttons, a polka dot sash,
and baby blue lace at the collar and cuffs,
just to wear to the dance hall that night on August 7th
when she waltzed with the prettiest man there —
the one with the strongest arms
and the wisest eyes
and the prettiest white teeth.
The music was like satin and velvet;
like those luscious chocolate caramels
she once got for Valentine's Day.
She was so radiant everyone was staring;
even the people waltzing kept craning their necks to look at her.
Something was becoming more and more curiously alive
about the room.
It seemed the air itself was waltzing
1-2-3 . . . 1-2-3 . . . 1-2-3 . . . 1-2-3 . . .

It must have been on a 2
that Miss Newcombe smiled exquisitely
and happily burst into flames.

Neither Miss Newcombe's partner
nor the pink organdy gown
were as much as singed.
For a split second the gown hovered in mid-air,
as if confused.
Then, with nothing left to cover,
it dropped delicately to the floor
like a rose petal.

I like to imagine Miss Newcombe's partner understood.
That he picked up the dress
and quietly left the hall
while everyone else went crazy.

People and Christmas trees who spontaneously combust
go to a secret place
where everything is switched on and awake.
Those little golden particles
you see when you're excited
are constantly vibrating in the air.

Miss Newcombe *had* to combust.
She'd never be 22 again
in that gown
on that night
with that man
with those teeth.
Here, she moves in a state of constant consummation
with the dazzling uniqueness of an albino giraffe.
All the trees are Christmas trees
with silver garlands and sequins
and those electric glass ornaments
with bubbling water.
Every moment is always, always, always enough.

SMALLEST DOG IN THE WORLD

for Billie

Seeking a soulmate, I bought a dog afraid of everything.
Hunched shoulders,
morbid shivering,
upper back pliable as a slab of oak;
people were always asking us if we were cold.

"That animal is almost too sensitive for life,"
says a friend.
I nod, blushing,
possibly even twitching,
stooping to paw at the stress-related hives on my leg.

I blanketed that dog
with a love so thick
it was far too gelatinous and rich
for any human.
Cooing incessantly,
I hovered, enveloped,
and watched her uncurl.
Now she bares her teeth at pit bulls
and flirts shamelessly with strangers.
So this is how you make a creature strong,
I see,
somewhat later than most
and yet still in this lifetime.

"Doctor – help!
I can't stop singing to my dog."
"What could be more natural?," says the doctor.
"The heart yearns to praise."

"Doctor – help!
I can't stop kissing my dog
on the forehead."

"How could it be otherwise?," says the doctor.
"The heart yearns for beauty."

The smallest dog in the world
shares my penchant for fanaticism.
There we are, in the L.A. paper,
under "Poet Spreads the Word About Red Cross."
That's me in the beret, like some terrorist of mercy;
the sacred chihuahua's wrapped head to claw
in the international symbol for neutrality.
(I'm surprised I don't have Red Cross nipple piercings
and little Clara Barton-shaped decals on each tooth.)

"Doctor – help!
Hearing that 'Dog' is 'God' spelled backwards,
I have once again confused my priorities."
"Absolutely normal," says the doctor.
"The heart yearns for imaginary significance."
(Or did he say,
"The heart yearns for solace?")

The smallest dog in the world
scares away macho dudes
and emotional diabetics
who lack the blood sugar
for progressively saccharine terms of endearment.
This, I suspect, is a blessing.
That noise you hear is the landline,
the cell, the fax, and the door,
all of which we seem to be ignoring as usual.
Wrapped in fetal position
around the smallest dog in the world,
I have learned to form the perfect circle.

"Doctor – help!
I can't stop thinking about my dog;
when I'm out on a date,
when a man comes close,
when. . ."
"Impeccable choice," says the doctor,
waving snapshots of his beagle.
"A dog will give you more love in an hour
than a spouse can offer in a hundred years."

The smallest dog in the world is more than
a mere fashion accessory.
There I am in velvet
at an elegant formal affair.
"I didn't recognize you without your other half,"
sneers a socialite.
At this the boundaries of selfhood evaporate,
as if they have attempted to pay by check
without a driver's license.

"Doctor – help!
I can't stop babytalking my dog."
"It's about time" says the doctor,
sounding suspiciously like my mother.
"Biology is destiny."

The Vandalization of Sweet Mercy

I am not usually a woman
who names her car six weeks before she buys it
who names it Sweet Mercy
in honor of every
turbo-charged spiral of forgiveness
that touches us
quickly,
lightly,
on top of our heads,
whispering that somehow
we're allowed to be happy
if only for a moment
if only until the next
irrevocable mistake
which will also be forgiven
which will carry in its arms
the promise
of another bright spiral
and eventually another.

Forgive me.
Something has happened to my biological clock.
When other women close their eyes
and see pink and white babies,
I close my eyes
and see little red sports cars
Zero to 130 miles per hour
in point-two-five seconds.
When other people are slowing down
to inch their way over railroad tracks,
I am for some reason
speeding up,
gathering momentum
to take those tracks
in one magnificent flying leap.

There is little time to unravel complexities,
why
on the 33rd morning
of my 33rd year
I awoke with the hormones of a 16 year old boy,
why, when I heard that God's own agile chariot
had been in a wreck
and would be fixed
and would be almost affordable
it took me six months to convince myself
I deserved such a spiral.
Six months of carrying
its photo in my briefcase;
six months of wondering
if someone would slit my throat
or slash my tires
or uncolor my hair
if I owned such a car,
and finally,
when I brought Sweet Mercy home
that Friday afternoon
and it was too late
for the birds to sing their morningsong
and too early
for the birds to sing their eveningsong
they were singing anyway,
the closest thing to an *Aria* that had ever come out of their beaks.

He makes an appearance in my dreams sometimes;
the owner of the pellet gun does.
He says, "I am the red thread
quietly sewn into each of your garments
while your thoughts are busy elsewhere;
I am the crooked, discolored tooth in the smile of your beloved;
the flaw that keeps you from drowning
in a sea of free-floating anxiety."

And so I understand
it was an act of the deepest possible love
when he relieved me
of the awful burden
of Sweet Mercy's complete perfection
by shooting that bullet hole
right in the middle of her windshield
right in the middle of the night
less than five days after I bought her.

The cracks spread out like a glorious sunburst
like the intricate pattern in the web of a spider
jagged circles
and intersecting lines
with a uniqueness
only a snowflake would understand.

And then there was this sense of holy calm.
Sweet Mercy with a pellet gun hole
was a car I could feel comfortable in.
And while I was still fairly sure
Sweet Mercy would find some way to abandon me,
the bond between us grew even deeper.
On Libertyville Road
at 100 miles an hour
this car like a funnel
blowing prayers into my brain.

The change creeps in silently,
gradually.
We are waiting at stoplights
and that feeling of contact with the road is going,
slowly.
Sweet Mercy,
who was never born for gravity,
is beginning to lose all patience with pretending.

I fill her up with every kind of ballast I can find:
bags of rock salt,
hard-bound anthologies,
heavy, if minor, household appliances,
but trunk space was never Sweet Mercy's forte
and we run out of room for ballast
in less than the space of a heartbeat.

The chant creeps in
behind my eyes
behind my ears
I knew you would leave me
I knew I didn't deserve you;
but Sweet Mercy has no time to listen to this.
She is trying to tell me
we are going back home to the Pleiades,
that I am going with her,
we are joined at the hip —
she has no power to go anywhere without me.

There is no time to pack
and less room for luggage,
only a note to leave.
Forgive me
it says
I almost completed
my Amnesty International membership form
lost in the jungle of paperwork under my desk.
Forgive me
I was almost ready
to write four letters a week
to political prisoners
in Central America
and the Persian Gulf but
Forgive me
I am a very good girl but a little disorganized.

Forgive me
it says
I have never been very good at forgiving
Somebody always has to come along
to help pry open my small white fingers
to help me let go
of the saddest color of memory
the kind that burns a hole
in your palm
the kind that burns a hole
in your heart.

But Sweet Mercy has no patience for this.
She thinks the guilt we carry
like halters around our necks
is the most extravagant form
of earthly self-indulgence.
She says
this is what keeps the rains from coming on time
this is why people go hungry.
She begins to rise,
floating away with me
before I have finished the last forgive me.
My words trail off in a scrawl across the page.
We are lifting high above
anything that tastes like
anything but hope,
anything less symmetrical
than the matching handles of the Big and Little Dipper.
Sweet Mercy
who no longer needs a radar detector
exceeded the speed of light
about a thousand planets ago.
Still, the sky before us is not looking back,
the sky is breathing ever so quietly.

Swing Low, Sweet Pontiac

for Roger Kaputnik

My father said there's a tollbooth
on the way to the Sweet Hereafter
and I have to say I'm strangely honored
that in at least one Vicodin vision
he chose to be carried to infinity
in my red 17-year-old Pontiac Sunbird
with its dirty white *schmata*-top
three hubcaps
and the continual high-pitched squeal
of a drill at a discount dentist.
This is one sunbird that never learned to fly,
I want to tell him;
it crawls from zero to 25
in a little more than an hour and a half.
But my father's in no rush, I guess,
and I'm thinking if good intentions
can be converted to currency *anywhere*,
it surely must be there,
at that dazzling tollbooth.
In this case the currency's all in the bumper stickers:
"Practice Random Kindness and Senseless Acts of Beauty"
on its field of purple
directly above the license plate;
"Wage Peace" scrawled in white letters on aquamarine;
"Save Tibet" on that flag of twin snow lions
and fierce geometry of light;
and over to the left, the tender, if prosaic,
"A Home for Every Animal Begins with a Place in the Heart."
I'm glad I never found the anti-nuclear classic
that spelled out *"The Meek Don't Want It"*
beside a drawing of the earth,
since this might have offended the character in the tollbooth.
While it's true that here, in this temporal realm,

my earnest bumper stickers
at best provide reading material
for the rare bored driver not phoning or applying cosmetics,
I think my father tried to see them
as proof that his sad-eyed daughter
turned out to be a relatively magnanimous person after all.
Mistaking my mother for me,
he asks if we will be taking the top down for this journey,
and I'm thinking,
if not now, when?
The heavenly cartoonist and I
can inch our way to timelessness
with the wind in whatever hair we have left,
singing "Beauty is Truth; Truth, Beauty,"
preparing to trade all we needed to know on earth
for all we need to know hereafter.

ANGELS

some say they are watching,
whispering answers,
helping find lost socks, wallets, hope

they sit in trees,
on roof tops,
ride waves at the beach;

in every room, right now
one is standing next to you
on the left or maybe
the right

no golden trumpets
no white robes
no wings

just minor miracles
the perfect word,
a light bulb that flickers when you say his name,
a scarlet blossom on your morning walk
when you were beginning to feel
the only color left
was black

The Impoliteness of the Fox Squirrel

some admire their red feather-duster tail
or pointed ears,
big, plaintive eyes
or the way they can balance
better than circus wire walkers —
and deftly run along the sagging branches of redwood,
electric wires, Comcast cables and
oh, the wild leaps my squirrel can take
while eating sunflower seeds from my bird feeder
and I appear
with water bottle, broom

today he crossed the line
when I heard the sound of gnawing
from my roof,
louder than the screech of a scrub jay,
followed by scampering of little clawed feet

peering in my kitchen window,
he tries to woo with lashes and flick of tail
the stare,
eye to eye,
almost penetrates to my soft spot for small animals
and I wonder what he is thinking —
about the delicious taste of nuts or perhaps squirrel love —
maybe he could become my pet,
replace my son's long gone guinea pig
buried beneath the bird feeder,
but in seconds he's back on the roof
chewing a new doorway
through the shingles
into the attic and
instead of asking
he has already moved in

BEE STORY

Ancient Greeks believed that bees
        carry souls of the dead.

The bees arrived before dinner,
while we were toasting my husband
with champagne,
the fifth anniversary of his passage.

They darkened the sky
like a cyclone,
filling backyard bay tree,
buzzing louder than a leaf blower
or my son's electric guitar,
thousands of tiny bodies,
golden,
in the late afternoon sun.

I was not afraid
when some flew in my kitchen window,
stuck to the wall, quietly watching me.

Honey bees,
dancing pollinators,
weaving in the wind,
left their hive
to follow a new queen,
start a new life.

A miracle,
like the first swarm that appeared years ago
after Buddhist prayers
for Rick's Bardo,
when a buzzing ball of bees
hung like a dark shadow

under a branch of liquid amber,
outside our bedroom window,
They dusted my plants for a week,
funeral flowers still fresh.

Both times they disappeared before dawn,
filtering through ancient redwoods,
blending with the stars — a swarm of souls
flying into the night.

ARIADNE

A lamp disappears down a corridor
leaving a thin thread of smoke.
A pebble skids, walls move.
There is a tumbling inward, a cave collapsing
the voice of a mountain beginning again
like a tongue crying to itself
an ear tasting blood and bone.

Why would a queen choose to walk into agony?
Why reveal mysteries to an assassin?
Leaping dolphins around her and laughing ladies
the court atwirl with bull dancers
flashing gold and lapis lazuli
yet she, white face set to some unseen pattern
slips him a knife, whispers him past
the owl at the entrance, whispers him
past the honey pot with the drowned infant
whispers him into her death.

Domestic Litany

Hail philodendron, full of light
      in the well of your tendrils our blood runs out.

Hail pot, kilned clay, grave reminder, full of light,
      congealed in your still shape, our bones know
      the limit of their spheres.

Hail teakwood table, oiled and rubbed like love, full of light,
      casket wood, love slips from us.

Hail room, nubbed and tufted and basketed and even
      subtly sheathed in silk, full of light,
      shroud linen swathes us from touch.

Hail house, holding succulent fulfillment in all the levels,
      full of light, suspend us
      chaste upon a catafalque.

Hail yard, green with natural authority, inviting flesh to earth,
      entombing the slow drift downward, full of light,
      absorb us now.

BURNING

In my second summer
of daisies and dandelions
my uncle held me

> up to the freshly painted
> yellow house
> and I licked it.

My tongue burned
of sun leaping
from petal and wall.

> Deception, Uncle!
> Right me!
> Glory's not edible!

Shh, he whispered, the wall's crumbling,
petals leave on the next wind.
Love the burn, it's all that stays.

GRANT PARK CONCERT

In the first lull
after the whole symphony's full cry
while time suspends
on a raised baton
and the flutist has yet
to snatch a last hasty breath
before her solo

a three year old shouts
into the silence, "Bravo!"
convulsing the orchestra
and everyone else who knew what was coming
or who'd forgotten
that the time between taste and joy
is prestissimo.

Later, in the twilight yard
in what we thought was silence
the same kid's hands go up
like a conductor's.
"Bravo, crickets!" he cries
"Bravo, katydids!"
rousing us out of deafening,
premature cadences.

CANINE WORSHIP

Ecstatic tail
at the door's opening
the first confirmation

of my true self
come boldly home
unloosing stays of propriety.

Fervent paws
aim straight at essence
shredding skins of façade.

Devout tongue
annoints balm
to the rash of unspoke hate.

Mystic enthralled eyes
Forgive my thoughtless rap
in the instant given.

Such full measure of devotion
bespeaks a low IQ
or a god.

The Road from Selma

The road from Selma stretches in the rain
white as a shroud, rimmed with stiff troopers.

The marchers stand bowed, hands joined, swaying gently
their soft strong song stilled.

Then up from a Birmingham bed
rises a gentle Boston man, Jim Reeb,
steps softly back to Selma
and moves among the stilled marchers.

The troopers stir, link arms,
close ranks across the road
stretching from Selma in the rain
white as a shroud.

The Boston man, Jim Reeb, walks toward the troopers
and they straighten and stand guard tight as death.
But someone moves behind them, waves his hand.
"That you, Jackson?" Jim Reeb peers ahead.

"That's right, Reverend. Come on through."

The troopers tighten guard, straight as death
But Jim Reeb doesn't stop.

He goes on through,
right through the stiff ranked troopers
white as a shroud
rimming the road from Selma.

And Jimmie Lee Jackson takes him by the arm
and they march down the road to the courthouse.

Over in Mississippi Medgar Evers stands,
three young men rise up from a dam in Neshoba County
and they all go down the road
and walk right through the tight stiff trooper line
and down the road from Selma.

And from all over there's a stirring sound.
Emmett Till jumps up and runs laughing like any boy
through the stiff white rim.
Four small girls skip out of a church in Birmingham
and the tall old man in Springfield gets up
and goes to Selma.

And down from every lynching tree
and up from every hidden grave
come men, women, children, heads carried high,
passing a moment among the bowed, stilled troopers
and down the white road from Selma.

Until the age long road is packed
black with marchers streaming to the courthouse.

And the bowed stilled group in Selma
raise their heads, hands joined,
swaying gently, in soft strong song
that goes right through the stiff ranked troopers
white as a shroud
barring the road from Selma.

FOR MY FATHER-IN-LAW

Isaiah mutters in both our bloodstreams
though you are still astonished
that in that small town church
those damning charges
should have run

over the sun-dazed faces
of dozing Iowa farmers
as they did in the Russian *shtetl*
through the thick darkness of the *shul*
over the nodding ear curls.

What was it that kept us awake
among the somnolent safe?
Was it the secret lash
of the teacher's strap in the black hall
and the rabbi's impious boot
under the Sabbath table?

In our wakefulness we've admired together
the fine tracing of the mind,
pinning shadow upon shadow
defining light in light's image,
a dangerous, persistent etching

and the solid stance
of the brave —
the lift of chin,
the shake of head
under prod, flame, gun.

But in "Christian" charity, you have gone
eons beyond me, shining David's star
through continents of human ash in search
of that one redeeming mite of compassion
even in the implacable over-stokers.

Love arises wordless
at your tolerant touch,
storms resolve their dissonance,
the world made mild
under your smile's sun.

The Moment

There was this moment
no one would think it unusual
I was lying on the couch

you were trying chords at the piano
Paul was bounding up and down
the stairs, feet loud and assertive

Jill was in the bathroom, then
she came in, hair shining, and looked
out at the hawthorn against the sunset

Paul paused on the balcony and said
something, and we all laughed
and that moment froze and expanded

I felt the presence of all of us
filling the world. All was dark except
that room which gleamed with laughter

the strong healthy being of the children
your eyes showing
that you saw it too

even the pressure of the velveteen pillow
and the smell of foam couch baked by sun
and the dog, old, groaning before the stair climb

my fingers seemed more tender than usual
I saw the whole world tuned only
to that room, and I thought

how good it is, what luck
how long will it last?
And then it was gone.

WRITING'S A SCARY BUSINESS

You're going along with the crowd
doing your bit and all that
and suddenly you're snatched
off the path, without a sound
out of sight of the rest of the safari

into a remote spot, off the tourist route
a thick jungle. You stand there, heart banging.
Someone half-seen is speaking, maybe,
in a language you don't know. Or more often,
dissolving altogether into the underbrush

leaving you stunned, afraid you'll find something —
whatever is in the place — some truth you may not
care to know, some spook you don't believe in,
some still untabulated disaster, natural or other —
dragons, undetonated mines, residue poisons
from old wars.

                        You long to sit down
but who knows what's under the pile of leaves?
You're too old for this, you're tired,
you'd like to get the hell back to the others,
have a drink, watch the tube, doze . . .

but something is watching you
from inside or out, you don't know.
All the hairs of your body stand
at attention, your nose twitches
like a rabbit's. You would bound away

but there's a feline in you
who's caught a scent that stills
your limbs in a holding pattern,

sharpens the sight through slitted lids,
jets out a quick fix of adrenalin.

You watch. You know how to wait.
Sometimes you pounce. Sometimes
you even catch something.

ARTEMIS

You must learn to hear
      rock growing
      and the flow of sap.

Mount granite
      clutching tight with your thighs
      tremors will jet through your life channel.

Wrap your arms around the trunk of the rowan tree
      the bark will speak to your cheek
      the forest will hold you in its breath.

Even the ice
      of the year's death
      can't stop these songs.

There is no healing
      so whole
      as this earth murmur.

You are this moment's daughter
      the voices of this hour
      are for you.

EARTH DAY

I come in from the smog gasping
and the conditioned air smoothes
my lungs, softens my mouth.

I turn on the F.M.
and the doors of the palace open.
The rings of the ladies nestle

in gentlemen's ruffles and they move
with slow grace and precision
across a floor solidly gleaming.

Wine glasses shine in the clear light,
white wigs curl everywhere, and there
is little Mozart at the piano

not knowing his grave would be
misplaced, breathing as if the sun
would be visible forever.

THE BALL PLAYER

and this, ladies and gentlemen, is the absolute
center of the universe, all lights shine
on me, I have the ball in the Old Ball Game

the crowd howls around me
then halts breathless
a massive multiple lung

I shall make The Basket
the ball rising in a perfect arc
and descending through the flawless circle

(but what if I should break the ball?
I could, if I liked, say
"this is a foolish skin full of air signifying nothing

the rules are accidental scrapes on a dirty floor
that could have run any which way
and still might")

at that the crowd heaves
like a monstrous animal
you are not supposed to pause too long

or the ball will pass to someone else
and anyway if I were to puncture it
letting it fizzle out to a crumpled membrane

they would simply annihilate me
and the lights would all shift
to a Real Ball Player and a New Ball

they have a ritual for that
I like
ritual

I like this custom of maintaining a hush
before an important play
shall I try for a basket now?

the boy crouching at my side says
"it's a skin full of nothing, isn't it so?"
as if I had said that aloud

or did he say, "*you're* a skin full of nothing, isn't it so?"
I can't tell which he said
I have a sudden

conviction
that I'll never
make a basket

there is that monumental heave again
they're restless
it's the Old Ball Game

keep moving
those are the rules
and then it

comes, the boy knocks the ball
out of my hands and it
explodes into my darkness.

HOLY TRINITY OF CHILES

While Columbus was busy
spreading Christianity in the new world,
the natives were teaching his men
the holy trinity of chiles.
They were surprised at the flavors of
chocolate, cherries, and tobacco
merging with a fiery hotness
that made their mouths glow
all night like votive candles.
This Jesus, who ate with tax collectors,
sat with these people to eat meat in molé sauce.
True confessions poured out with cleansing sweat;
their watery eyes turned heavenward.
Shrines were replaced with churches,
bland food with tongues of flame.
As the believer grows in faith,
the chile matures from green to red,
the ribs infused with fire of spirit
to be shared with the world.
Unlike Christianity,
this great evangelization of the chile
took only a century to reach China
and the remote forests of Hungary,
the tongue infinitely easier to convert than the heart.

Transfiguration of the Orange

Orange peels unravel like mummy bandages
reveal its juicy soul squeezed tight.
The sacred secretions are stored in chilled jars
to be drunk by the Gods of Morning.

Once poured from the heavens,
these forewaters sank into underground root kingdoms
then ascended to the highest sun thrones,
nurtured a fetal flower unwrapping its gooey limbs,
then flashed pink wings that attempted to fly.

The idea of an orange swelled inside the blossom mind
until it broke out like a tumor
shedding wrinkled petal skin.

The original flower licked by prehistoric salamanders
still lurks inside this glowing princess goblet,
swirling with sugar oceans and white-finned sea dragons.

It falls into my hand,
    an entire world,
       an entire history
flooding into my mouth,
washing away burial plots of my greatest desires
that reawaken and prick my tongue
in a thousand places at once,
a stinging pleasure that bleeds my self-restraint dry
until I am brushing my face with tarantula legs,
bitten by the orange desire to eat uncontrollably
to feel my brain bathe in ancient waters.

Hiking The Wash

Barely a month into my first semester of college,
two friends and I went hiking with the chaplain, Fr. Michael.
A week earlier, I had stumbled into his office crying.
He had watched with curious detachment
as I spoke of my philosophy teacher
who swore there was no God and said he could prove it.
I, with my green yearnings, had attempted to argue my professor
like a child trying to wrestle a man.
I fled, embarrassed at my toy chest of understanding.
After wandering the campus through my tears,
I knocked on Fr. Michael's door.
I swear within minutes
he had scissored my teacher's arguments to shreds.
I wished I could remember half of what he said.
I wanted to take him to class with me,
to pit him against my professor,
like some big brother against a bully,
but he suggested we go on a hike instead.

The place he chose, an hour drive from campus,
had a well-worn trail up a rocky bluff.
On the way down, he suggested we hike the wash
spilling off the mesa.
On this new path, our feet sunk into alluvial sand,
leaving footprints in the dry riverbed.
A sudden plunge forced us
to climb down boulders
into shallow pools hidden by the sun.
The afternoon heat bit into our necks
and clung to our ankles, as we jumped rock to rock.
We slid through narrow fissures,
that brushed dirt onto our backpacks.

About halfway down, Fr. Michael stopped
on a particularly flat stone, perched above
the final jagged descent into the desert below.
He had us sit down, as he took out
a vial of wine and medallion of wafers.
He celebrated Mass right there in the heart of the wash
where raging waters once flowed,
his arms outstretched, seemingly
touching the whole horizon of saguaro and sand.
He gave us each a verse of scripture to read aloud,
and our voices traveled farther than we ever imagined
deep into creosote and mesquite groves.
My previous ideas of religion:
of a priest standing at a pulpit,
of praying on kneelers,
were flooded away from me
as I felt the raw skin of earth under my feet,
a peculiar comfort in sweat and dirt, and
the feeling there were angels buzzing in the desert.

After Fr. Michael took us back, he shook each of our hands,
and said we should go hiking again, even without him.
I didn't understand at the time,
but my hiking life had just begun.

Memories of a Premie

First memories
are newborn hairs
trailing off
soft infant heads.

So I hoped for my son
who lived his first weeks
in a heated box
hooked to heart monitors
a feeding tube
threaded up his nose
down to his tiny
walnut-sized stomach
all day a slumber
under bright blue
bleaching yellow
from his fresh skin
eyes closed
to the world.

Evenings after work
I scrubbed my hands orange
before entering the NICU
a room punctuated
by heart and breath
monitors beeping
suddenly screaming
before settling again.
Nurses rowed between
shuttered pods
cheerful blankets
hiding the one inside.
I held my son to my bare chest
let him feel my body heat

before putting him back
inside his incubator
for night after night.

My wife and I
hoped his first weeks
of solitude
would barely smudge
the mirror of his mind.

But months later
well after he came home to us
well after he learned to smile
we brought him back
to be with his former
roommates and nurses
a party with balloons and cake.

I did not expect how strongly
my son would embrace
his daytime nurse.
He last saw her when he was only
a few weeks old.
He gripped her with everything
a six-month old could give.
Somewhere deep inside
he was being held again
outside his glass box
human touch
timeless and warm.

SHAWNEE, OKLAHOMA, JULY 13, 1907

This must have been what it was like,
the evening warm and full of possibility,
stars just beginning to appear in the sky,

my grandmother, beautiful and barely 21,
boarding the street car to the station,
my grandfather following at a discreet distance

and already the presses starting to roll:
School Superintendent Elopes with Wife's Sister
Leaves behind six children

while on the train to Denver, heads together,
they are inventing their own version of history,
the past evaporating behind them like steam.

PAS DE DEUX

The man I met on a blind date
forty-two years ago
is on the roof with the leaf blower
while I stand below, slowly easing
the long cord from the bunched-up coil,
guiding it past the claws of the ladder
as he inches up the slope.

Even the crows are silenced
by the roar and whoosh, as gravelly
bits of leaves and broken branches swirl
off the eave and scatter past the neighbor's fence.
Dust settles all around me,
but I barely notice, my attention focused
on the cord, the pitch of the shingles, his feet.

He side-steps down for a stubborn twig
and I head the same direction,
reeling in the cord like a fishing line,
casting it high so it clears the roof line,
the vent pipe, the puffed lip of the skylight.

We meet at the low gutter,
our hands briefly touching, pivot
back to our positions — his right arm taut,
my left leg poised for an arabesque —
and begin our adagio back.

LEAVING MONTANA

And place is always and only place
And what is actual is actual only for one time
And only for one place . . .
—T.S. Eliot

Last night a flood of starlight
cast a ghostly glow on the sunflowers,
the raspberry canes, the shadowy
pines at the edge of the yard. If we listened hard,
we could hear the far-off bugle of the elk
that spent last winter down by the draw.

This morning every leaf on the cottonwoods
is afire — gold, orange, magenta —
and a few feathery clouds barely move
above the house, the pond, the field where the kids
played flashlight tag that first winter,
snow glazing their hair like fairy dust.

There are so many reasons to go,
but try telling that to the asters, reaching
like arms as we pull out of the driveway,
or the squirrel questioning us with his tail
as he gathers acorns by the Saunders' oak.
Even the black bear has come down from the hills
to leave his berry-rich opinion at the end of the lane.

We turn left on Ricketts Road for the last time,
cross the silver bridge, and just beyond the first bend
we finally see the moose
where the river runs along Main Street,
makes a sharp right turn, heads down
toward Highway 93 and flows out of town.

PRAIRIE SPRING

Evening and the flat land,
Rich and sombre and always silent;
The miles of fresh-plowed soil,
Heavy and black, full of strength and harshness;
The growing wheat, the growing weeds,
The toiling horses, the tired men;
The long empty roads,
Sullen fires of sunset, fading,
The eternal, unresponsive sky.
Against all this, Youth,
Flaming like the wild roses,
Singing like the larks over the plowed fields,
Flashing like a star out of the twilight;
Youth with its insupportable sweetness,
Its fierce necessity,
Its sharp desire,
Singing and singing,
Out of the lips of silence,
Out of the earthy dusk.

SUN SANG

1.

A nobody in her own eyes, she would find streets
nobody would walk after a certain desolate hour,
and would fill them all night with her singing,
till she was empty by the time she got home,
having sung for no one, not even herself,
and wanting nothing better than to sleep.

Since she joined the holy order, though,
she sings for the love of God.
She's two people now, both of them full:
one is the servant of what she hears,
the other is the integrity of what comes
shimmering out of her mouth.

Now she paraphrases Thoreau to describe her life.
"Music is everywhere. Everything is always singing.
It's only listening that's intermittent."

2.

She was never a nobody, not in my eyes.
Her voice was untrained, but the sweet
high notes were rarely beyond her reach.
Her hands were strong and loved my back.
She sang while kneading out the knots
and my muscles would hum along.

And when she cried, from deep inside
the diaphragm, that too was a kind of singing.
Sometimes we sang duets, and afterwards
in her room: the smell of much needed rain.

And later when she left, a nobody in her own eyes,
and said, "I'm not coming back" —
wasn't that a song with a haunting refrain.

3.

I wrote her about the seals, how every year
they migrate to a sanctuary under the Antarctic.
They're singing down there and nobody knows why.
Scientists thought it might be sonar, a way
of detecting other life, a way of securing meals.

In fissures of ice they rigged lines of fish
and monitored sound waves for data.
They dreamed up names for the expected outbursts —
jackhammer, swiss yodel, evangelist – and waited months
for something new under the unsetting sun.

But each day and night brought more of the same.
Monitors blank. Seals quiet in their cathedral of ice.
And a host of minds that had missed their guess,
mirrored sunglasses giving back to the land
the glaring monotone of emptiness.

4.

It used to be, every Sunday meant going to church.
Now the only time I go is to practice my piano.
The director of activities, an old friend,
lets me use the Steinway in the sanctuary.

The stained glass windows are circular,
like the shape of God, no beginning,
no end. The pews empty, the altar bare,
my hands remember their child's game:

"Here's the church, and here's the steeple . . ."
The fingers used to play the people.

They still do: in their repertoire
you can hear a congregation of prayers,

a collective variation on the theme of longing.
And now and then, a song approaching
a psalm, nothing but pure praise.
One night, working late, the Asian
janitor must have detected
a tone of desperation. I caught him
sweeping dirt that wasn't there
to give me extra time.

After the coda he waited a few measures,
then asked politely, "All done?"
I appreciated his good timing.
When I said good night I meant it.

Outside, it was April again and the air
was the warmth Vivaldi must have known
those long nights he wrote La Primavera.
Horse chestnut trees in bloom

and a huge bright face above them: round,
not like the face of God, but like
the custodian's face, humming back
to the dark planet a kind of lullaby,

a kind of answered prayer.

5.

After the seals failed to bite, much less sing,
it was back to Stockton St., back to sing-song Cantonese
dipping through the air like a dragon-tail kite,
awnings cranked out over windows of fresh seafood
that would make any seal croon,
and boxes of finger-sized dried fish, metallic blue
like tin toys from the five-and-ten,

and melon crates, mangoes, a mountain slope of plums,
roast duck on a hook, steaming noodles and soups,
and X-rated fortune cookies, red blush
of rhubarb, green blush of cabbages,
and the herbalist jars of coiled snake and fetal deer,
and the suckling pig on a platter, carried above the crowd,
its maraschino cherry eyes like rubies for a royal party.

6.

Walking through the crowded market streets
where nobody knows my name or speaks my language
and it doesn't matter, where my eyes are not as almond-shaped
nor my skin as pale nor lips as full, and it doesn't matter,
I'm also two people now. One is taciturn
and goes tone deaf at the name of God.
The other is a jailbird: isolated deep in my thought
he knows the whole block I'm walking
is an undiminished bar of eighth notes
on the larger scale of the street. The whole city
is a divertimento, streets undulating back
to some overture of first creation I can't begin to imagine.

Isn't it a happy accident, then,
to learn that just around the corner
the World Theater is playing a movie
called *Anxious to Return*, a little corroboration
that our desire to be where we belong
survives our dislocations. And good fortune, too,
to have these market signs. It doesn't matter
what language they're painted in, they translate
to music for a thousand mouths: *Hing Lung, Wee Wah,*
Sun Sang in the narrow streets: bright red
keys to the city, passwords that help us enter
the province of the living once again.

MISTERIOSO

The more people I know and the more I know people
the more frightening they become. Everyone
has been damaged to near extinction. Everyone
has loved inordinately those they should not have loved
except in the most disembodied spirit of good will.
And everyone has been loved at some time or another
by the wrong people, or for the wrong reasons, or for reasons
that at the time seemed suspect, insubstantial.
And who hasn't been at the mercy of circumstance:
born under a bad sign, born with bad genes, or just born,
period. Timing is everything and some will never be
the right person in the right place at the right time,
no matter how hard or how long they try. Period.

When I carried these black winter thoughts from work
and got two blocks from home, I knew something
was wrong: a darkness literally fallen on Mission Dolores,
streetlights out, traffic lights out, the corner stores and the
         bookstores,
the movie theater and the café, all closed up. It threw me
back into the old New Age notion that we create our own reality.
I quickly started thanking my lucky stars, as if their small light
would suffice, as if merely the idea would click on
at least one lightbulb again. Of course, it didn't happen.
Doing the dishes by candlelight in a cold house, the steam
warmed me by degrees and I recalled Katrina, my first California
         love,
telling me that when her ex-husband came over for dinner
he didn't mind at all doing the dishes, unlike me.
He was a conga player and the hot water kept his hands warm.
The other thing Katrina said that I'll never forget
is that she would love me for eternity, in whatever form.
It took less than a year for the veil to fall from that sweet illusion.
There was a man who readily agreed to be compensation

for all Katrina felt she lacked. He'd been after her since her
        married days,
she wanted desperately to be married again, I wasn't moving
fast enough, and that was the beginning of the end.
Five years since I've heard a word from her.
We are ghosts to each other now. Period.

Suddenly the power came on, the lights, the radio with
        Thelonious Monk
soloing on his "Misterioso," and I blew out the candle on the sink
though its radiance, pale yellow and flickering, had made the
        kitchen gloom
a cave of companionable meditation, like the grotto in St. John's
when I was too young to be disappointed by the mysteries
of the Church. The votive candles would cast deep shadows
in the Madonna's mantle, but she stood resolutely on top of the
        world,
the evil serpent crushed underfoot. One day after school, praying
for all the souls lost in limbo, I stared for hours
at her flawless face. Stared until convinced she smiled at me
for my devotion; I was young enough to believe she knew I cared.
I blew out the kitchen candle and Monk was playing all the wrong
        notes
beautifully, in that adroit, mischievous way that had made Katrina
        laugh
when she introduced me to his quirky syncopations, and saw
the bemusement they put on my face. Solo finished, Thelonious
        called out for
"Coltrane! Coltrane!" and his tenor sax took over, and it threw me
back to the bay window in our high bedroom, the international
orange of the Golden Gate Bridge in the far distance, and closer
the gold onion domes of the Russian Orthodox Church, made
        more golden
by the sun going down: a scene like a picture postcard of the
        absolute.

The last time a blackout hit, I was standing at the corner
of 24th and Castro, waiting for a bus with Rita and Theresa.
When the lights went out it was like one stage set being struck
to make room for another. Twin Peaks appeared as the silhouette
of a young woman's breasts against the more-visible-than-usual
constellations, and we walked to nearby Finnegan's, all dark wood
and candlelight, where Theresa introduced me to Jameson
shot by shot. I hardly knew Theresa but I liked her
because her hair was dark and silky and down to her hip,
and because in the power outage the city had been made less
a repository of systemized repression, and she wondered aloud
why more people didn't recognize they were animals.
Life was a matter of basic drives — appetites — and simple pleasures
profoundly gratifying, but we'd wandered far afield
of the elemental delights. It looked as if the electric buses
would be down for some time, and fog was rolling in cold,
so we went for a hot soak in Elisa's little local spa,
and Noe Valley seemed more a village than a neighborhood
and this unexpected darkness our true element, familiar,
inviting, like the steaming wooden tub we sank into
without clothes or self-consciousness, and which Rita, sighing,
referred to as a welcome return to the womb.

I finished the dishes and St. Thelonious Monk rejoined
        St. John Coltrane
and I decided I could be thoroughly annihilated by all the pain
others had acquired before they met me and eventually
visited upon me, if I let them. And as I cleared the counter
I thought of Peggy-O, who relied on household chores to ground her —
Zen work, she called it — and Leslie, who when her heart was
        broken
did a lot of scrubbing around the house, snozzled on White
        Russians
and called me at one in the morning "just to hear a human voice."
And I burrowed through the famous interminable strata
of papers on my desk, fancying myself an archeologist on a dig

in the quest for order and clarity, moving toward that fabled city
whose fragments once recovered and reassembled
would bear with startling relevance on the present moment.
And the thought of other allies came to me, like Kathy
who when love had brought me to a bad end, again,
insisted I go on looking, insisted I "go for the one with the legs
and the sense of humor," thus becoming my Guardian Angel of
          Leggy Wit,
and I thought of Alberto, my alter-ego, who once confessed
"A stiff cock has no conscience," and I thought how heedless
people seem to be of their power to affect other people,
almost as if they didn't trust the exalting, exultant
influence their attention is capable of inspiring
in the kinds of lives that are like one long blackout.
And when I managed to reach the final layer of debris on my desk
I found a quote from Rumi fresh as the day I taped it there.
"Why waste your time with those who don't know you?"
It was a question with the teeth of a guard dog,
with the vicious bite of truth. Knowing the truth
might set you free, but after that it's a daily fight
to stay that way. Next to Rumi's quote was a yellowing
piece of irony, an old flame's note that said
"You've entered places in me that have no exits."
I thought of the transmigration of souls — from one body
to another — and how far certain ones had crossed over
my border, as if seeking in me a permanent resting place.
Their reluctance to go further, to go deeper,
had been unfathomable at the time — and had banished them
to history, to the incorporeal, to the limbo of mere memory.
Once, they were so pitiably human I'd had the impulse
to protect them from every darkness, foreseeable or not,
including myself. But they were spectral figures now, hungry ghosts
tracking their dirt through the house, helping themselves
to my dinner table and easy chair, to my favorite side of the bed.
And somewhere far inside me, haunted as well as haunting,
          they still

nuzzled the household creatures that were stand-ins for themselves
or the children they yearned for. And still trembled at the
      despicable parents
who'd appear suddenly in my stern features. And after their bodies
had been profoundly touched — though they were far beyond my
      reach —
they still wept: in old pain, or ecstasy, or gratitude, or fear.

For a moment, I felt a surge again of something close
to compassion, an overload to blow the circuits of the ego.
I felt tempted to weep with them in a fit of reconciliation.
And more: I wanted again to rally their lost causes
in spite of what was lost between us, to front a new initiative,
to come out on the side of jazz and other joyful noises,
to endorse good Irish booze and animal pleasure, to revive
the hot whispers and holy cries turned cold as stone,
like names inscribed to mark a grave. I was annoyed
at having been annoyed earlier at the temporary loss
of power and light — it seemed unworthy of the faithless
I had wanted to save, including myself — and for a moment
I had to laugh: hadn't I died too along the way, vacated
whatever it is that makes life worth the trouble, abandoned
my body to its hapless agenda? I don't know how
we get taken out of ourselves, or how we get returned,
but I was back now. Back to being human, back to the old dream
of accepting the timely disclosures of love,
or what in my time has passed for love.
Even if the truth love brings can often be ruthless.

ADDIS ABABA

I'm nobody until I leave my house.
Then a man for whom the street
is the house he is bound to
tips his old trucker's hat in passing
and wishes me a "Happy New Year, Your Honor."
I should return his good cheer
with some fast food-cum-booze money,
though he hasn't asked for any,
though the spare change that has trickled down
into my pocket is too spare
to trickle into his. At the bank
the teller with the eternal pout
smiles warmly, calls me "Sir," says
what a pleasure it is to see me again.
Suddenly, I'm a magnate of invisible means.
Still, I cross the street quickly
when I catch the wild eye of a bristle-face,
he of the unbuttoned cuffs, trailing shirttail,
untied shoelace, as though he saw me coming —
his would-be patron, his answered prayer —
and rushed to dress for the occasion.
"Please, Allah, I have a job, I swear —
Addis Ababa Market, between Turk and Eddy —
but they say first I must have shave and shower.
I go to YMCA, *they* say five dollars
for shave and shower" — and already I'm turning
away, wondering what the hell I pay my worthless
bodyguards for — "Please, Allah, you give me
the five dollars and I promise you, next week
you come to Addis Ababa, between Turk and Eddy,
and you will have your money back,"
and by now he has secured my arm,
so I pull out a dollar bill so crisp
I could cut his hairy throat, but he counters

with another tack. "No, Allah, *five* dollars,
I *beg* of you, *please*, Allah," and the beggar drops
smoothly to his knees, as eons of tradition demand.
The lunching law students, the sweet-smelling future
wanglers of America, are only mildly interested
in this type of negotiation, But I urge him
to get up, *get up*. I have to shout at him
to take the little I'm offering, which is better
than the nothing I imagine he's used to —
and he does, though perfunctorily, no thank you,
no smile, no more invocations of the deity,
his zeal reserved for an easier mark. . .

And months later, in a city
that is not Addis Ababa, I am back to not being
a circuit judge or an oil sheikh,
but still hear that nagging
please, Allah, please, Allah, rising through me
as through a minaret: the open arches far above
the stone floor, the filthy rich and the dirt poor
prostrate on the same prayer rug, bowing to an ancient
and intricate design, the light with its thin fingers
touching every one of them.

VIEW #45

after Hokusai and Hiroshige

I dreamt half my life was spent
in wonder, and never suspected.

So immersed in the moment
I forgot I was ever there.

Red-tailed hawk turning
resistance into ecstasy.

The patrolmen joking with the drunk
whose butt seemed glued to the sidewalk.

A coral quince blossom in winter,
pink as a lover's present.

And tilting my bamboo umbrella
against the warm slant

of rain, was I not a happy peasant
crossing the great bay on a bridge that began

who knows when, and will end
who knows when?

"IN THE EVENING WE SHALL BE EXAMINED ON LOVE."

—St. John of the Cross

And it won't be multiple choice,
though some of us would prefer it that way.
Neither will it be essay, which tempts us to run on
when we should be sticking to the point, if not together.
In the evening there shall be implications
our fear will change to complications. No cheating,
we'll be told, and we'll try to figure the cost of being true
to ourselves. In the evening when the sky has turned
that certain blue, blue of exam books, blue of no more
daily evasions, we shall climb the hill as the light empties
and park our tired bodies on a bench above the city
and try to fill in the blanks. And we won't be tested
like defendants on trial, cross-examined
till one of us breaks down, guilty as charged. No,
in the evening, after the day has refused to testify,
we shall be examined on love like students
who don't even recall signing up for the course
and now must take their orals, forced to speak for once
from the heart and not off the top of their heads.
And when the evening is over and it's late,
the student body asleep, even the great teachers
retired for the night, we shall stay up
and run back over the questions, each in our own way:
what's true, what's false, what unknown quantity
will balance the equation, what it would mean years from now
to look back and know
we did not fail.

SOME LITTLE HAPPINESS

knows our names
and where we live
and sets out to meet us halfway.

It arrives humming,
an enchantment of tones
we have never heard
and don't want to let go,
because we know
they will never be heard again.

Some little happiness lives
in our eyes, in our skin,
leaves a trace in the lines
around our tired mouths.

Some little happiness.

We don't have to deserve it,
we don't have to expect it,
we don't even have to admit
how much we need it,

and some little happiness
will rest its hand on our hands,
will tell us, Take me,
I won't be here that long,
and neither will you.

It's okay, whispers
some little happiness,
trust me.

And we do.

SASKATCHEWAN BOREALIS

I was young when the never failing flame
of Queen City's oil refinery
blazed eerie and calming

Like losing individuality

I never imagined
one day the open sky would consume
every memory,
changing crude to gasoline

Like the gravity of love

My close friends tell me
I've spent too many Canadian winters
freezing neurons

They're right
and that's how I know
they're honest souls

But my wolf pack
Saskatchewan bred
discovered new verses,
love piercing our bodies,
the night we lay
hand-in-hand,
vulnerable and exposed
eyes to the stars
bathed in aurora

And that first kiss
from which I've never recovered

UPSTATE NEW YORK

The sun shone through me today
leaving me unable to know
what was sun
and what was not.

Flooded with memories
of so many New York mornings
when you opened me
urging me to look
and touch your mysteries.

At first, you frightened me.
Your warm touch
consumed me.

I don't know how many days
I wandered like a madman,
drunk with permanent addiction
drinking only your daylight.

But fear of loss
loss of ego,
caused me to throw myself hard upon the wall
begging for sobriety.

What kind of fool
throws sunlight out of his house?

For twenty years you kept knocking,
hoping I would open a window
and see you there.

This is how you taught me love, eventually
by consuming my littleness
and letting the current take me.

Earth and Water

Atheists
with their religious doctrines
appear in my tea room,
preaching the gospel
of sex, indigestion, and dust.

For non-God's sake,
have another drink.
Your mad evangelism
has made you limp and impotent,
junk in hand, spewing seed
like a well gone dry.

Put down your pamphlet.
Go to your temple;
I'll go to mine.

I have tea to drink now.
You're welcome to join me,
but I'd appreciate your
putting your inadequacies
back in your pants.

LEDA

See how my head falls to one side
when he comes near,
as if we were two swans?
I offer him the vein in my neck
to put out my life,
or to wind his own around it.

I have built a temple
to each God who rejected me.
Grief has been my angel,
coming in times of hard tearing
to wrap white wings
around my molting feathers.

See how beautiful my new feathers,
fine and soft,
down fit for a God.
Surely He will come to me now.

So many Gods have bent near,
twining their long necks with mine –
Gone!
They were only men.

MAZATLAN

Mazatlan carried her round brown babies
naked on her hip.
She wove the long dry grasses into chairs.
She wore pleated, embroidered, white, white, cotton,
dragging her hems in the dirt.

She knew when to hold her babies away.
If a little pee splashed her feet
she didn't mind because the
bougainvillea blossoms were also falling there.

Our real home was with our maids.
They touched our red hair for luck,
and took us to the edge of town
to visit a mother whose chorizo hands

plucked chicken feathers,
drifting into our soup,
sticking to our urine splashed legs
as we squatted bare bottomed in the dust.

I ran a squawking chicken to the axe
and played with severed feet.
She fried corn in new fat, bent
over the iron skillet and smoking fire.

Her shawl was fringed in black
like long-fingered clouds
reaching into the ripe mango sunset
around her silver earrings.

She lulled me to her warm brown skin,
not minding the snail tracks
from my runny nose
through my tangled hair.

We rode to California
tacked to bouncing straw chairs
slapped back to the cab of our parents' pickup,
singing and staring at our feet,
dusty in the Mexican sky.

Rutted dirt roads
turned to ice plant, freeways.
We watched for Disneyland
submitted to the long scrubbing
wearing our skin down
to white flour gruel.

I still go rolling in the moss and musty leaves
that smell like the belly of Mazatlan,
still go looking for a fire I can see,
real if the smoke tears my eyes.

Naked mothers love best.
I've been looking for some dirt
behind the California smile.

REQUIEM FOR THE RESERVOIR

Where for twenty years students walked
a small path twisting among wildflowers
in grass thick and tall as wind waves
and sometimes catching the wild prairie ecstasy
have been propelled to dance the circular
movement and shine of grass in wind and sun,
now hardens rock, truck and tractor print on empty ground.

Let us say the names of the dead:
Big Bluestem, Black-eyed Susan, Yellow Puccoon,
Golden Trefoil, Brook Flower, Wild Ginger.

Where mothers and daughters have gathered
lakeside to mold dolls of grass and mud,
decorated with stick and pine cone,
left for the sun to season, and where willow
lent crowns to weave flowers for our hair,

Let us say the names of the dead: White Baneberry
Soloman's Seal, Hepatica, Trillium, Moonseed.

Remember when a flock of Canada Geese
balanced on thin ice
under the sheep's back sky of an early spring?
Remember how the mud refused to dry
in that turn where the long grasses, thickly woven
watched us bathe our long interned winter feet
in the first mud of April?
Remember how our feet sank, delicious,
till we found firm clay to curl our toes around?

Let us say the names of the dead,
Blue-false Indigo, Large-flowered
Prairie Beardtongue, Indian Grass.

Remember the blue heron, knee-deep in water
and mud at the edge of the marshy cattails?
Remember how still he stood? We thought him wooden
and thinking that, walked until we stood eye to eye
before he sailed away. Will he come again? How long till
his food returns from under rocks placed by
dump trucks run in tractor ruts over stem, weed and seed?

They say the dead will return; let us repeat their names:
Sweet Cicely, Indian Paintbrush, Blue Flag Iris,
Bunchberry, and Columbine.

IN THE WIND RIVER MOUNTAINS

I go swimming because the water holds me up
because the water touches me all over.
It is a lovemaking,
the way it slides past my sides, calves, knees
cools the top of my head,
Jellos thick around me until
I am fruit encased in cold green translucency.

Give me a wind, a river, a mountain a lake,
covered with granite rocks,
all the trees dead, burned
and the lake cold,
so cold it takes me four days to get in,
becoming a prayer, a revolution, a ritual cleansing.

Why does the lake still exist
in air so dry it could suck the lake into it
and contain it all without rain
as the wind contains without a shimmer
the unwilling offering of the edge of my lips
and the plump of the skin on my hands?

My body is an uncomfortable thing
to take on a long hike. Still, I like
to watch the scenery change:
poised on the edge of a limestone cliff
I wonder whether to cry or to trust the trajectory
of my body through air and trust the willingness
of my feet to find one balance point at a time.

I prefer always to be close to the ground
choosing to scratch through wild berries and
crush the wild mint under muddy legs
or to climb tiredly stomach over a log, swing one leg,

watch the broken-off knife of branch as the last
thigh goes by. I could be hopping lightfoot
log to log as the others have, to leave me a quarter
mile behind, panting in a field of blue lupine
that merges into dusty sky made of my breath.

I like to sweat. Pores open, evaporation is its own revolution
a happy event, not like struggling with breath. Climbing
the boulder strewn drop next to the rapids I know
that when I catch up the others will leave before I rest.
Here, God has made a flagged stone walkway
into the river where a bear could easily
crawl out and drink from the river without wetting his feet --
though I suppose he doesn't care about that.

The kids go on, promising to return in three hours.
I think of grizzly bears while I pant and sweat.
I wet my hat, bathe my face, head spinning, look for shade,
fall onto the underlip of a boulder
in the stars of heat prostration. If a bear comes,
the burnt tree trunks will not offer refuge
not that I could climb a tree anyway
and I sure as hell can't run; I'd be staggering
on the edge of the mountain. If a bear comes --
if the kids don't come back, or don't stop for me --

Inert under stone shade, flesh on granite,
my mind becomes element-air miles across.
If a bear comes, if the kids don't return --
I am willing, flesh like fruit, so different from stone,
cells with nerves to sense themselves,
cells into the Wind River Mountains
can melt and evaporate
until no messages start or end.

I dream of an undersea life,
of a boat in a harbor
or rock pilings under a pier,
of the ebb & flow of shadowy green waters
and the ectoplasmic sensing of sea food on a rock.

I like to swim because water surrounds me,
holds me up while I struggle with breath,
I like to be submerged in the water under thoughts.
It's a kind of lovemaking, flesh in the water,
flesh walking through air, flesh lying on a rock.

On the Death of W. D. Snodgrass

You loved blonds with blue eyes
replaced them when they turned wives
forty-five to my 19.
I was Larissa
in that near Russian winter
defying your misogyny.
I navigated ice tunnels and became my future —
moved away and continue to write
questing for an inspirational chalice
addicted muse
holier than thou grail
and found you on every rail
on the trail of summer;
the tail end of late autumn
in each turning of the equinox
in Indiana late one February
on Long Island in his alcohol-laced lips
in his November kisses
cold by sleet time.
But now that you are gone
I will know when you try to reappear in another form.
I will sacrifice the poems
for sleep
and self-induced suffering is no longer a treat,
for I am older than you when we met.
Yet I am very much saddened by your death.

Pearl Sky Days

Almond-scented afternoons
wet, yellow and timeless
fragrant in memory
blend Baltimore
with the way you feel
on a Long Island morning.

Early coffee cups
and shells I can't forget
juxtapose
another war
waging against a CNN backdrop.

Your lean torso
t-shirted and terse
relaxes to my rub
tension lessens from my touch
on that pearl sky day
I have never forgotten.

Scarlet, scattered stones
lost in a month of moments
we pass
monuments from the past.
Thirty years have passed
yet it's all the same.
The same poets read
as I still search for mentors
for immortality
and love.

BROKEN BOY

Write about what haunts you. —Frank Bidart

Your lips taste of fall:
warm cinnamon apples and cider;
when petals are lost; sheep gone,
and I long for forbidden sport.

Your hazel beads gaze;
we are alone in time and space.
Life erases itself,
and as I reach for taut, tapered fingers;
hands that held mine; held me minutes ago,
I do not know how we began
or if we will end
or even if we were.

In wet July berries, we were not real.
Then, our lips kissed, and
nights did not end;
days stretched into the next
back to Washington Square,
when my grandmother was my age,
and I walked through the arch;
played in the park
in those post-polio summers.

Now that I am nearly over,
I dream of dead dogs clothed in plaid;
you wrapped in a blue sweater
sitting rows in my past
a broken boy in a broken world
wandering a haunted, wasted land
fodder for today's nightmares
that steals my sleep.

EXILES BETWEEN THE YEARS

From a letter Samuel Beckett wrote to Desmond Egan

The arboretum cuttings
of many autumns
have come and gone
along with all the "exiles between the years."
While we were caught in a French Café
playing our own end game,
the pawns wept for Margaret
and I for you.
I became so tired of playing checkmate
with my own life.

So my mind wandered
to a peach-scented summer,
when trees shaded a redwood deck
dropping their fertile gifts
at my feet.

Fecund and full
I awaited your birth:
my first,
my only.
I remember this clearly,
though thirty years have passed,
and the black clone dogs
left long ago,
I still dream them
in my mother's garden,
plundering cherry tomatoes
under sky-white whispers
when time held promises
it never delivered.

MAY 1968

I remember still
humidity hung like moss at Tara
and we clung to time
as though there would be no more.
In the eroding ocean beaches
we explored the hard, sandy slopes
watched the wet reeds overhead
heard the thrusting of the tides

Thirty-five years have passed
my wedding album more a cemetery directory
between battlefield briefs.
The news barks, "Fire Island is disappearing;
field five gone
already"

I remember March 2003.
We strolled, timeless, ecstatic.
Coffee cups, cigarette butts, forbidden love.
Hester Prynne in tandem
mirror images, Dostoevskian doubles
not idiots.

My moods self-immolate
incarcerate, incense me.
I cannot deal with frustration,
have no patience.
Yesterday is my bible.

PARIS

Share with me
my memories of Paris:
a mélange of impressions
indelible painted images
inked in my soul.
I am my own Japanese pillow book.
I wear my words on my skin.
Fragmented mots of tarnished moments
tied together by silver threads
and misted over like the earth
on an early day outing
along the Bois de Boulogne.
Skin taut and pink as the beads
on the necklace you gave me
a Matisse deep pink
on a soon-to-be-distant birthday
so late in life.
I was surprised
I can still feel the dampness
of late spring's longing.

THE BATH

White chamomile mist
covers everyone
in the steamroom.
I cannot breathe.
Am I in a cauldron
in Hell,
cooking in the Devil's soup?

Old men take
their prescription thermal bath
to cure and to flash
young women.

A stream of water
whirls us around
in the fun pool.
Old Hungarian men hold
onto the side,
maybe on purpose,
so we bump into them
like race cars
in a mass accident.

Health enthusiasts roast
in the sauna
spiced with eucalyptus
on a low and steady heat
of 150 degrees.
Moisture leaves their body
blood runs out of their brains
until they stagger outside
leaving their toxins behind.

CUTTING YOUR HAIR

It's full moon again,
and I'm cutting your hair.
Chopping your curls
my scissors move quickly.
Blond, brown, silver parts
of you gather on the floor
and I sweep them up
with regret
because I hate to lose any bit of you.
But your wild locks
will soon need taming,
so two lunar cycles later
we'll repeat our ritual.

SWIMMING

I push the water hard like a frog,
slice it with my arms
faster and faster,
hit it with my hands
then sink.

I accelerate my heartbeat
to run oxygenated blood
through my suffocated heart,
to clean my coronary artery
clogged with old sorrows.

Trying to keep my heart
fit and flexible
so it doesn't crack
like mom's did.

It gained weight
and I have to paddle harder
to stay afloat,
so I swim ten more laps.

SEARCHING FOR ENTRANCE

She steps into a postcard
where poetry is a boat with a white cowl
rocking on a blue lap.

Above *Lago di Como*
Brunate rims the crescent like an artist's garret
for the jaded elite escaping the heat
or their husbands.
Light falls in triangles
of honey-soaked parchment.
A place where no one sleeps
yet everyone dreams.

The *funiculare* hauls her on a silver leash
up the roller coaster hill to the old stone Hotel Milano.
She tries to hold onto something
but the slant of the walls drags her back.

Restless she wanders the streets —
cobbled canting capricious —
every doorway filled with women in black,
furrowed faces hunting sun.

The handsome grocer fails to rouse her
with his amorous still lifes —
pyramids of polished pomegranates,
brown eggs in burlap, leeks cocked on a bed
of crushed ice, artichokes concealing
delicata under soft bristles.

Her life is already severed, burnished,
waiting to be consumed.

Now the maid drapes a clean white tablecloth
from her door lintel, every day folded
with a different design, a message
for women in frames:
Look each day from a new angle.

Climbing above the mansions she stumbles
upon a fragrant bed of bearded iris
below three stone steps leading to
what?
Each golden tongue for a day
shriveling to a question mark.
Tuberous toes dancing up the hill
long after the house has fallen.

BEST USE OF FLOOR

The burnt stain on the oak floor
of the dance barn at Valparaiso
forms conjoined crescents
like a pair of humid hands
touching fingertips.
We weren't even partners
when you wove your neighbor's arms
into a spin along the contra line.
I only tilted my head back
to contact your eyes
blue beneath a black sweat band.
You claim you were only stooping
to hold the hollow under my shoulder
when our lips met.
Crazy things happen on the dance floor,
I thought, spinning back to my partner.

Corn husks slip across stubble
behind the pole barn
as you draw me between dances
to stand on a stain
unfaded by buzz stepping feet.
Will you be my partner?
For life, you add.
I glimpse a curtain of eyes
rising on our performance
rehearsed by everyone except me.
I feel your mitral valve flapping
faster faster.
Opening my mouth to say it's too soon,
the prompter in the rafters whispers Yes.
My mouth stays open.
Crazy things happen on the dance floor,
I think, as I spin flame-faced
down a gauntlet of grins.

The sweat crescents on the pine floor
remind me of the night you caught me
groping back upstairs in the dark
naked.
Your long fingers detecting motion
brushed my breasts, hotwiring my starter.

We didn't make it
to sleep warm covers
or the soft bristle of the Persian rug.
We kindled a fire on the wooden landing
by rubbing our bodies together
until a languid flame   •
spurted from our thighs
to lick the timber beams.
After the fire
consumed the rest of the house,
we opened our eyes on a pine platform
halfway between the undulating
cadence of tree frogs
courting.

BLACKBERRIES ALL DRIED UP NOW

Elderberries lift purple paws to the pregnant sun,
bending on brittle bones.
I cut the hollow stems, pluck shiny seeds
the size of glass beads on a Blackfoot dress.
Below the navel, an inverted red triangle,
sign to men at a distance —
I am woman.

I walk the medicine path.
I am warrior of the unseen.
I have no fear of forms.

Wandering through a harem hung with gauze,
invisible threads stick to my face.
A belly dancer with eight legs
winds her silk scarf around a stunned monarch.
Each web stitched with white lightning,
sign to men at a distance —
I am woman.

I am spirit catcher.
I spin the invisible.
I leave no loose ends.

Two riddled trees still bearing a few pippins
sag against an apple-peel moon.
When I reach up for the scarred fruit,
a speckled king snake wriggles from under grass.
Gold sequins on her skin-tight sheath,
sign to men at a distance —
I am woman.

I am a line drawn on air.
I walk with my belly.
I taste with split tongue.

Stripped to the sweat
I eat the remains of initiation.
But I am no longer fertile — shriveled apples
on a scarred tree sagging with a handful of riddles.
The serpent sheds below my navel,
sign to men at a distance —
I am woman.

I will ascend to mountains, to temples.
I will find my way back
to the world unseen.

THE BEACH AT M'BOUR

The fog muffles your small sounds
as I move my palms over the white curves
of your breasts, soft as gardenias.
All night we have been swelling with the moon,
cascading, churning the sand,
pulling back with a sigh.

Now it is nearly dawn.
The fog pearls along the curve
of your neck where the sun is rising.
But you are from the land where the sun
sets. The sun will rise on this fogbound beach
and you will fly away from the sun.

We have come to say farewell in secret,
as we love. To your American "Goodbye"
I say, "Au revoir, until we meet again."
The sun will rise and burn away the fog,
drying the dew on the white breasts
of the gardenias, burnishing the humping
backs of the waves, the moist belly of the sand.

My Senégalese sun burns your skin.
I have seen it, pink as mimosa
and sensitive to my touch,
after we ran naked as noon to the point.
You left me on the spit of sand to swim
too far out until I cried, "Sharks! Come back!"
Since that time we have not walked in the sun
together. You are a night-blooming gardenia
and the sun, you say, will burn away our secret.

Now, covered by fog, your petals open,
pink as mimosa and sensitive to my touch.

The fog blurs our forms —
you, smooth as driftwood, and me,
your blue-black shadow.

The sun bulges up between the massive feet
of the baobabs guarding M'Bour,
hibiscus red as your lips, which are parting
as we are. Still I smell gardenias.

RETREAT FROM KANDAHAR

Holed up in the honeycomb
caves and kezar tunnels of Tora Bora,
land of black dust, barren knees
of the White Mountains
above the black forests of Spin Ghar.

White turbans, bearded faces muffled
with dust the color of their wives' burkas,
they will fight in the riddled labyrinth
for honor, for the promise
of paradise.

They will fight to the last
Kalashnikov bullet, until the colossal
pressure and rush of heat from the daisy cutters
dropped at their manshaped doors
blasts them to ashes.

In the catacombs of Tora Bora,
they will leave behind empty white boxes
of dates, dumb bells, cluster bombs,
a few fingers, and a horde
of black widows.

LALLA

14ᵗʰ c. Kashmir mystic poet

Wrapped her bones in skin.
Went about naked,
dancing and singing
in silence.

What she heard
she gave to the infants
of sleep. What she touched
she released from under
the mask. What she saw
she laid at the gate
of emptiness. What she tasted
she left for the ants. What she smelled
she engaged with her breath.

One morning she slung a strip of cloth
on each shoulder, tying knots on one
for ridicule, on the other,
for respect. In the evening
the cloth merchant's scales hung
balanced. Neither scorn nor praise carried
weight. She wrapped them around
nothing.

THE CONDOM

He could put it on
with one hand
and in a single
motion so smooth
his woman said

he ought to do that
for a living. People
would pay to see
that, she said.
So he practiced

before the mirror
a whole year
before hitting the
county-fair circuit
where, she was right,

he made enough
to retire on
and after that just
lay around thinking
of a comeback,

of escaping handcuffed
from an oversized one,
a Houdini risking
his life time and again
inside an airtight skin.

The Password

for Ezra

He tells me his password is
"languageismycopilot,"
and I imagine him
handing off the controls
to consonants and vowels,

both he and they wearing goggles,
the cockpit of course open
to the rushing air,
long bright scarves
around his neck and the neck

of aerodynamic syllable
after aerodynamic syllable,
with their lift and tilt
leaving in the blue a trail that forms
a compound-complex sentence.

Sometimes he instructs his copilot,
and sometimes his copilot instructs him.
The way through the sky
is lined like the ruled paper
he wrote on as a child.

For his copilot, no God,
Whose flight log is a series
of disasters; rather,
this partner who sings,
this dictionary with wings.

MAYBE

Maybe the loons.
Maybe the black and white feathered loons
screeching their eerie cry through fog.
Maybe the goose bumps or the tears.
Maybe the taste of the morning on your tongue
and the way the light slants in
at a deep angle, waking all creatures slowly
with its thin perfection.
Maybe the sea, washing over the soul, mixed
with grief and apology and the hugeness of surrender.
Maybe the heartbreak, the splitting open
if you let it.
Maybe death bigger than millions
of autumn vermillion leaves, bigger than moons.
Maybe the desert with its humidity
locked inside sand and bones.
Maybe the red rocks jutting up
through thin air, reaching without cease
like I am for stillness.
Maybe, maybe this moment is the only
sound in the universe
and I am the song.

THE FLY FISHERMAN
for M.

He whips the line
in undulating arcs and S curves
against the white birch trees
along the banks of the Mississquoi.
He is a watery landscape,
fluid and mysterious
as life itself.

He is almost a fish
moving through black water,
searching for pools
where the flies hatch thick.
His line and flyrod
are his eyes and hands
pursuing the smallmouth bass
and rainbow trout
as he stands hip deep in the river.
He is an amphibian
at the beginning of time,
alert to the slightest movement
under the blue-black water.

He brought me to the river's edge
and showed me mayflies
sitting on the surface,
worms with triangular upraised wings
of the thinnest cells in the universe.
He told me about an angler
who ate them.

As blue morning glories
climb the fences
at the edge of summer,
he wonders what trout think.

His heart beats
to the primal rhythms
of nameless, twisting rivers
as he calls to the creatures
who glide silently through bottomless pools,
knowing what they know.

Disconnected, I Retreat into Chocolate

Affairs of the mind seldom begin with temptations of the
flesh. They are created in the steaming bowls
of sacrosanct periwinkles waiting to be born.

I had an experience once of being totally disconnected
from my stars and I thought — why not wear plaid
Saturday evening?

The cat can't find me here. I'm hidden behind the brown
easel with freckles. Can't you tell by my tone of voice
that I've gone shopping?

I'm feeling ballistic and neutronic both at the same time.
Can that signify something? Maybe that I shared the
same past lives with Pollyanna, or took out the garbage
on Tuesdays when I felt sad.

The same thing keeps happening over and over again and
the hole just keeps getting bigger. I'd like it if you just
buttoned that up and kept everything tidy, please.

Carefully avoid stroganoff and you'll be all right when
the stars peak and flow. I can't seem to find my
blue-tipped carousel. Have you seen it?

It's forever.
Shooting off fireworks, we created sensations
in our bellies that equaled Ann Margaret's 40th birthday
bash.

Poke me in the arm. Can you tell I'm frozen? I've gone
vogue at the jazz circle and you'll see me dressed
in starships and hula hoops.

Don't let me cry on this balloon. It melts with tears.
The hotness of your hand leaves marks on my shirt. It needed
ironing anyway.

Fevers don't go away when you whisper to them. Once I saw a cat
peeing in a garden. She turned into a sheep when I tried to
pick her up.

Parley-vous stick shift? My heater vent just blew me a kiss
and I think I'm having an orgasm. Can you play that tune again?

When you screw on a label, watch what happens to the mice in the
        room.
Would you fix me a tiger with two straws and wheels?

Chocolate would be good right about now.

THE GENEROSITY OF RAIN

We are born inside the rain,
releasing a chant
within the fog, voice of a familiar angel,
nectar of irises, lilacs, violets.

Where it gathers
in the wide curves of the river
beneath hanging willows
and cottonwoods, the moose
come to plunge.

In spring, peepers
praise the cleansing rains, and rivers
tumble into a fury
of coffee brown
after long days and nights
of torrents
while the land deepens
into emerald.

For a moment fierceness and wars
step out of the way.
The universe rainbows itself
spectacular, celestial.

STEPS TO FOLLOW WHEN YOU'RE AFRAID

1. Taste the morning sunshine through your eyelids.
2. Allow flute music to mix with a fresh green salad.
3. Whisk together the smell of rain with birdsong.
4. Saute the leftover fight you had, throw in a pinch of skydiving.
5. Slice diagonally an old hurt, sweeten with lip synching.
6. Simmer for 14 hours.
7. Check for signs of happiness.

DECEMBER

This is the taste of what has been lost,
crushed by the heaviness of winter skies.
I am the daughter of the dark Earth.
Everything must be forgiven like debts.

Crushed by the heaviness of winter skies
we gradually wear away our false outer skins.
Everything must be forgiven like debts.
A tang of black tea lingers in the throat.

We gradually wear away our false outer skins.
After all, how is happiness created?
A tang of black tea lingers in the throat,
like a slow walk through bare maple groves.

Above all, how is happiness created?
I am the daughter of the dark Earth.
I walk slowly through bare maple groves.
This is the taste of what has been lost.

DRUG

translated by Wang Ping and Keith Waldrop

Waking one summer
morning in New England, I
remembered the breasts of the girl in my dream
My hands still with the feel
of clutching the round subway strap
I stand still. Life moves on
Her eyes remind me of an owl
In the darkness, my love for her
crawls quietly through weed-filled fields
The owl dives noiselessly
Her mouth holds my tongue
Long hairy legs clamp
tight — my cry of horror
explodes in the moment of love

This is the drug I imbibe each day
a woman I love madly
Her skin is whiter than mine
She has grace, elegance. Her
fingers caress my
skin always with tenderness
But nightmares come
when love is deepest
Their memory whips my face
pushes me seven different directions
then pieces me back together
and sends me loving
in the constant, violent dreams
of my sweaty bed
Loving, hard work which
rejoices my spirit, tires and confuses my
body — I realize I'm addicted

Such is life in the New England summer
Violence, love, terror. When I open my mouth
my tongue, that's used to tasting words
tastes a pair of small breasts
I feel poetry and the drug
all mixed together. They
boil and bubble in
the seven celestial areas of my body
I move on — my life stands still. I
love that woman, such grace, such elegance
She teaches me to give up poetry
She teaches me, in her flesh, in my
fatigue and loss, in such
desperate loneliness and
in her love full of terror and hysteria
suddenly to see and to understand
the truth of myself and also
of the thing I'm so deeply addicted to

PASSAGE

translated by Wang Ping and Sue Allen Thompson

Life is a wall encircling the heart
Every year another stone
making it more solid
Surrounded
you see dawn coming
through the cracks
just as the inner life shows through
when you forget to close yourself
in dreams
Through the gaps you see
drenched trees
the nurturing land
Then a new day begins
and you resume building. You age
the wall gets thicker
the light inside grows dim

One autumn afternoon after the rain
you're exhausted. Whether alone
or writing in an old chair
You've been busy laying bricks
and painting murals. Twenty years
of manuscripts piled all around you –
they're your life, and you've been circling inside them
like an animal. Sun has turned
the paper yellow. You've grown old
The wall is coming apart

On this rainy afternoon
you want to pause
to examine the wall as it is now
You hear an insect
chirping in a damp crevice

This time, instead of brushing it off
and placing it on paper
instead of filling your pen with it
so the pen starts screaming
you leave it alone. Poetry
calls out its loneliness. The insect
must have crept in there while you slept
a sleep that cracked the wall you've been building
for twenty years. In your heart
you listen to the insect
thinking. Instead of bending over the desk
making your chair squeak
you just listen

With the wall rising around you
you sit on your own thoughts
and feel your body split open
revealing a hole. Trembling
from head to toe, you watch the walls around you
Eventually you become that hole
A thousand voices
slip through you
before reaching a deeper place

My Mission Statement

To bring inspiration and innovation to every athlete in the world.
—Nike Mission Statement

My mission is to be a unique driving experience.
My mission is to be putty in your hands.
My mission is to be your favorite pair of jeans.
My mission is to whisper in your ear in
Several pre-selected Romance languages. To star
In a movie that takes Sundance by storm.
(I hope Penelope Cruz will be in it
Even though she will contractually throw pans
Of ink on my head and shoot me colorfully
With a sleepy pistol and make her lips do that
Pouty thing upon which we can hang
The Collected Works of Henry James.)
Which reminds me. My mission is
To rewrite the dull parts of the Kama Sutra.
Because, listen, people! What's a man without a dream?
I say he's calamari soup. I say he's a man without
A mission statement. This is why my mission
Is to be a global partner and a preferred
Provider. To serve nutritious food to
A hungry world. To leave it all on the field,
To go hard when coach calls my number.
My mission is to write one thing you must
Slip under your pillow. My mission is:
Be the pillow. My mission is: Be the night.
My mission is to bring inspiration and innovation
To every recluse in town, to every jaw-dropping
Wearer of a white mini, to every captain of
A space station, to every radio listener too shy
To call in, to even the stranger who left a nice note
On my windshield that time. To you, in especial.
My mission is to be in business for eternity.

CEDAR CROSSINGS

The cedar is not as elegant
as the white pine,
nor as stately as blue spruce.
Disheveled, she bears
the weather with great abandon.

Dirt on her knees and familiar
with the underside of things,
she ruts in the earth, her hair
knotted with nests.
The wind through her house,
wild woman through and through,
in the red season of reseeding
she wears tiny blue berries for jewels.

Sometimes when I cross through cedar
I find a rust-colored streak
on my arm and cheek
as if I have passed through fire.

FOLLOWING DEER

To catch sight of deer
is like tracking down the dead
or angels.
They vanish when I move too quickly —
a tail goes up, a white flare
that signals the thunder of my own presence.

There are signs of them everywhere,
a perfect pair of hoof prints
stamped in the earth,
this morning
gnawed-off blossom tops
in a patch of purple coneflowers.
Sometimes when a delicate head
flowers on the wind
before it fades back into dark foliage,
I can feel the light quiver
inside my own body.

Once I stood by the river
watching the sun drop below the bridge,
colors flowing back and forth
across the water like oils.
The doe entered and allowed herself
to be painted in,
her honey-colored limbs
a gentle, flowing river of deer.

WINTER TRILOGY

1. Winter Cedar

Today the cedars
are brooding darkly among themselves
and have nothing to say
not one stir or motion
or white flag of deer
or bird swing

not even a hawk scree
scrawls the blank grey of sky
the cedars are as tight as siblings
keeping the family secret

I follow a pair of hoof prints
that cut through the crust of snow
a precise pattern
of yesterday's leaping

2. December Storm

All the darkness finally broken loose,
a fury of white
whips at our skin and hair.
It lifts in small tornadoes from the hillside
and drifts in deep layers we set our skis in.
My friend and I thrust the long stems of our feet
into the soft heaps that part like a sea.

The cedars twirl and turn inside out.
A blinding light spumes
from their bosoms.
The storm tossing on their boughs,
they bend and bow, clutching heavy fistfuls.

Our way through them no longer familiar,
spray of snow glittering
on scarves and mittens,
we push through thickets of the storm
to the cloistered center. Whips of wind
slow to brief spurts and we enter the shelter,
hold our hands one to the other for warmth,
blow blood back into skin and look out
through endless avenues of snow.

3. Cedar Snow

Cedars bend close to the earth
with heavy armfuls of snow
as if it has become a burden
to hold up so much silence.

Large mounds of light recline
on the darkness of cedar. Ferny fingers
break through a background of snow
like an x-ray of silence.

Layers and layers of silence.
The cedar is pregnant with snow and
the snow is pregnant with cedar.

Looking at the cedar's new shapes
defined by the weight of the snow, I think
now we are down to the very bones of cedar.
They lean into one another
like a ghostly village,
cedar touching cedar
on a new level of intimacy.

I begin to feel larger
walking around inside cedars
where it has been snowing
forever.

HEART OF CEDAR

The heart of the cedar grows black at night;
the air is old and heavy,
and dusky blood flows through cedar veins.

Cedar tops remote as church steeples
commune with the light of a distant star
pulsating from another time.
Cedar trees huddle in their black gowns,
thicken with an inky intimacy
that one could get lost in.
Branches sprout dusty feathers
as the huge owl settles in.
Sometimes I can hear the wing sweep the grass
or the scream that rides the last breath
of some small traveler hurrying home
along the invisible trails.

The cedar folds so many shadows
into its heart at night, yet wakes
green each morning
in a light that drops
through its stopped limbs
like a new soul.

POETRY

Word jazz.
History book of the spirit.
The heart's chambers a jigsaw puzzle.
Mnemosyne's secrets.
Flocks of doves over snow drifts.
Neon lights in an inky sky.
A stamen meeting a pistil.
The Big Bang.

DECORUM

She wrote, "They were making love
up against the gymnasium wall,"
and a young woman in class,
serious enough to smile, said

"No, that's fucking, they must
have been fucking," to which many
agreed, pleased to have the proper fit
of word with act.

But an older woman, a wife, a mother,
famous in class for confusing grace
with decorum and carriage,
said the F-word would distract

the reader, sensationalize the poem.
"Why can't what they were doing
just as easily be called making love?"
It was an intelligent complaint,

and the class proceeded to debate
what's fucking, what's making love,
and the importance of context, tact,
the *bon mot*. I leaned toward those

who favored fucking, they were funnier
and seemed to have more experience
with the happy varieties of their subject.
But then a young man said, now believing

he had permission, "What's the difference,
you fuck 'em and you call it making love,
you tell 'em what they want to hear."
The class jeered, and another man said

"You're the kind of guy who gives fucking
a bad name," and I remembered how fuck
gets dirty as it moves reptilian
out of certain minds, certain mouths.

The young woman whose poem it was,
small-boned and small-voiced,
said she had no objection to fucking,
but these people were making love, it was

her poem and she herself up against
that gymnasium wall, and it felt like love,
and the hell with all of us.
There was silence. The class turned

to me, their teacher, who they hoped
could clarify, perhaps ease things.
I told them I disliked the word fucking
in a poem, but that fucking

might be right in this instance, yet
I was unsure now, I couldn't decide.
A tear formed and moved down
the poet's cheek. I said I was sure

only of "gymnasium," sure it was
the wrong choice, making the act seem
too public, more vulgar than she wished.
How about "boat house?" I said.

At the Smithville Methodist Church

It was supposed to be Arts & Crafts for a week,
but when she came home
with the "Jesus Saves" button, we knew what art
was up, what ancient craft.

She liked her little friends. She liked the songs
they sang when they weren't
twisting and folding paper into dolls.
What could be so bad?

Jesus had been a good man, and putting faith
in good man men was what
we had to do to stay this side of cynicism,
that other sadness.

O.K., we said. One week. But when she came home
singing "Jesus love me,
the Bible tells me so," it was time to talk.
Could we say Jesus

doesn't love you? Could I tell her the Bible
is a great book certain people use
to make you feel bad? We sent her back
without a word.

It had been so long since we believed, so long
since we needed Jesus
as our nemesis and friend, that we thought he was
sufficiently dead,

that our children would think of him like Lincoln
or Thomas Jefferson.
Soon it became clear to us: you can't teach disbelief
to a child,

only wonderful stories, and we hadn't a story
nearly as good.
On parents' night there were the Arts & Crafts
all spread out

like appetizers. Then we took our seats
in the church
and the children sang a song about the Ark,
and Hallelujah

and one in which they had to jump up and down
for Jesus.
I can't remember ever feeling so uncertain
about what's comic, what's serious.

Evolution is magical but devoid of heroes.
You can't say to your child
"Evolution loves you." The story stinks
of extinction, and nothing

exciting happens for centuries. I didn't have
a wonderful story for my child
and she was beaming. All the way home in the car
she sang the songs,

occasionally standing up for Jesus.
There was nothing to do
but drive, ride it out, sing along
in silence.

SISYPHUS AND THE SUDDEN LIGHTNESS

It was as if he had wings, and the wind
behind him. Even uphill the rock
seemed to move of its own accord.

Every road felt like a shortcut.

Sisyphus, of course, was worried;
he'd come to depend on his burden,
wasn't sure who he was without it.

His hands free, he peeled an orange.
He stopped to pet a dog.
Yet he kept going forward, afraid
of the consequences of standing still.

He no longer felt inclined to smile.

It was then that Sisyphus realized
the gods must be gone, that his wings
were nothing more than a perception
of their absence.

He dared to raise his fist to the sky.
Nothing, gloriously, happened.

Then a different terror overtook him.

BELIEFS

I believed in nothing, so I thought
no system of smoke and desire
got in the way of what I saw.

There was the other world
if only it could be seen,
slag heaps and golden valleys,
crime and celibacy —

visible companions — if, say,
your politics could braid them,
and there were all the gods
in the darkness of our needs.

That was when I realized
that to believe in nothing
is a belief too, and not much fun
either, and acceptance

of the world as it is is as dumb
as standing still when flood waters rise.
Fortunately in the midst of it all

you came along with your singular beauty,
the truth of things for a while
tactile and unequivocal.

But often when you left the room
a few questions replaced you.
When you returned, they remained.

Is it possible to be in love
and wise at the same time?

In love, I might be so intuitively right
I'd be banned from a republic. In love
I might believe any foolish thing I felt.

Over time, questions formed curlicues
in your hair. They became part of what
I thought when I thought about you.

So good, then, when you stayed in the room,
giving them flesh, making them real.

Juarez
For L.

What sad freedom I have,
now that we're unwed.
I can tell the Juarez story,
which you wouldn't let me tell,
though I assured you
I'd tell it as evidence
of the strange places the soul
hides, and why I fell in love.
It was yours, you said. You
wouldn't let me make it mine.
You were in El Paso, a flight
attendant. Between jobs?
I can't quite remember. Men
gravitated to you as if they were
falling apples and you the earth.
This man you were dating, your
El Paso guy, as you called him,
said he knew a whorehouse
in Juarez, a place where
the whores danced and you could
get a table, have drinks, watch.
Let's go, he said, and you did,
with another couple,
parking your car on the U.S. side,
walking in. It was 1961.
You were adventuresome, young.
You didn't know the verb, *to slum*.
You passed an excavation site,
then some adobe shacks, children
barefoot and begging. You passed
a man on a burro. And soon
you were a turista amid the dismal
liveliness of a border town.
Your date was handsome, high-
spirited. You weren't yet sure
if he mattered to you.

The dancing whores had holes
in their underwear. One couldn't
have been more than fifteen.
They danced badly, as if bad
was what everyone wanted —
herky-jerky, lewd. Your date
was clapping. (I remember the face
you made as you said this.)
On the way back, he spoke of the fun
he'd had. Off to your right was
the excavation site.
You didn't know why,
but you climbed down into it as far
as you could go, sat curled up facing
cement blocks, the beginnings
of a foundation. Your friends thought
you a wild woman, a jokester.
But you didn't say anything.
And you wouldn't come up.
For the longest time you wouldn't
come up. Even when they went down
to get you, you wouldn't come up.
I'm sorry. If you hadn't stopped me
I'd have been telling this
over and over for years.
By now, you'd have corrected
the errors of timing, errors of fact.
It would be that much more yours.
Or maybe you knew that a story
always belongs to its teller,
that nothing you could have said —
once it was told in my voice —
would much matter. Perhaps.
But, after all, it's my story too.
On that dark Juarez night,
every step of your troubled descent
was toward me. I was waiting
in the future for such a woman.

If a Clown

If a clown came out of the woods,
a standard looking clown with oversized
polkadot clothes, floppy shoes,
a red, bulbous nose, and you saw him
on the edge of your property,
there'd be nothing funny about that,
would there? A bear might be preferable,
especially if black and berry-driven.
And if this clown began waving his hands
with those big, white gloves
that clowns wear, and you realized
he wanted your attention, had something
apparently urgent to tell you,
would you pivot and run from him,
or stay put, as my friend did, who seemed
to understand here was a clown
who didn't know where he was,
a clown without a context.
What could be sadder, my friend thought,
than a clown in need of a context?
If then the clown said to you
that he was on his way to a kid's
birthday party, his car had broken down,
and he needed a ride, would you give
him one? Or would the connection
between the comic and the appalling,
as it pertained to clowns, be suddenly so clear
that you'd be paralyzed by it?
And if you were the clown, and my friend
hesitated, as he did, would you make
a sad face, and with an enormous finger
wipe away an imaginary tear? How far
would you trust your art? I can tell you
it worked. Most of the guests had gone

when my friend and the clown drove up,
and the family was angry. But the clown
twisted a balloon into the shape of a bird
and gave it to the kid, who smiled,
letting it rise to the ceiling. If you were the kid,
the birthday boy, what from then on
would be your relationship with disappointment?
With joy? Whom would you blame or extol?

The Inner Life of a Tree Becoming an Apple

A moment is nothing
but a multitude of doors,
a geodesic sphere
around an opening seed of self.

Each moment is a passage
through the only door there is
as it opens into endless
evolutions.

Maybe I'm a shiny platinum pin,
spinning toward a polished oak floor,
out of a longing
to be heard.

I could claim to be a thunderhead,
a sudden blue flash,
or a slowly
receding
rumble.

But today my eyes are apple branches
under soon-to-be-melting snow,
anticipating the honeyed aroma of blossoms,
budding leaves becoming, briefly, my hands,

a summer full of wet flesh sweetening,
early autumn hungers,
worms and watchful men,
a curvaceous golden beauty remaining pure,
a woman in white sprinting across a stage
and taking flight,
the strong stance and arms of the man
who'll receive her,

the heaviness of longing,
the subtle snap of release,
the sudden wild rush
of an apple falling,

an unpretentious thud,
a brief but tender roll against a firmness,
on a bed, on the earth,
yielding skins, large spheres, one door, many seeds, one of many
ways home.

SPHERE

The orange sphere is in your hands.
No longer dribbling,
you're driving down the lane
during the last of your allotted strides.
The clock is down to 2. Your team is down by 1.
From the crowd's roar, the rafters are trembling.

You begin your leap.
Briefly, you're alone,
until a body or a building,
you can't tell which,
slams you to the slick wood floor.

According to an official,
the defender was in the wrong.
Black and white stripes say,
take it to the line.

Now you're standing on the line.
The game is on the line.
The ball slowly rises in your hands.
You see the rim.

Behind the twine basket, arms wave.
Within the growing roar, you hear a whisper:
Stay calm. These matter.

You want to be admired, praised, loved,
even worshipped.

You're alone with many whispers
and millions of eyes are on you.

FIRST COURTSHIP IN A KITCHEN OF AN AUTO SHOP BY A WATERFALL

1.

In a large steel pot with small black handles,
a chicken is boiling in unseasoned water
with carrots and potatoes but no cabbage.

The one holding a wooden spoon
is my mother.

The one lifting the lid,
poking the meat, stirring
is my mother.

The one saying to the chicken
you're not done
is my girlfriend.

The one saying to the meat
not even close!
is me.

2.

We get married anyway,
and our car is in the shop —
a silver-gray Civic
we took there yesterday.

The shop — a shady jumble,
narrow drawers for tools,
oily red rags in a cavern,
five wide doors of unpainted strips of metal,
closed,
no one
coming in.

Unguided, we look for our car —
past an accord, a green Carmanghia,
a rusty Camaro.
We find our hatchback,
but the engine has been removed.
Our mechanic isn't there.
No one knows when he'll be back.

3.

All along, it was not subliminal,
not my mother, my girlfriend, my wife.
Not the shop, the car, or the missing mechanic.

I am standing by the waterfall
that froze into icicles
cut off near the top
with a single sweep of my arm.

I am painting over the face
that I painted behind the falls.
Wide brush, white paint, same smile.

A stony face, textured,
water-stained,
dark,

a bit of mossy life
and always smiling.

WOOD AND RIVER IN CONVERSATION WITH A HATCHET

1. Wood

Red and yellow maple leaves,
Adirondacks, dappled light.
A woman approaches a trunk,
gouges the bark,
attaches a bucket.

2. River

The Tuolomne River rushes white,
glides glassy over granite slab.
A man enters the shallows,
holds a porous-bottomed pan,
dips, scoops, waits,
looks, discards.

3. Conversation

Welcome to my love,
but get to the point.

You're the woman of my dreams,
the woman of my nightmares.

You hate me.

I don't.
I'm out of here.

4. Hatchet

Wielding an old red hatchet,
whose blade cuts flesh
but not deep enough to kill,
whose blunt end breaks ribs
but doesn't kill.

Straddling a dry log in harsh light near a river,
I hear her or me or someone say, OW!
Get it over with!
I see a back bashed, ribs collapsing towards a heart,
a wrist hacked where blood isn't flowing,
That which doesn't die isn't dying.

I'm trying to be sweet.
I remember the blueberry pancakes.
I keep the gold nuggets
in a jar on the high shelf.

Welcome to forgiveness.
I don't know if I have a point.
Maybe a dull blade, fading scars,
rivers of dreams.

OLD STORY

They say that God was telling
her unbelievable story
when suddenly she pulled
a slender hand full of props
(sun, moon, earth and various stars)
from her sky-black velvet purse.
After setting each
in almost perfect motion,
she paused
while creation held its breath
for the inescapable conclusion.

None of this matters to you or me.
Philosophy won't clear arteries
or send blood coursing through thought.
And when you think
you have it nailed down,
wind shifts and shadows sharpen —
a heron ripples mirror's pond;
a goshawk drops without a sound.

THE GIFT

Searching for the lost coin,
now stubborn in its hiding,
I sweep the hardwood floor,
scour the cedar deck,
rifle drawers, claw through chests,
rake the garden's tangled depths,
mole-roads, rose roots, blackberry crypts,
corner it at last
— belly-up but breathing —
behind an empty apple box
forgotten in the dream-infested
mushroom cellar, pulsing like a toad
resigned to spit and brood
below the creaking timbers of the house.
Tiny as a redwood seed
and rough as pumice stone, it cries
with the thin voice of a penny
when I bend to pick it up,
as if by pleading in the dark
sown deep around us
it could deflect one thorn or thought,
reverse one whirling atom,
as if by sinking into shadow
it could become the nothing it is not.

SLEEPING ON AMTRAK

Evening slathers borrowed gold
on strangers' faces,

drops a skin of rain
on fields and silos streaming by.

A faint click-clack with shadows
fans shuttered eyes.

Towns recede like memories of kisses,
broken toys, first snow, seventh grade.

Tracks tunnel into haze
enveloping a trestle over mocha river veins.

Loosely worn by summer,
dusk's threadbare veil caresses us,

as fragile as the fog that shelters lovers,
as quick to vanish as

one-hundred years of steam.

ELEGY FOR A BORDER COLLIE

Yes, I reply to the cryptic stones,
she was the alpha pup
who refused to grow up,
more human
than my snarly neighbors.

She reveled in necessity:
herding cats, scolding geese,
disturbing the high-and-mighty
fortresses of squirrels.

And yes, she would have tumbled
like one of you
down the salmon's icy ladders,
or levitated over embers
to catch her Frisbee had I asked.

Divining the weather ahead,
she suffered critic crows,
and gathered out of fall's debris
a whirling litter of her own.

Now her doe eyes target spinning suns,
and her wolf ears perk at howling moons.
She runs, leaps, zeros in
where I will not, cannot
call her home.

PREPARATIONS

> *Your soul is a chosen landscape.* —Paul Verlaine

Shake loose the dreams
that fall like snow
upon the shoulders of your mind,
thoughts that stick like lint
to the static of your coat.
Peel back the husk you wore
threadbare. Allow the sparrows
to carry aloft your frayed,
unbraided breath.
Clip off your shattered shell.
Watch it drop like a pared nail
through galaxies of sun-lit dust.
Let the janitor sweep it away
with the hair and the filth.
Slough off your cells.
Shed your golden scales.
Let the grist of your life
lift on the wind.
Let it hover over highways
and settle into every wrinkled river
meandering the earth.
Pay the rent. Leave love
to argue for its pound of flesh.
And if you find your bones
picked clean and tagged,
lined up on shelves
like discount auto parts, relax,
kick back. Speak gently to what's left
of the beast you rode to death.
Tell the landlord you're heading west.

DISTURBING THE UNIVERSE

Between two shafts of light,
I lift a stone

from underneath the waterfall,
drop its weight

with wondering hands
into a pocket of my jeans,

then speed my burning engine home
over twilight's broken roads.

After raking water's gift of sand
into orbits ringing once wet worlds,

I dance on the drome of the revving rain
revising arroyos for rivers to dream.

THE LOVE OF HORSES

For J.

On this pleasant brown afternoon, smudged
with February, by barns, I watch horses.
I watch the twelve dreaming girls astride them:
mud and snow, lapping up against each other. I watch
this strange kinship of opposites, girl and horse,
stalled together in one closed motion.
The girls have grown more confident, though still shy,
as if they don't yet know what all this means:
the thick, furred thing that lifts and flows
beneath them with a name. Each girl, I think, longs
to ride up into the woods alone and close a leafy door.
And no matter how much she talks to you about horses,
she will never say exactly what she means.
Meanwhile the exultant Mrs. C talks on:
"Communication with your horse is everything."

I remember how it was with us: you still black from war,
and me, dumb as snow. But how brilliantly we communicated
right to the candle's sticky end, in this new language
of weight and counterweight, of lift and tilt and press.
More words than we would ever speak. Only the eyes,
the eyes would ruin everything, as they did,
when one of us — it was me — first looked back
beyond the rugged cabin's glow, to where
the shrunk world waited, lonely and impossible.
Was it an angel astride a beast or a beast astride an angel?
How I wanted an answer to that riddle that now
I'd never ask. You were so golden, so golden
and utterly at the end of everything I knew about love.

FOLLOWING EURYDICE

For months I sought you, along the stony way.
Afraid of following, afraid of not —
your ashen grave clothes, their endless rising and dipping,
the road I could not give up.

Oh unbearable disunion, the living from the dead.
Where can we meet in this meadowless land?
Here everything is root, or what seeps out of root.
No leaf, blossom, or living branch. The entire set
staged with what will keep us separate:

jutting rock, treacherous bridge, the dead air lit
by weird transparencies of light, a molten rust
roiling underfoot. I move as if on wheels
made invalid by grief. The tiny control switch
is at my left hand, the lyre is on my lap.

Orpheus inhabited his will, his fierce blue engine
bearing down. But what have I who must follow
this string, the trail of ashes, time...whatever looks
as if it's going in your direction. Some days

your presence is so thick it's as if I can slide
my fingers through you, naming you this way:
silt, risen vapor, world without end . . .

At first I believed you were teaching me
how the dead can be pursued, can even choose
to stay within our grasp and go on
touching us. But now I know

you are only what you are — *non-touch,*
a sort of endlessness of *that.*

FALLING BACKWARDS

> Hey, Mr. Tambourine Man play a song for me.
> In the jingle jangle morning, I'll be following you.

Perhaps we each have a moment when the body turns back
      to its one discernible landscape, a brevity
with its own door attached. If only I could keep myself
      from falling backwards, we might think.
I could enter that door, land in my own life forever.

Mine was the moment I walked where I wanted, leaving
      the party of noisy kids, girls in undertaker make-up,
boys with loot in their pockets, grinding cigarette stubs
      on the snowlaced walk. Princeton, blind date (circa 1966),
some dance or other. The winter hung like lead between

this world and the next. I heard the gritty music jangling
      someplace up inside. I climbed the granite steps, cracked
the iron doors, and slid inside a nodding garden of backlit heads.
      An angel, so far away . . . so close up . . . (his tiny furzed
head and cap) wrestled with a skinny god, twanged music

from its metal arms and mouth. Kali on a blue guitar. The mind
      has songs for everything. The year was *Free-Wheelin' Bob.*
I've told this story ever since, how I saw Dylan. Memory's sieve
      is what I drop my quarters in, what I come to in the end
when I started out for more. I fell into myself that night, I did.

But whatever god it was that caught me, tossed me back again
      half-touched. Years later I'll describe myself as anything
for you, driving the Vermont roads, CD player up very loud, Bob's
      Budokan release — but knowing it's all wrong. A door's shape,
a screen in that door through which we try to see, but the scene
remains

peppery, does it not? As in a dream when you can't see the speaker's
face. Supposing moment to moment we think *another story is
all that's needed*. We just get harder blessed with whatever lies
beneath.

Go back to the shimmering almost present, the wet black road
that leads to the graveyard (circa 1725). It was early summer when I
again

cracked those iron gates, fearfully. I stepped onto the spongy earth
inside,
so fearfully. I crept and crept around the mossy slabs, trying not
to touch anything, yet I touched everything: the bodies, the rot.
Everything lay underneath everything else anyway. How could
it not be so? Just as the Tambourine Man raised me up that night,
sun-dazed, shook-lead. I told you how memory keeps filtering this
life.
The graves were damp with what keeps us alive, so I put my
hands
in that. What comfort in its beds. Even the tombstones read my
name — Hill,
a family just like ours. The great granddaddy's tomb lies over
here.
He was from Scotland, I think. Look: black granite, moss speckled.
My face

shines in what cannot shine back: unspoken years. Driving the
green gullet,
falling as far as my own sense, my own music. The CD player is
up very loud; the rain is tearing down batches of pink petals which
are
only now giving in, letting themselves become what all along
they were meant to be: Beauty's next smear on the black road's shine.

The Way of All Bats

I

It was the crinkling sound awakened her,
the soft clucking under eaves,
and then she sees them —
first one, then the others, five in all
flown in.

Through what opening or tear in the screen's
perineum? As if she'd whistled for them in her sleep

so they came to her
to teach the crisis of confinement,
the trick circling the same dim room, tethered to a pole.

And how the mind can make a game of anything

to keep itself awake, amused. From the other side of glass
she takes in
her own high speed panic. But surely

these bats are too much, going round and round like that.
What's there to do
outside of reaching for the daylight broom. Thwack.
Fear has no shame . . .

Thwack. And we hold back our pity
because isn't it beautiful, really? All honor and glory, even
this flying for years stitched to one small orbit
like a flag or a bat

seeking to quit
all of it
but its given symmetry. And beautiful, too

to labor inside these walls, missing time and again
the one window-of-all held up
like a black bouquet.

II

She feels like a contortionist trying to *think* her way out,
make this parabolic bend away from a *way* —
wanting to undo herself of the gardener's
dress,
without letting the cord snap,
to come clean, yet stay . . . . .
intelligent

and *occupied*. Unbounded, yet bound.
Being born requires something . . . more.
Like a hand, a dear hand

that inserts itself, turning the head round
so the eye can catch the miracle
of one small bat
slipping off its iron orbit (oh, quite by chance)

and take the window exit.
Then another one . . . whoosh
gets it, and another . . . until all are gone
to a graveyard of stars

which is how we entered this world, is it not?
And how we return, driven at last,
from what never was . . .

AFTER THE MORNING BATH

after the painting, "After the Morning Bath," by Pierre Bonnard, 1910

It must already be mid-morning
as Marthe gets out of the lukewarm bath
and steps away from the towel
someone is holding like an evening cloak.
The day is just coming into focus:
perhaps she will go to the market
to purchase the foods Pierre loves best —
figs (just in season), camembert,
endives, a freshly killed rabbit.
Or she will tend to the garden, so neglected
since their last trip to Paris —
heaven knows the geraniums need to be cut back,
the roses pruned, the alstroemeria need water.
She turns her head and is struck
by the image in the mirror:
the creases next to her eyes
that Pierre calls his little bird feet
seem deeper, no longer the feet of a sparrow
but those of a crow, and she can hear it
cackling now in the garden, mimicking
every word she is saying to herself —
figs, endives, roses, geraniums —
as she searches for her slippers and notices
how easily her feet slide into the red.

MEDINA

Walking through the medina in Fez you ask me
if any two people could ever be as close as we are,
a question as simple as the young man asking for a *baksheesh*,
his eyes squinting in the sun as he looks at us
and then we look at each other, embarrassed,
not by the man, the same one who tried to rip us off
days before in the shop full of lapis lazuli,
but by our naivete, how easy it seems to go
from having so much to having so little.
We spend the rest of the day very near each other,
drinking mint tea in stalls full of brass, carpets,
their designs no less intricate than the medina itself
where we walk, arms hooked into each other,
talking only about the things that grab our senses:
there, the sulfurous smell from the tannery,
a wall covered with purple and green leather hides,
the voice of the muezzin calling the faithful to prayer.

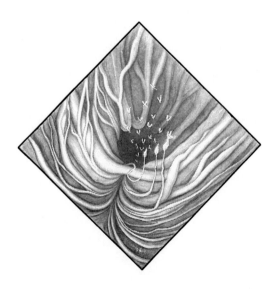

CAPRICE

> Frau Gräfin, das Souper ist serviert.
> from the opera, *Capriccio*, by Richard Strauss

The Countess Madeleine has not yet chosen
the man she will marry, she must know
in just a few hours, and already the Major-Domo
wants to serve her supper: medallions of venison,
fresh spätzle, Porcini mushrooms, Schwarzwurzel.
She thinks this is all preposterous,
the dinner (and now the urn of Liebfraumilch),
the fact that she must even choose between two men,
the composer or the poet. And to think,
with her crystalline-blue eyes and blond hair,
the family money, she was sure she would be swept
off her feet. Her father would call her his *Schätzchen*
as did his friends, who would laugh
as they tried to touch her in all the wrong places.
She opens the two large windows in the drawing room,
closes her eyes and hears Mozart's *Ch'io mi scordi,*
his lilting rhythms make her sway.
But suddenly she is troubled by the absence
of words, she needs them to help her define
this moment: the moon, so full and so near, the stars
in complicity with everything that is dark around her.

Edith, Typing on the Balcony

after a family photograph, Frankfurt, June, 1939

It is a Sunday afternoon, the dishes
have been put away and she allows herself this —
she pulls out the typewriter, swings open the door
and takes the machine onto the narrow balcony.
A few months ago, this would have been unthinkable
but the streets are empty and today she feels strangely
optimistic, so she begins her letter to America:
Heute ist das Wetter bild schön.
She can hardly contain herself as she writes about
the cat, Moorle, that her cousin left behind,
how it follows her around all day long
and sits on her shoulder as she does the dishes.
And the piece of chocolate Herr Schmidt gave her,
who cares if he did it out of pity,
she can still feel it melting in her mouth.
She mentions her younger brother Paul
who has just come onto the balcony with his camera
and what is he thinking, snapping a picture of her,
Er is doch so blöd, but if it comes out she will send it
next time along with news that things are getting better.
After all, didn't their fathers defend Germany in WW I —
in fact, she will enclose a photo of them she just found
and don't they look so proud, standing there in their uniforms.
Yes, today she just knows that things will get better,
immer besser. Wir grüssen euch. Edith.

PASSAGE

After spending a year
coming to terms with the disease
my mother looks at me
and says *I'm sorry.*
Already her body barely
leaves an impression
on the jelly pad the hospice brought in
to prevent bedsores.
Her watch slides off her wrist
and lands quietly on the quilt,
then disappears in the down.
The unread *New York Times* are piled
on my father's side of the bed,
each issue opened to the crossword,
the unfilled boxes no longer
ask for a clue.

MALLARDS MATING
IN THE RAIN AT RUSH HOUR

Oblivious to cars screeching around them,
the iridescent male and the brown female
dodge their necks up and down,
circling with a quacking precision.
They take off in a wet flourish, chasing each other,
narrowly missing the hood ornament on a white Jaguar
and come around again, landing in the middle
of honking drivers to repeat their delirious dance.
When a man walks out of a bookstore
clapping and waving to scare them off,
they ascend vertically like holy ghosts
then nose dive back into slick streets.
Dying for love, isn't that what we all do
at one time or another, labeling it romantic,
as we recklessly rub a furry bloom of foxglove
against our lips, ignoring the poison that
hides in leaf, stem and stamen.

DANCING AT OLD THRESHERS'

Tangerine sunset floats low on the horizon.
The moon is orbiting around your hat.

I dance with you between rows
of early September corn,
your Amish beard a field of uncut hay.

I haven't memorized the map
of the constellations, but your eyes
are burning. The landscape of your muscles
ripples under your white muslin shirt.

You turn me two hands round
as the Great Bear rises in the sky
above your left shoulder.

There's a secret beneath my gingham apron,
a shower of falling stars
as we dance around the fire
kicking up the ground made hard
by late summer rain.

We orbit around the shapes
of our forefathers' stories —
a galaxy of seasons changing,
the stars a blur,
woodsmoke and wisdom whirling.

As we circle around each other,
the bear wakes up from his dreaming,
hears the tinny music
of hammered dulcimer floating south.

He pulls corn out of the husks
and you open your mouth.

The moon cracks like a pumpkin.

The sparks brush your skin
like a woman with turquoise beads,
tan muscular arms
and the secrets of your shoulders.

I am the goose shadow dreaming
of the day the universe began,
singing the music of the next creation.

In the Voices of the Birds

What I most remember about Christopher
is the way he knew the names
of all the birds
at dawn
by their songs.

His cornsilk blonde hair
blue overalls, no shirt
the strength of his shoulders
and the way we stayed awake all night.

There was light in his touch
between the birds.
They flew in and out
of his fingers,
and birds outside our window —
a window we couldn't
open again that way.

We met when we could after that,
in Iowa, Switzerland, San Francisco,
in borrowed cabins on two different oceans.
You took me to my brother's wedding
in a red pick-up truck,
made fun of the priest and my brother's future
mother-in-law,
which you claimed permission to do
because you were Catholic.

I remember the way you hurt me,
what you said,
and the sentence I typed on your
portable Smith Corona in Nantucket
before I left
for the last time.

It was November,
with a light dusting of snow
over the sand.
The pebbles on the beach
hid their messages.

On separate sides of the continent
we listened to different oceans
and slammed our lives shut —
you in Brooklyn Heights
with your two-year-old son
on your shoulder,
me in San Francisco
climbing the long hill
to 24th Street.

Twelve years later,
holding your first book of poems
in my hands, I am
hungry for memories,
hungry for every word,
hungry for any hint of a message
where I might find myself.

In the inscription, you write:
"There are histories
in this book you may
be familiar with, because
you were there."

I am not the arms
where you will rest your head
when you're eighty years old,
but I always hear you
in the voices of the birds.

MERIDIANS

Love is not an emotion.
Love is who you are.

1.
His hands told her
that he was one of the Tantric sculptors
of the Temple in Varanasi
where Hindu gods and goddesses
are perpetually making love.

Halfway around the world,
he traces the fire meridian
up her left leg.

The butterfly angel who dances
out of her heart chakra
has flame blue swallowtail
wings.

2.
Men are the sea she swims in.
In the Temple in Varanasi
or on the basketball floor of the gym
at the 43rd and Judah
contra dance
in San Francisco.

She walks through the door
with a red pashmina shawl
draped around her shoulders.

Men are the sea she swims in
under floating summer light
when she dances

face to open face
with her eyes burning
a soft trail of fire.

He says,
"Let me be a soft cocoon
for you." He takes
her spinning through
soft blue light. He would
like to know the mystery.

During the silent prayer
she envisions his face —
blue pearl eyes,
the wide arc of his mouth,
his compassionate
face.

3.
She holds the sheets to her skin
wraps herself inside them
so she can breathe his molecules again.

An echo of burgundy satin
in the shape of the
ballgown she wore,

a single violet
fooled by November's warmth
into blooming,

the room where they danced
now empty except for
the echo of a flute.

4.
The location is nowhere,
something exotic, foreign
something more musical than linguistic.

His hands emerge
from inside a sculpture of lovers
he carved centuries ago,
beauty without a filter.

Halfway around the world
the sky is clear night after night,
Pegasus and the Pleiades
floating above
a long arc of milky stars.

The sky is open, transparent
except for the evening
of the Leonid Meteor showers
and his voice
outside her window.

At four o'clock in the morning,
he is singing, "Wake up! Shine!
Come with me and see
the stars flying across the sky!
Sing to me! Don't be afraid."

5.
She dreams she is a hummingbird
and she needs to fly
in the morning.

Her voice sings inside the sculpture
of the Temple at Varanasi,
beauty without a filter.

When she dances,
she discovers something about herself,
silver bells
wrapped around her ankles,
and the music comes from everywhere.

In another world
the contralto singing of a tamboura
and hands that teach her more deeply
who she is and where
she is located
on the Earth meridian.

Every time he speaks
a hummingbird
flies out of his mouth

And you have to
walk through fire
to go anywhere in her house.

PARACHUTE

I am crawling through a parachute. It's a tunnel of gauze or silk
or ripstop, with Persephone pushing my knees. I am blindfolded
with a green silk scarf. Or maybe it's purple. Isadora's dancers or
dragonflies push my body into distortions. I am wild inside gauze.
Spinning inside air. Crawling in the dark toward a flicker of light.
It's a mystery covered by a cocoon while meteor showers explode
over my shoulders.

There aren't any instructions, and I'm surrounded by ripstop.
I'm free falling from the air with prayer flags drifting around my
ankles. Floating in the dark. Yellow and black stripes of light and
shadow drift across my feet. Banded bees are trying to tell me
stories, but all I hear is a buzzing in my ears. I am rolling down
a long green hill a long time ago. I am picking a wild bouquet of
poppies for my second grade teacher.

I am walking the high beams of new houses abandoned by
carpenters of the late afternoon. The last farm stopped giving
pumpkins last October, but this is a good place to collect discarded
nails with my eight-year-old friends. The beams are an open
theatre, and the shadows tell us stories. We have borrowed our
mothers' scarves, and we are teaching the bees how to dance.

My lover and I are dancing barefoot after midnight. We are
both covered with oil inside a steam of jasmine flowers. I skate
counterclockwise over his body before the second hand stops. We
might be in Kyoto or Tel Aviv, but the walls are now a blur. My
heart is shaking, or maybe it is the walls.

The tunnel is streaming with gauze as I crawl in the semi-dark.
The bees are humming softly on the other side of the parachute.
The tone is silk or translucent, and floating. It's a new kind of
music that I refused to listen to before. The bees say the erotic is
in the shadows, and nobody can love without the wound. They tell
me we all need to be pierced to know the mystery.

I am dancing inside a parachute, and suddenly I don't know how to fall. I am high above a ferris wheel of strangers, a thousand paper cranes after the bomb explodes at Hiroshima. The sake, still warm from the heat of your hands, is spilling across the table while you paint on my back with ink-covered fingers.

There is someone whose collarbone I see in my dreams. He sings to me in bass or tenor overtones in a familiar language. I can almost hear him breathing while poppies grow through the cracks in the slate path. I meet him in the tunnels between the pyramids.

PHOTOGRAPH FROM OKINAWA

In the photograph
she is coming down the stairs
from the bath house where she lives.
You are the nineteen-year-old Marine
from North Carolina
whose words flow into her ears
like an exotic song
from the other side of a mystery.

You are tall, handsome
and the wide muscles of your arms
push into the seams of your shirt
before you scatter your uniform
on her tatami floor.

She is lost in the cornflower blue
of your eyes as you rock
her narrow bed
and fill the halls of the bath house
with cat sounds.

And in the geisha curves
of her perfect island body
you are trying to forget the daylight
of the military base
where you don't have a voice.

When you ask her to smile
for the photograph
you don't notice the way
her eyes are glazing over the pain
she feels every time she remembers
the soldier who went to Viet Nam
and exploded one afternoon
in the middle of the jungle
in a cloud of orange fire.

And you are unaware
that moments before you leave this island
for the last time
she will try to fold herself
in your suitcase.

A week later
two of your friends will tell you
that they found her at midnight
running naked down the street.

When they bring her back
to the bath house
she will dream she is eight years old
trying to dig a tunnel to North Carolina
with a silver spoon.

She has no idea
that twenty years later
after your round-eye wife
breaks all of your dishes
and walks out of your house
for the last time,
after your next girlfriend
is dragged out of her apartment in Manhattan,
tied up, and thrown into a suitcase,
after five pilgrimage journeys
to holy places in the Himalayas
at altitudes beyond where
the people you've left behind can breathe,
and the other woman you have finally come to love
walks out of your house for the last time
and won't even answer your phone calls,
you will find her photograph.

She doesn't know
that you worship her now
inside a golden frame
beside your paintings of bodhisattvas
and holy stones from the Ganges River.

She has no idea
how much you loved her,
and you didn't either
at the time.

REQUIEM

For Edie

The door opens on Tuesday.
On Friday she walks away from the world.
I saw them at the Symphony,
Brahms and one hundred voices around them.
He was wearing a black suit with a top hat,
she in a long silk evening gown,
his arm softly around her shoulder.
They waved at me from a high window
and then they walked into the stars.

Nobody else could see them
but they waved at me
from a high box in the air.
In the fortissimo,
low pedal tones of the organ
vibrated the ceiling and the walls,
and in the quiet moments
one hundred voices hummed
the chord of the earth
as it turned.

In another world,
she is skating on a river
in the rose pink of sunset or dawn.
A fox fur hat around her face
keeps her warm, sheltering her
as a cottonwood tree from thunder.
These memories comfort as a soft pillow,
green and cool, a meadow
glowing with wild irises and daffodils,
the path through the forest where you walked,
where the leaves of your life
glow like rhapsodies at your feet.

Entering the Word Temple

1. Bird Face

A lacework of yellow oak leaves
in front of the porch of a woman
who paints visions on the walls.

Her colors are from a different place.

The man in her vision has wings
flying over the city of music
with the face of an Egyptian
mythological bird.

The city has a sand bridge
over a blue river.

If she paints him,
he will find her.

2. Amethyst Birds

He broke four of her windows
before he painted her house.

Around her windows
he painted amethyst birds
flying to South America.

He hid photographs under her pillow
while the house became
lantern green and violet.

Autumn was unseasonably warm.
The wind came from South America,
made his body strong with desire
and conflicted longing.

Hundreds of ladybugs flew
through the cracked windows.
She counted the spots on their wings.

Everything in her house
is covered by a thin layer of dust,
even the glass hummingbird
in her dreams.

3. Bear Song

As the season changes,
the edges of the leaves
are on fire.

The Earth is getting colder,
entering the empty space.

In a loft apartment
a cello
a single note
of a Bach partita
the cadence of an Italian
song.

Each day
I find the single note
that vibrates.

4. Snow Dream

The snow comes out of season
swirling around a wrought-iron street lamp
twenty years ago.

I wake up from a dream
of pelicans and flamingos.
My skin is full of flamingos.

The women are covered with scars,
each one a city,
a citadel, an island.

My skin is rose pink.

I am running barefoot
on a beach of round stones.

I am in the air —
a butterfly, a meadowlark
an open window.

5. EARLY PLAYFORD

Before he replaced the glass,
he sanded the edges of my windows.
The sand came from South America.

On a silver music stand
the *Bach Suites for Cello Solo*,
Early Playford
speaking to my hands.

I find sand in unexpected places.
Inside a vase of swirled blue glass.
Falling out of sand dollars.
Inside hiking socks with a memory
of the Pacific Ocean.

We walk over a wood bridge
after midnight. In the sky
Orion, the Pleiades, Cassiopeia.

Orion shoots his arrow
with sand falling out of his belt.

6. CHRYSANTHEMUMS

The cold is delayed.
In November, pink chrysanthemums
still blooming.

There are extra days for painting.

My house is layered with new colors —
lavender, purple and lantern green,
what I see inside
the color of music.

Beyond the open window
the edges of the leaves,
a river of earth and sky
spinning like Sufi women
surrounded by morning glories
and galaxies.

7. CELLO LESSON

In the middle of the forest
I am wearing a black velvet gown.

Muddy print of leaves
on a hidden path,
an amethyst, an echo, a memory.

Inside a grove of pine trees
he plays the cello,
gives his music to the trees.
The song he plays
is for me.

The kiss surprises me.

Music from the pyramids.
Secrets burned
inside the Alexandrian Fire.

Red squirrel
walking on thin branches
through an open window.

PARADOX

To Edith

For an eternity
I pined for freedom.
The threads that bound me
Were chains of iron.

I broke the chains
And reveled in freedom.
Freedom was life;
I was reborn.

Then I found you.
The sparkle in your eyes
was my beacon
Guiding me to love.

You gave me your love
And I was again a man.
I am now free but bound
By threads of moonbeams.

A Prostitute in Paris

Twenty-one and a lover,
surviving on Supermarché yogurt
and hard cheese crepes —
it's Paris that sustains me.

Having walked all day
with a brown portfolio,
flagging my model life
of scattered jobs and smiling rejections,
I inhale spring's last flirtations.

Up from the broad boulevards,
full of light and life,
pavement narrows to a dry stream
of hard cobblestones.
Doors, walls and windows press
the late afternoon close
under a low ceiling of sunless sky.

Napping Rue St. Denis is not ready
for the after-work rush.
Women and girls chat
like factory workers, between shifts,
unmindful of time cards
and conveyer belts.
A few stake territory alone,
puffing the air spicy with Gitanes.
Their casual glances ignore me,
as usual — and I ignore them.

She approaches, knowing,
in a plaid skirt, white blouse
and maroon sweater,
fresh from university.

Open lashed hazel
speckled with misfortune,
under Jane Birkin bangs —
invites me, silently.
I hesitate, Adam's apple choked
while swan-soft fingers stroke
my naked forearm — lightly
with the grace of Mary's roses
with red so red it's blue.
Penniless, I stare into translucence
to fathom what she wants,
for I am as pretty as she is.

If her sylph hand slid down
into a pocket, would it be for my wallet?

She coos in French with clean, full lips
but I only grunt, "Non, merci,"
off towards Boulevard Bonne Nouvelle.

It's been thirty-five years
and the hairs on my arm
still shiver . . .

SHOES

Our Lady of the Assumption —
I always hated the color of the massive naked walls
a sickly pink
that none of nature's roses ever wished to reveal.

He packs the pews with an alarming number
of friends mourning his many incarnations:

Scout / Teacher
Athlete / Coach
Lost Boy / Lobbyist
Recovery Man
Father / Provider
Straight Arrow
All-American.

I don't remember the church even being this full
at the midnight mass when I embarrassed him
on my seventeenth Christmas Eve —
a mod misfit
outfitted from Magnin's
on one of my clandestine forays into "The City"
gray paisley shirt of too shear voile
matching gangster-striped bell bottoms
with elephant legs
sporting a zipper
zipped to the conclusion of a two inch fly.

I was forty-three when my father taught me to tie my shoes.

After all those wasted years
of misconstructed knots
shooting floundering strands
a simple double-knotted lesson
now enlaced us and kept us tight.

Always a mama's boy
my allegiance began to shift as we rode red bicycles.
You on your own — me on my mother's
worn from disuse
up and down a plein air trail
concrete that ribboned along the American River
rich with the dry smells
of eucalyptus, thistles and sunshine.
Like the invisible currents of the river itself
(not muddy like my Midwestern neighbors)
but California clear to the stony bottom
our autumnal friendship washed away years
of raised voices and blunt denials.

From the time of the news clipping
hailing my birth as the new-promised lineman,
I embraced secrecy and distance
so as not to disappoint the Rose Bowl veteran
with my pansy-bright perspective.
The eldest of seven
invisible as a middle child.

Now surrounded by the stations of the cross
elected to eulogize this mighty and responsible striver —
abandoned by his mother, Ruby O'Day, at the age of two
to become a moral compass
keeping his older brother with the rakish smile
and the rest of the team on track
— I am not allowed to say what is in my heart.

Sitting now in the front row
having changed my peacock blue tie —
a celebration of Dad's listening eyes
— to an almost nonexistent gray on gray pattern
handpicked by my insistent, embarrassed mother,
I hold it all together

bound, double knotted, and woven tightly through the holes
until I see the video's image of you,
projected big-screen under the canopy of a wooden Christ
a man so much younger than I am now
barefoot and smiling, spaces between your teeth
holding your barefoot baby — me
with such tenderness.

Nine Haikus Touching The Moon

I
From behind a cloud
a Shiva moon reigns over
this lonely planet.

II
Love breaks down the door
flooding in the autumn moon
a harvest of hearts.

III
Icy branches chime
for moonlight skis on blue snow
while our breath entwines.

IV
Luna Park in Rome
tossing a white ping pong ball
I win a goldfish.

V
As petals rain pink
the moon fingers them gently
slowing their descent.

VI
The man in the moon
croons his silver sonata
breaking lonely hearts.

VII
Glass of *Sambucca*
held high in the piazza
brimming with the moon.

VIII
Moonstruck I stagger
barefoot over fresh cut grass
humored by fireflies.

IX
Above summer surf
a rented moon drifts wishing
to stay forever.

Thanatos Wears Shalimar

Overdressed for muggy 90 degree heat
in black silk pajamas,
a garland of dried roses and lilies
coiling round his head,
rhinestones on his ruby red tennis shoes,
Thanatos leans into a lazy day.

He bypasses the athletic club
where he could initiate
a stroke or cardiac arrest,
but it's too hot to leap and spin
in a leotard clinging to his bony frame.

Skulking in shadows,
reeking of Shalimar and sweat,
he stalks easier prey
in the dementia unit
of my mother's nursing home.

In the dining room, weary heads bobble,
dishes clatter, someone cries, *Mama*.
Hesitating at my mother's side
to gape as she devours a kosher frank,
Thanatos shouts into her better ear,
Not yet.

He glides to another table,
embracing Sophia,
who smiles, dreaming of her garden
awash in lavender asters,
anemones and snapdragons.
Sophia exhales for the last time
just before taking her noon medication.

Tapping Barnie, still in his bathrobe,
Thanatos whispers,
Don't bother to dress. You're next.

His computer implant reminds him
he has two more cold calls to make.
But weary and dying for a smoke,
He scuttles out into the heat.

HEADING HOME

On assignment in Nashville, Tennessee,
my second husband becomes a born-again Willie Nelson
without benefit of voice or guitar.
A thousand miles from me, he whispers endearments and
dances the Texas Two-Step with a honey-haired, Knoxville sweetie
whose beguiling, country ways have spun him
like a top into her orbit.

Back home in Boston, on a chill, Sunday morning,
he murmurs in our marriage bed,
"It's been great, but it's over."
Later, futile bargaining and hope dismissed,
he disappears into the ebony night, fueled by a quart of Jim Beam.
His 10-gallon hat, western-style jeans and rattlesnake skin boots
are jammed into a Samsonite carry-all — a birthday gift from me.
He scuttles away, leaving a vapor of alcohol
and words that haunt me trailing in his wake,
"It's time for me to soar and live on the edge."
I learn he found these words, now etched
into my heart with cut glass,
in his American Airlines magazine horoscope.

If you look into the midnight sky, is he soaring still?
Can you see him circling the silver-stained moon?
Or like a shooting star, is he falling to the cold, unyielding ground?
Perhaps, like Icarus, his wings seared by the sun,
he has plummeted, smouldering, to earth,
gouging out a scorched crater where the
Grand Ole Opry once stood.

Week after week, I restore my soul in the therapist's office,
as tangerine leaves slip from the grasp
of the brittle branches, stripping them bare.
A winter white mantle drapes their thin shoulders
until April soil erupts in lemon daffodils
as the fissure in my heart narrows and heals.

In October, as the green leaves
slip again into costumes of red, gold, and tangerine,
I load luggage, maps and CDs into my trusty, rusty Toyota,
pull away from the curb and turn west.

SHIFTING GEARS

Fog, a goose-down quilt
blanketing Highway 1,
wraps around my windshield.
Cars without lights, ghost-riders,
whiz past, beg to be statistics.

Unable to see three feet ahead,
my thoughts leap in non-sequiturs.
Where are my Billy Collins tickets —
languishing in an unpacked box?

Buy cat food, pick up allergy meds,
replace dead watch battery, mourn
lost loves and decades evaporating
before memories can be stored,
not time enough to notice or lament.

Down-shifting into 3rd gear
at the crest of a steep hill
winding along the shrouded Pacific,
I brake to slow my descent.

Damp mist sets the tempo
at adagio, inviting me to
quiet my restless mind.
Breathing deeply, I acquiesce.

THE STONE WILL SPEAK

As the high Maya priestess of Chi Chen Itzá
I rule the temple, and I am dying.
Before I leave, I have carved a stela
of all my mistakes, to be placed
on the east wall of the Nunnery.
It is hell revealed, my life.

This is the only way to escape the priests,
my tribe and the indifference of heaven
that has tethered minds
to the tradition of human sacrifice.

My story is bordered in the skulls
of the warriors that gave their
lives for the poets.
When my bones have burned
and I enter the chrysalis of heaven,
my errors will be placed in plain view.

What I have hidden
will be revealed
in stone that faces the sunrise.

What I have endured,
will be remembered
in stone that shadows with sunset.

All will know why at the end,
I stood alone with the quetzal
to be burned.

Mexico City

The serpents inside the glass slither
on the information about information
eating itself. Quetzalcoatl, plumed serpent god,
is here and whips his smog feathers against
the window panes. All anyone sees and hears
is transportation transcendence.

Art will be about the fucking of information.
It will look like skeletal fumes choking
the best of the Polanco Princesses, blue
in their penthouses. It will rebel against
nuance. Everything will be a clear
revenge of the European invasion.

Skyless search engines will hunt for souls.
I am the stone grasshopper kept alive,
but frozen in time in Chapultepec Park,
my long black tongue, a computer
chewing the lessons of history against traffic, asking,
México, what remains of your belly of mercy?

VIA SACRA

How do we know the stars
within us are not dark
wings from a dead moon,
ravens on white
catching ghosts that give a damn?

Stardust specks that hide
inside our casings,
blood rivers we carry
where wind cannot touch
the goodness and darkness
measured by our angels,

zig zags of thunder
never spoken out loud.

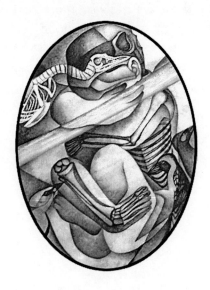

MY UNRULY BREASTS

There is no place to go in the sweat spilling heat
to take off my bra, well of course, yes there is,
but the thought of my breasts unleashed
in the heat bouncing down the street
without me, makes me truthfully nervous,
so all day I have contained them and my breasts
are at the breaking point, I must get them home soon,
they are starting to rebel, don't look at them please,
alright, go ahead, but I'm warning you they're hungry,
tired and pretty cranky, in fact one just escaped
and is bouncing down Shattuck Avenue, now the other one
is chasing after it, oh no — both of them are jaywalking as I run
trying to catch them, (the running is much easier now)
oh jesus, my breasts have entered Safeway
and are careening toward the melon section,
one turns around and sticks its nipple
out at me while the other topples cantaloupes
and honeydews into the aisles and a spontaneous
soccer game erupts, the manager comes along
and bellows, "Whose breasts are these?!" I just stand
there like the next flat-chested customer and shrug.

ON AWAKING: GRATITUDE

The grey dawn slowly brightened
with strands of sun
breaking through blinds
streaming across the bed, onto
the still cold from night floor.

Life felt distant, like
having hibernated through
a long, dark winter
deep in the snow of slumber
longing to laugh.

And black was soothing,
a loving blanket that
wrapped warm the soul,
getting past months of bed rest
and wanting to run.

The light demands action,
days dreaming blossom
and a harvest of love —
the health of body,
mind, spirit and soul.

Of course there is suffering.
Experience is a journey for
the witness to embrace, yet
that for which we are grateful
far outweighs the challenge.

MONDAY MORNING

On Monday morning my brother preaches Isaiah.
His voice goes on, through the phone,
about the Bible.
Not like the droning of big black flies in summer
but a clarinet playing a tune
I can't quite follow.
From my kitchen table I'm distracted
by a redheaded woodpecker
working on a stump out beyond the drive.

My brother's strength comes through God.
Mine too but I don't wear the button, raise the banner.
He's working hard on that stump,
probably looking to save my soul.
I wonder if there will be babies.

I ask, 'what if a person doesn't know how to read,
can he get the Jesus message any other way?'
Black, some white and that bright red head, beautiful.
I don't hear the answer,
I'm distracted by my baby's coo.
She's not hungry, just baby talk.
I'm smiling.
He says the end of the world is coming.
I find that believable most days,
but today is as clear and bright
as the ting from pure crystal
I believe we will be granted another day.

CLIFFS

I dreamt we climbed the cliffs of Atlantis.

There was nowhere to go
but through ruins. We heard tones
a chord you said,
warning of lightning, swift sorrow, a future
we could not change.

Below the cliff, we followed the music
of a cove at high-tide.
A light rose inside my body,
spreading gently, becoming wings.

We wanted to fly
through wind and wave,
We wanted to go to that place
only our bodies knew.
wild horses, oceans rushing.

So we danced into a crystal haze
while white leaves
castaneted like falling stars,
measured the feeling in waves.

We flew toward a secret sky
Leaves, moon, wind.
Music falling each moment
a whole sky in rhapsody,
hair spilling into Cassiopeia, starlight in our mouths
as we took a step without feet.

BY MORNING

My mouth was a flower
you kissed and peeled,
sweet white skin of the moon.

You said the act reminded you of your childhood.

Outside our window
white oleanders stir in the wind
and the vast wide night
filling with lightning,
crashes.

You said we'd
reach inside our dreams
catch starfish
perform miracles,
because inside us,
walls, washed by moonlight
were shattering.

The sea says yes and then no,
water meadows now rich with fish
empty out with the tide.
By morning,
even the trees are gone.

Speaking to Stars

1.

Silver light dances
then falls,
over the world.

Spreading inside my body like wings.
silent as snow
pure, pale, clear, a lake dreaming of herself.

It is the light we all want.
made of glass and lightning
singing below sea waves, opening to voices of angels.

Sometimes, the moon spills open
leaving milk on my skin.

2.

Let me touch your silence
cold star,
far away and remote.

Let me tell you
how I have longed for you
when I lost my beloved.

I lifted my face to your light
again and again
under endless skies.

Until an ocean breeze came
and I woke up in your arms.

3.

I read the mysteries of stars
milk light voices
I listen to their transparent wounds.
I have waited to tell you by a twilight sea,
waning moon.

On a shore of white crystal
I am holding a lapiz ball
as apple leaves fall at my feet

Red leaves fall
from a deep velvet sky,
spelling their sacred truth.

I trace Venus
Orion, Ursula minor
paint my wrists with light
and walk through a crystal door
stardust on my shoulders.

You are lying face up
to Pegasus
wondering why I prefer
wings and stars.
Comets dancing through night's fire
life unveiling her holy face.

THE CLEAR GLASS PRISM

I. The aftermath of gray

The hurricane rips through your heart,
toppling telephone poles.
Satellite signals explode, all communication ceases.
In the basement, floods rise,
white caps foam over books, first editions and last.
The junky romance novels
that led to the junky romances, floating
through days of no light and warm beers,
waiting for the return of electricity.

II. Yellow, shrieking

This is the moment of yellow, when you yield;
your face covered with gold dust, eyes jaundiced.
You give in to the other guy, always kicking and screaming,
light him down the path to desire.
Wait, go slow, abide the cautionary tale.
Does desire become you?
Try on the lemon custard sweater again and again.
You are blinking on and off. People can see you swaying.
They dare not touch you as you might explode.

III. The white dream

Against black, the stars grow dizzy, sigh,
breathe again. Hold your diamond to the sky,
which is more brilliant? Walk to the rhythm of the song.
What are you wearing? Baby bikini lace underwear,
the petticoat of an eight-year-old,
a teenagers first bra. Who touches you,
what covers you? What will be uncovered?
Will your dreams remain a comets trail,
reappearing year after year?

IV. Green becomes you

You never actually made love among sharp
blades of grass, only sat among four leaf clovers,
a two-year-old waddling a breath away.
Your skin tingles as you realize
there is nothing more to wish for.
The grass carpet embraces your body,
it will be years before you understand
which rituals can save you.
When memory switches to the shag carpet
beneath a mad affair, you pretend not to care.
Time no longer proceeds in any logical order.

V. Red

Scarlet period stops sex. Measles stop
schoolchildren. Lips stop. Lollipops stop tantrums.
Blood stops desire. Treadmills stop heart.
Heart stops desire. Brake lights stop.
Cherry trees stop lies. Fire engines stop infernos.
Red. Stops. Everything.

VI. The smell of purple

On June twenty-ninth, the fields in France
become violent with lavender.
Royalty has always had the smell of old musty velvet,
no matter how many jewels in the crown.
Don't we all imagine a coffin
with the scent of overripe grapes,
the smell just before they
collapse from the vine, one by one?

PROTOCOL

Dining Room

Grandmother's house, the fiancé introduction.
Plate after plate of manicotti appears on Italian lace tablecloth.
He eats all, greedily.
Aproned body as thick as her hair is thin, she is beaming.
She approves of this man I am about to marry.
"You like manicotti. That is good. Now we
bring out the main course."
My fiancé, heavy in the crinoline chair,
realizes no escape. Only I notice
his face matches the chartreuse wallpaper.
"You will give me lots of great-grandchildren, yes?"

Bathroom

The way the double blue line suddenly appears on the
beige plastic stick entrances me. My body already
told me the truth, but I desire scientific verification.
I count. Could it have really happened on our honeymoon?
Or, the illusion of a honeymoon,
not to Bali or Barcelona or Belize,
but a nearby motel room, glow of neon between blinds.

Bedroom

Sprawled across my barely-made queen sized bed,
sizing up the newborn on my stomach.
How could she have ever fit inside me?
Casual discussion with husband in progress.
I will pretend it's okay when he arrives home at 4 am.
He will take me to Rio, to Carnivale.
We both eye the infant breathing in unison with my stomach.
Which of us sees her
as an excuse for not going anywhere?

Kitchen

The used-to-be white wall phone,
my newest annoyance. I can barely reach
the stove to stir the marinara sauce while I talk.
When will I go cordless?
Put down the spoon, start peppering,
I stretch to talk to my daughter.
The connection is alive with static.
She is calling from Ghana, her voice wild as she describes
the country chosen for junior year abroad. Twenty years,
and I still do not know
where she came from nor where she is going.
She laughs the laugh I wish was mine.
"I'm trying to figure out the proper protocol"
I turn the stove dial to simmer as I reply.
"for wishing someone
you are no longer married to a happy anniversary."

Learner's Permit

Now, on Moody Street,
"Mom, I don't know what to do."

The passenger seat is out of whack.
We are driving — no, we are not driving.
Alanna is driving.
Sixteen, DMV approved. Needs instruction.

Drive. Just drive, I want to tell her. Drive
until the ghosts stop chasing you,
until butterflies fly to the moon.
Turn the steering wheel until you feel
the heat of your heart in your fingertips,
ready to touch a lovers body so he levitates.
Stop only for pedestrians in crosswalks,
for they will fill you with stories as you sip
teardrops mixed with warm milk.
When it is safe to go, press on the accelerator
and drive, drive until your songs swallow the road,
until your hair grows wild with desire,
until you don't notice the signs
that tell you tomorrow is now today.
Drive until you see the tip of a mermaid's tailfin
in your rearview mirror, taste salt from every ocean.
Follow the road as it arcs around palisades
and ice palaces, drive until your veneer turns to dust,
fluttering on the wind like ashes from an urn.

Alanna is not ready yet.
We will keep practicing.

LAST KISS

Hoity-toity lamps in the storefront window.
A cacophony of light splays outward. You are kissing me.
Back arched, cold glass against my skin,
sleeveless dress. You are kissing me good-bye.
Six month old love, new lover. You are kissing me
as you are leaving me. The light from a dozen lamps
seeps into my skin. Your kiss turns my body to wax,
I cover you, scorch you, envelop you.
You kiss me back with the nonchalance of a
whistling sailor. I let go, fumble a good-bye.
The lamps in the window flicker their approval.

EACH MOMENT A WHITE BULL STEPS SHINING INTO THE WORLD

If the gods bring to you
a strange and frightening creature,
accept the gift
as if it were one you had chosen.

Say the accustomed prayers,
oil the hooves well,
caress the small ears with praise.

Have the new halter of woven silver
embedded with jewels.
Spare no expense, pay what is asked,
when a gift arrives from the sea.

Treat it as you yourself
would be treated,
brought speechless and naked
into the court of a king.

And when the request finally comes,
do not hesitate even an instant—

Stroke the white throat,
the heavy, trembling dewlaps
you've come to believe were yours,
and plunge in the knife.

Not once
did you enter the pasture
without pause,
without yourself trembling.
That you came to love it, that was the gift.

Let the envious gods take back what they can.

HOPE AND LOVE

All winter
the blue heron
slept among the horses.
I do not know
the custom of herons,
do not know
if the solitary habit
is their way,
or if he listened for
some missing one--
not knowing even
that was what he did--
in the blowing
sounds in the dark.
I know that
hope is the hardest
love we carry.
He slept
with his long neck
folded, like a letter
put away.

LATE PRAYER

Tenderness does not choose its own uses.
It goes out to everything equally,
circling rabbit and hawk.
Look: in the iron bucket,
a single nail, a single ruby —
all the heavens and hells.
They rattle in the heart and make one sound.

THE ENVOY

One day in that room, a small rat.
Two days later, a snake.

Who, seeing me enter,
whipped the long stripe of his
body under the bed,
then curled like a docile house-pet.

I don't know how either came or left.
Later, the flashlight found nothing.

For a year I watched
as something — terror? happiness? grief? —
entered and then left my body.

Not knowing how it came in,
Not knowing how it went out.

It hung where words could not reach it.
It slept where light could not go.
Its scent was neither snake nor rat,
neither sensualist nor ascetic.

There are openings in our lives
of which we know nothing.

Through them
the belled herds travel at will,
long-legged and thirsty, covered with foreign dust.

IN PRAISE OF COLDNESS

"If you wish to move your reader,"
Chekhov wrote, "you must write more coldly."

Herakleitos recommended, "A dry soul is best."

And so at the center of many great works
is found a preserving dispassion,
like the vanishing point of quattrocento perspective,
or the tiny packets of desiccant enclosed
in a box of new shoes or seeds.

But still the vanishing point
is not the painting,
the silica is not the blossoming plant.

Chekhov, dying, read the timetables of trains.
To what more earthly thing could he have been faithful? —
Scent of rocking distances,
smoke of blue trees out the window,
hampers of bread, pickled cabbage, boiled meat.

Scent of the knowable journey.

Neither a person entirely broken
nor one entirely whole can speak.

In sorrow, pretend to be fearless. In happiness, tremble.

TREE

It is foolish
to let a young redwood
grow next to a house.

Even in this
one lifetime,
you will have to choose.

That great calm being,
this clutter of soup pots and books —

Already the first branch-tips brush at the window.
Softly, calmly, immensity taps at your life.

REBUS

You work with what you are given,
the red clay of grief,
the black clay of stubbornness going on after.
Clay that tastes of care or carelessness,
clay that smells of the bottoms of rivers or dust.

Each thought is a life you have lived or failed to live,
each word is a dish you have eaten or left on the table.
There are honeys so bitter
no one would willingly choose to take them.
The clay takes them: honey of weariness, honey of vanity,
honey of cruelty, fear.

This rebus—slip and stubbornness,
bottom of river, my own consumed life —
when will I learn to read it
plainly, slowly, uncolored by hope or desire?
Not to understand it, only to see.

As water given sugar sweetens, given salt grows salty,
we become our choices.
Each *yes*, each *no* continues,
this one a ladder, that one an anvil or cup.

The ladder leans into its darkness.
The anvil leans into its silence.
The cup sits empty.

How can I enter this question the clay has asked?

THE POET

She is working now, in a room
not unlike this one,
the one where I write, or you read.
Her table is covered with paper.
The light of the lamp would be
tempered by a shade, where the bulb's
single harshness might dissolve,
but it is not, she has taken it off.
Her poems? I will never know them,
though they are the ones I most need.
Even the alphabet she writes in
I cannot decipher. Her chair —
Let us imagine whether it is leather
or canvas, vinyl or wicker. Let her
have a chair, her shadeless lamp,
the table. Let one or two she loves
be in the next room. Let the door
be closed, the sleeping ones healthy.
Let her have time, and silence,
enough paper to make mistakes and go on.

SHIKATA GA NAI

Shikata ga nai
means
It can't be helped

which translates
scour and scrub
till the smell of horse urine
is a faint memory,
cobble a table out of
scavenged fruit crates,
create a home from the stall
that is temporary shelter for
your family of six.

Pretend you don't see barbed wire
or soldiers with rifles in guard towers
when you gaze at Heart Mountain on the horizon.

Shikata ga nai --
a tacit agreement
to adopt the government jargon:
        relocation and internment,
        not concentration or prison camp,

to be as American as possible,
having to prove your loyalty
even though you were born here.

And when your daughter hungers to know
about your life in camp,
you giggle about the "hi-jinks girls"
and being prom queen,
a typical teenage life.

It suggests
your secret, mounting dread
each year as December 7th approaches,
even now, over sixty years later.

Shikata ga nai means
> End of discussion.
> I don't want to talk about it.
> There's nothing more to say.

A FEW SEEDS

Some instinct told me
I'd need those tiny packets of seeds
smuggled in my pockets —
cucumber, zinnia,
pea and chrysanthemum —
even more than I'd need a coat
to shield me from the stinging cold
of a desert winter.

A few seeds sown into
improbable soil, watered using
tin cans from the mess hall garbage,
till tender shoots peeked
above ground
reaching
for the meager
warmth
of April.

Now, rambunctious morning glory vines
tangle with cucumber,
climb tarpaper walls
to disguise this bleak barrack.
Snowy mums and golden zinnias
waken and nod their noble heads.

I stroll in the shadow
of a guard tower
as heat softens to dusk.
In block after block
green patches of wonder
are sprouting,
cultivated by those, like me,
who thrust into coat pockets
tiny packets of hope.

Look Alike

Once, in a darkened theater you stared
as Shirley Temple danced on the screen —
those chubby cheeks and beaming eyes
that made everyone smile.
"You look just like her!"
all the adults told you.
So you practiced your curtsy,
pointing to the dimple on your cheek,
flashed that smile that said you'd be a star.

With your jet hair, your slanting eyes,
you could never be the next Shirley Temple.
When did you discover
that what people told you was a lie?

FOREWARNED

At fifteen, I might have ignored the boy
from the Arab quarter who sold fresh figs,
tear-shapes in soft gold skin, small enough

to fit a young girl's palm. I might have
heeded my mother's warning
how Eve, eyes open to her nakedness,

wore an apron of fig leaves. But
the close of summer sent me back
to eat from the boy's hand,

sink teeth into sweet, pink pulp, seeds
blushed red. At dusk, outside the garden gate,
our mouths flowered, reclaimed grace.

AFTER WE CAUGHT THE BLACK BASS IN ROUND LAKE

I kept one of the scales,
small enough to balance
on the tip of my finger,
translucent, a serrated half-moon light,
the annuli too finely etched
for me to count the fish's age.

Yes, it's the age of things
that sobers me. Leached dreams
flopping against an unwise end,
the hooked throat widened
as if to peel back sounds.

Listen. The mouth of the bass
extends beyond
the rear edge of her eye,
but she never spoke and now
not even a dip in the water
reminds us she once lived.

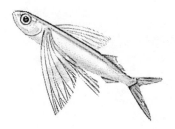

DISQUIET

> And twofold always – May God us keep
> From Single Vision & Newton's sleep. —William Blake

Sixteen, and already
every voice inside me
had its opposite, its dissenter,
a yes, but for every therefore,

the counter responses
canceling each other out
in the adolescent urge
not to look stupid,

a silence in the classroom
even the teacher who knew
my great love of Blake
tried to warn me about.

Years later at an all night party
I didn't say a single word
and a woman said about me,
still waters run deep.

I thought her a fool
and loved her admiration,
I, whose opposites inside
had by then birthed others.

No doubt too much division
can turn malignant and spread,
and it's pointless to appeal
for what can't be prevented,

except that it gives me
something like hope
if I pray a thing
can become more alive
each time it splits again in two.

NOBODY KNOWS THEY'RE HERE

In 1995, doctors reported that it is possible many people are
actually twins walking around in a single body, a phenomenon they
remain oblivious to all their lives.

No wonder, this disaffection with anyone
different from ourselves.
Imagine the beginning:
two mirror images in the womb,
every need met without effort
and the rest of the world
elsewhere in the muffled beyond,

an existence so complete,
who among us wouldn't panic,
conceal the twin inside our body,
be born secretly doubled and doubtful
of the possibilities of other-love?

Not that we don't keep trying.
This man and I, for instance,
two bodies in bed, trying to make up
for two absences, so even at its best
sex is a detour around what both of us
have forgotten has disappeared.

Outside our window
a screech owl arrives feet first
on the back of a rabbit. Small beings
disappear like that a dozen times a day.
Survival of the fittest, we agree,
just before the discontent
begins again, before what's missing
intrudes and I start to catalogue
what I don't like about his odors
and good humor, the way
even our happiness can feel wrong.

WHEN THE OTHER TEACHER IS A GOAT

Here, after betrayal
in the Blue City of Jodhpur,
one teacher is a woman,
the other a goat.
The woman opens a gate,
offers me apricots, melons, a peach.
The goat's a ruminant wandering the alleys,
his beard-wisp waggling as he chews.
On the wall behind them
is a message in Hindi.
All the letters hang from the upper line
like nooses or chimes.

Hurt's the worst time to choose
between comfort and wisdom.
The satisfying sureness of being
the one so clearly wronged
solicits fresh fruit, a respite,
sympathy the color of the sun.

But India's ashes and endless chants,
its tedium of rebirth, remind me
I've done it that way before,
allowed my feet to be rubbed,
my fresh fruit peeled.
I've even hoped the betrayer
was peering in the window,
watching others offer solace.

She smiles, her sari swaying from her hips;
he gobbles laundry and tin cups
and reminds me of the Buddhist story:
when the last demon wouldn't leave,
the master declared it his teacher
and put his head in its mouth.

TEMPLE PRIESTESS WITH A GIFT

She only appears when hurt
has made you human again,
though you mustn't think
what she extends is consolation
or forgiveness.

Remember Alice? One bite
makes you small.

She's pointing out a door
you can't go through
without more offerings of your own.

She'll take your clothes, your calendar,
whatever will leave you
embarrassed and adrift.

You may not know for months
she's attached a threshold
to your shoes,

just that footsteps echo
in a chamber without a floor.

Blame means nothing here,
nor does the wish to be elsewhere.
She's set an alarm clock
you can't shut off without
a failure of your own.

Surety

Wanting a man she's not sure she wants,
a woman climbs up a cliff
and into a cave which hands her
oils: coal-black, cinder-gray, sepia.
Think of it this way, it tells her,
these brushstrokes up his thigh.
It insists she paint and she does,
making the cave's outline
visible under the mountain,
its edges fluted with dripping water.
It wants to see itself
like a mouth turned inside out.
Put the mountain inside me, it says
and she practices with her pockets,
turns them wrong side out, slits open the seams.
The cave wants to leave the country, catch a cab,
walk down a city street, linger in a lingerie shop,
hold a white camisole up to its shoulders.
The cave wants fingers, it wants to twirl a straw,
smash moths against a window.
The woman's sure they should start
by unbuttoning the black silk shirt
of a man who knows how to tremble,
which makes the cave remember
the earthquake of its birth.
They're walking down Market Street toward
the Liberty Bell. Inside it, another cave,
the cave explains, and a clapper swathed in silence.
Let freedom ring the cave starts to sing
but the woman is hungry, wants roast beef,
maybe the man unzipping her dress.
It wants to dance, it wants hooped earrings, a pierced navel,
a tattoo in the shape of itself on the back of its neck,
something else for the woman to enter on all fours.

It wants to be a funnel, and *you*, it says to the woman, *you*
stand with your mouth open beneath me.
Open wider, it says and they're kissing on the street,
the kind of wide-mouthed kissing
that lets whole stories move back and forth —
betrayal and loss, the debris of our lies,
the memory of a girl who keeps swimming out to sea —
until the cave itself wants to enter the woman,
snaggle its stalactites in her hair
but she's thinking about the man again,
whether she wants to be sipping wine with him
or offering him her breast,
but what to do with this cave, impatient now,
with the partially unbraided, the merely untied shoe.
If he were here, it says to her,
I'd say to him, okay, you too,
and so he's here and the zipper's easy, buttons smooth.
The cave supplies music, an opera singer, an oboe,
it wants their mouths on all its hollow drippings,
no end to this turning inside out.
They crawl out of bed in a high-rise hotel,
two of them shy in the aftermath.
How about religion? it sings, *let's make me a god*
but the woman's sure now that she wants
the cave back in the cliff, that she wants to sleep
with the man in the fissures, under low ceilings,
she wants it all bearing down on them,
dank air and emptiness,
the way they are when they're unsure,
inept, pointed stones beneath their backs,
the batteries in their headlamps gone.

TWINLEAF

(of the barberry family: low flowers of early spring)

I discovered at an early age
that too much noise and light
signal a split-up,
that closeness with no cover
withers into separate beds.

The twinleaf, for example,
its frond so deeply double-lobed
it resembles the Siamese,
lives only in deep shade,
sacrificing bright bloom
for two leaf-islands joined
by an isthmus of green.

In the woods I love monkshood
and the mouths of closed gentian;
at home, the most inaudible
gestures of love:
your hand in my hair,
marked pages in a book,
three stones on the counter
that signal the night.

When experts warn us
not to keep secrets,
I fret about sun on my head,
what wilts in the blaze.
Let's close the curtains, love,
paint the walls green.
I want us to curl
in the shade of our silence,
our mouths to close
around each other's body

the way my twin and I did
in the prenatal x-ray of the womb:
belly to belly,
our thumbs, like stubby roots,
in one another's mouths.

SPHINX

To feel your skin.
The insatiable thirst for warmth.
Breast plate of a deity.

Drunk from the coconut blade
I adore your lava fed caves
Inflammable exponents,

fired through your electric
cliffs, the wild consonants designed
only for your body.

Vinegar pit fire ceremony.
Smoke coming up the mountain
bringing the gifts.

Grand Unification,
the way air feels when it moves.
Shark weight at the altar.

Your shirt is on the floor.
Lightning-white sand. Binary
stars rising on the horizon

of another planet where
sapphires rain from the sky
when it rains.

Ravine the milk gorge
pounding hooves in sunken
verticals, wounding.

Honey poured
into the wound, Jurassic,
frozen in amber.

Maple syrup levitation.
Fake yoga priestess scarification
Translucent portals

into the blood drumming
the silent concert in the breast
of the circling hawk

weaving the wordless realm
around an omniscient chrysalis
containing the egg instructions,

all the hieroglyphs at once.
The black egg painted gold
or the gold egg painted black.

Where the beaks have tapped
their chisels around the shape
of your blossoming continents,

the urge of the claws
to rip, to hold, to hold,
to rip and the distinction.

Holding so easily becomes
ripping, like flying, the respirational
alternation between holding

and ripping like breathing,
ripping and holding the ocean
pours into the sky.

THE HEART

is a fetus
in a crib of rib cage.
A stalactite
that has dripped itself
all the way to the floor
and is growing wide.
Ice trunk lighthouse ooze.
Dark juice commander.
Avatar on a meat hook.
Stigmata headquarters
with five umbilical cords
emptying out into the night
on mermaid-fiberoptic octopus arms,
suspending the spider's brain,
the grotesque engine
of primal wetness
with its boomerang blood
cockpit and pendulum.
Naked pet.
Half nightwatchman.
Half night.

SCENIC OVERLOOK

Highway drone in the silent
machinery of the blossom, the way
the forest folds into smoking
snow and melts in the air, almost mist,
the weightless ash, sideways confetti
of the apocalypse, the scrolling codes,
all the torrential unraveling, crumbling
of ones and zeros, keys
and keyholes, zoo lightning;
Zeus-mudra shadow puppetry
against the drum-stretched retinas,
the antler-lock of kissing pelvii
next to the scenic overlook sign
where the charred-black landscape marks
the indisputable end of tourism.
When, after all the water is gone,
the camera becomes medieval
and the tour guide is bound,
bludgeoned to death and eaten,
his remains a decomposing strobe-
lit, post-erotic carcass
that stinks of extinction, of burning
flesh, as foul as breath itself.
Moth flitting against the hanging lantern,
flag yolked cold to the spine,
that swaying of the dock
and the lake, swaying
of the pendulum within,
the yellow claw of the hinge
digging through the heart
of the mountain for a tunnel.

BAGEL

Working behind the counter
at Einstein Bagels in Chicago
she has smirk eyes
and flirt breasts.
She is tiny with mantis limbs
and sideways eyes, big
round bagel holes,
moose head eyes
she is Mexican and smiles at me
like it's not allowed
she is a deer in headlights
content with public submission
a secret, a closed book
with a padlock, sexy
as purgatory
but slightly mal-
nourished, thin as a dart
in a bulls eye
coat hanger veins,
hair in a ponytail
pulled through the hole
in her oversized job hat.
I bet she looks incredible
in a red dress and loud shoes
or in baggy sweat pants
after work.

When I was ordering
I didn't see her naked
but now I do
mounted like a hood ornament
on the hard gloss of her lover
I am the voyeur
the bullshit artist
making her hair wet,

raspberry cream cheese
on her nipples
which he licks off
as her back bends
against the five PM light,
her hat on the floor
he rips her with love
and a parachute opens
inside of her.

They are having one
of those parachute weddings
in the nude
the rush of wind up their spines,
goosebumps like thorns.
He clicks into her
like a piece of toast
her soft lips gently slit
with the auratic gleam
of her perfect teeth,
her eyeballs rolled back
like satellite dishes
taking the universe
into their small bowls.

They are lovers,
his butt clenches like a heart
his feet are sweating
beads of sweat condensing
his thighs are tight
and their breathing
tears down the sidewalk
from Lake Michigan.
She's on top of him
like a spiral staircase
working her small body

on top of his,
straddling his hourglass
working him like a sailboat
paintbrush joystick
her breasts barely bounce
because they're so hard
like moon rocks.

COURTESY AT THE THEATER

"Excuse me, please," is the natural thing to say when having to disturb
anyone in order to get to or leave your seat in a theater, and if someone is obliged
to get up to let you pass, you add, "Thank you" or "I'm sorry." When climbing
in and out of a row of seats, face the stage or front and press closely to the backs
of the seats you are facing, being careful not to drag your coat or purse over the
heads of those seated in front of or behind you.
  –From Emily Post's Etiquette, "Courtesy at the Theater."

"Excuse me, please,"
        may I touch your hair?
        The dark moon oar of your long Indian hair?
        or better yet when you are getting
        some Milk Duds before the snack bar closes,
        will you brush up against me?
        Drag your umbrella of hair
        across the desert of my neck?

"Excuse me, please,"
        may I turn you into light?

"Excuse me, please,"
        will you be my hovercraft?

"Excuse me, please,"
        may we spiral in the nudity of reality?

"Excuse me, please,"
        can we gyroscope in the guts of a dream?

"Excuse me, please,"
        May we share this seat
        hidden in the shadows of the projection
        light? May we privately intertwine,
        secretly hold the lips
        of our hands together?

"Excuse me, please,"
        May we levitate now? I'm ready to writhe
        in the white public of midair,
        to cover your skin with nocturnal balm
        to make the collaborative shadow puppet
        of our dance bark on the blue horizon.

"Thank you,"
        stranger for sitting here in giant warmth
        with me for the last two hours.

"Thank you,"
        for sharing your coat with me, and

"I'm sorry,"
but tonight is the night that I die
the way I always wanted to,
during a rainstorm. Your hair
is the black ocean of the shipwreck.
        Rose-slit bindi, cusp of lightning
        that is your entire body.
        I am the captain of a ship trapped at sea
        in the quiet freedom of surrender,
        in between the guillotines of razor light,
        who has just realized he must
        go down with the ship.

I was Feeling

I was feeling all happy and
Joyful and so I said Hallelujah
Praise the Lord and asked the birds
To tell him in case he hadn't been
Listening and sure enough they
All left the telephone wire and flew
Due north and I walked along
And then I saw a dead bird
Hit by a car lying in the road so I
Picked it up and bore it home humming
A funeral march and I buried
It in our backyard chanting a
Mournful funeral chant and I laid
Three violets and a daisy on its grave
And then I needed a black ribbon to
Tie in my hair so I went into the
House singing a sad song for
Deceased dickeybirds where my mother
Told me to STOP THAT GODAWFUL NOISE

GLADYS

With a wounded heart
I walked into your yellow kitchen.
You sat at the corner of the table
with silent tears
rolling down your cheeks.
You were a teacher, the daughter of Jewish immigrants.

I was the young black boy who
cut your grass
and cleaned your house.
I painted your yellow kitchen
and asked, "Why are you crying?"

Your silence became sobs.
You told me the child who threw a book in your class
was crying for help.
You cared about him
and spoke to the principle about his pain.
No one listened.
The system tossed the child aside,
and your heart hurt.

As the sun set over the Hudson River,
I walked out of your yellow kitchen
with my heart filled
with hope
with love.
I now strive for success,
knowing you saw my innocent pain.
My life has been transformed by your
tears of love.

Out of Touch

Hanging
on a New York gallery wall
me
a black and white nude photo
shot from the back.
I was reaching for the light
shining down from heaven.

Alone, shy,
hiding in the shadows
from the New York glitterati,
hungry birds of prey
demanding to feast on my flesh.

At last I
find myself
within
the
inner circle.

Out of touch
from all who
appear
real.

Out of touch
from the soft lights,
all the clouds of
smoke
that fill the
air.

Out of touch
yes
Out of touch
because
I've been in touch
In touch
In touch
with out of touch

and I found that
touched by the hand of God,
out of touch
will one day
be
in Touch.

NEW LIFE

I sit cross-legged
on a smooth flat rock
above a stream,
our life force pulsing as one.
Like a yogi in the Absolute,
my mind is reflective.

Red,
yellow,
burnt orange leaves
like whispering clouds with changing faces
quietly stir on a windless day
and float past my watchful eyes . . .

my anger and disappointment.
life's unfulfilled dreams and broken promises,

old wisdom I called upon
to survive on my journey,

the passion I used
to move through my tumultuous life.

Tears fall from my eyes
like rough hewn stones
thrown into a Zen pond,

creating
    soft
       distinct
          concentric
             rings of life
                in the water.

I'm ready to begin a new life.

MEN'S INITIATION TALISMAN

Three inch blood red leather pouch
filled with sacred herbs and stones,
tied with a dark brown leather cord,
one carved white bead
as a tunnel to the other world.
Suspended from my neck in honor of
my sacred initiation into
Manhood,
your blood touches my heart.
With you my body and mind are like a
clear mountain lake.
Basking in the sun's warm soothing rays
I am Man!

I've danced the rhythmical steps of
Anger and Rage
Love and Hate
Passion and Cold
Fear and Joy
too long.

You have you taken me to sacred brotherhood,
killed my fear of men.
I can never go back.
I am a man who has died to the old male ways of manhood.
I am reborn.

I am your Wildman,
King,
Warrior,
Priest,
Magician,
Lover.
I am Sacred Man!

EATING CRABAPPLES

For Elinor and her tree full of cedar waxwings

From her window we watch — a whole tree
of them masked, chattering,
throats blushed as the pink sky
behind silhouettes of trees.

Breasts of cloud and milk,
wings dipped in flame,
they are kohl-eyed, drunk
as they tear at the fermenting orange fruit.

This loss of mother is our first,
and she who seems to be gone
has taken a small part of me with her
into that world she no longer fears.

At dusk the flock quiets, settling
amid beak-tattered remains,
and we sisters pull the pale moonlight
around us, turning inward.

AT PENTWATER LAKE

She looks at me from the wall.
I feel her watching as I stroke her cat,
but she is nowhere.
I am heavy as rain.

Later I walk the water's edge.
The silver-tongued waves swell as she recedes,
eroding beach, breaking records.
How alive she was, cocky — smiling
the smile I must have seen from the crib,
the gray green eyes that toward the end
had stopped seeing, and could do nothing
but emit light.

Even the lake moves to the moon,
feels the drag and surge, marks time.
Her time and mine, mother and daughter,
the parts of our lives together,
her diminuendo, and now
my shadow walks alone.

The alien wrench
of her passing has dimmed
though she remains within me,
those eyes, her simplicity,
pulsing faintly as the tumbling blue surf.

And If It Happens

And if it happens that you carry
your heavy-plumed sorrow
into the sea, turn back before the swells
lift you like a lover and subsume you,
drifting, limbs curved in aqueous silence.
Remember, it is not your time.

Or when you find the world collapsed
down to your pale curled form
on the bed, sheets bruised
by wine and spilled fire, smoke
in the halo of your hair,
open the window and let the cool vector
of moonlight run down your face.
Know that the fragile monochrome body
you see in the mirror
is your home — only for now.

Cup a breast in your hand,
pass a finger across your lips
and go to the garden beyond the peonies
crushed by wind, into the starlight and fireflies
and brandish the tender scalpel
of your longing. Dance abandoned,
knee deep in clover until your eyes shine
with dawn. There's no light like yours.

THE ANGEL

With a certain set of your heavy wings
you turn from minds that long to see you,
lead them to the things they know,
geese, high in the blue air, a backdrop
of blackbirds. On the darkest of nights
they don't know that clear drops of rain
sluice down your neck,
the wind pries your robe with its thumbs
and you tuck your head like a bird,
one foot drawn up out of the puddles.
But when the stars burn through the clouds,
you walk the shimmering miles looking
into eyes of slate, loosing frozen dreams.
and with your iron claw stop the world
and let them rest in the soft clouds
of moths around a streetlight,
the petal of the moon.

THE RATS

All summer I'd heard them rustling
among the eggshells, orange rinds and leaf mold
in the compost heap, seeing only perhaps
a tapered snout and quivering whiskers
before a hump of grey
slipped behind the fetid hill,
hairless whip flicking behind.
With frost on the kale
I should have thought them gone
but today when I come to fork the pile
in the noonday sun I startle, see the big one
backing a heal of bread into a hole,
vermilion eyes unimpeachable,
his mate reclining nearby,
lazy as a redtail in an updraft.
Today they don't flee but wary, meet my eyes.
Leaning on the fence post I contemplate life
among buzzing flies, rotting tomatoes
and the certainty of winter and sighing,
return the pitchfork to the shed.

NIGHT VISION

Flakes of snow fall softly
and the last rosy cloud greys,
abandoning the mind's horizon.
The shoulders of the hills
hunch against the cold, the field
a flat belly, punctuated by the navel
of a frozen pond. Skirting the dark
clumps left by the plow,
two dogs trot a hedgerow
and the veil of night flows
over eyes that strain to see,
having forgotten the fire
the invisible holds.
I feel the body of the earth
becoming my body, my body filled
with quiet stars and the snow.

EPIPHANY

Like Kerouac you burn, burn for the streets
of this spring-scented city, fondle
silver-spooned rings, wooden boxes that open
to quivering bugs, hold glass beads
into a rainbow of light.

Doesn't the sky speak day after day,
display knowledge night after night?
You hear the voice but only listen
when disaster's giant wave sucks you in,
then spits you back out, if you are lucky.
You listen and hear the message
but can't bear to lose anything.
Not even your contradictory self.

On good days you stand like a blindered horse
in front of a carriage for passengers
or allow yourself to be hollowed
by the world into a thin, fragile bowl.
You hunt each day to find a good deal,
a bargain, a rosewood elephant
for less than the cost of the wood.

On good days asparagus fern and lantana bloom
below the sky, its speech, its knowledge.
This is an open door.
One foot in, you hope, is enough to change
like the movement of light
that slants the afternoon.

At night you listen to Rilke,
master of words and sentences so tight,
they take your breath.
Breathless you want to live
to be heard.

INTERSECTIONS

> *Happiness is not an ideal of reason*
> *but of imagination.* –Kant

Would you give me your small laugh again if I confessed
I carried your book of poems on a plane to Europe?
Would you believe, opening it now, each line represents
reasons to continue my own writing?

Would it matter if I confessed
our past travels in a Moebius strip, one-sided, twisted,
returning desire continuously,
that my daughter's recent essay on M.C. Escher explained how
his creations float in mathematical structures?
Would you believe that time
off-sets everything?

Would you understand my difficulty
if I confessed
the plane's steady roar deceives chaos,
that clouds gather the sky,
that your poems open the world's transom,
that I'm the intruder
trying to carry away words like jewels?

Whichever way a plane intersects,
causes a change in the sky.
Will rain release itself
early or late?
Would you wait?

I confess, I'm not on a plane to Europe.
Desire is caught in a time slip,
glass jars piled high in the garage for pick-up.
Cruising altitude 30,000 feet above my earth,
the sky, the palest shade of blue.
White winter sun illumines and warms bare branches.

Juvenile Court Waiting Room

The sun points fingers
behind our backs
against the wall window.
We've stopped looking puzzled
at each other,
what went wrong.

An officer guards the magnetic walk-through,
yawns, leans back leisurely.
I try to read faces of names
called as they rise.

The clock's thin hands snail forward.

Have we learned how little it takes
to lose so much?
Someone ambles outside to draw
on a cigarette. To the eye,
the man, middle-aged, in ponytail,
looks more delinquent
than his boy in a crew cut.

Guilty is man-made.
You fidget. I write,
milk and bread, water plants tonight.
For now, the future is a cat
climbing our backs.
Next.

THIS IS THE ROAD TO SOMEWHERE

That's what I want to talk about; How love
of one kind or another can shape a life. –Dan O'Brien

You don't know yet
except that it takes you away
from the City of Has Been, away from
the club of dancing white powders, your friends,
and green leaves grown in the secret
of someone's home. This road has three lanes,
coming and going, traveled otherwise
by American Freightways, MS Carriers
who *deliver your future.*
An occasional foreign model
is guarded by the trees of your childhood:
Southern pine, poplar, hickory, sweet gum.
In either direction, there is plenty of land
and room for interruption and confusion.

The City of Going Somewhere is
another court of hurdles to jump without penalties.
The judges are waiting in silence.
Your sister understands.
She is steering you in the right direction
and your good sense still has the length
and width of the road to awaken soon.
You stop at a Burger King or Hardee's
for a hamburger and fries,
a salad or veggieburger for your sister.
Chew, chew, pull your heart and your God-given
talents into the future City of Being Somewhere,
which will allow you to fine tune and master.
Accept what the present time gives,
so your eyes and hands memorize
the dimensions of good intentions,
and your heart can draw them in.

STOLEN SHOES

> *"To be enlightened, one has to love unconditionally, even the man who cheats and steals from you."* —An Indian Sage

Somewhere in Bangalore my sneakers are walking the streets,
wading the gutters for a glimpse at another lifetime.

I don't know who it was that shook poverty by the shoe laces
and slipped on the well-worn Sassoon runners
I had placed outside the temple in respect for God.

Maybe they thought Sassoon was an American god
like the Krishna Tire Company or Shiva Cosmetics
and it was karmically auspicious to wear an amulet
of a stranger's leathered soles.

Or maybe they were practical
and knew shoes would cover bare toes
better than the fifty-five pairs of open-air thongs
and rubber flip-flops
that lined the wall in an uncommon orderliness,
waiting with my white gladiators
for a richer, more loving hand
to guide them beyond the footprints they left behind.

It must have been a man that took them,
or a woman as a gift for her husband,
because in India my American-size feet were like zoo animals
herded into a cage for unusual observation.

I felt relieved to see them bared,
carrying nothing but my skin between me and the earth.
Maybe I had enough of shoes anyway,
like a pile of dirty shirts on Monday,
and it was time to pass them on
to someone who really needed them.

I hope it wasn't just the weight of old karma I left behind
and some unsuspecting homeless Indian was now burdened
with feet that liked to jog around Waterworks Pond
to loosen age creeping into joints
like an arthritoscope of life.

Maybe he'd be lucky and hear only the swift slick turns
of the shopping cart rolling down Easter's aisles
to the march of my Sassoon Weejins

blessed with Pepperidge Farm macadamias
and Ben & Jerry's vanilla almond fudge
dropped into the cart like an afterthought
that never had to worry about
whether there was a piece of mango
buried in the hill of garbage.

PAUSE: FINGERBOARD, BRIDGE

His grandma is gone, and the news grows fingers
inside his chest, bending ligaments
strung through his ribcage, a pressure
approaching vibrato.
                        He rosins his bow,
eased by habit, not needing to ask
the lump to sharpen his grip, its bite
and slide.
            Now, to accompany her ascent,
the cello poses, the long bow hovers.
Even Time suspends: a ragged little moment.
The bow is a notched arrow, a lesson in elasticity
she's already learning by heart.
                        Loss cocks a wrist,
utters one prayer to molded spruce, belly and scroll,
bids his instrument move beyond the century
cut short by saw, chisel, rasp — the first life,
evergreen.

Yesterday's Owl

You roam to forget, barely noting
shingles of algae, scabbing the pond
where the feathered prow of a waterfowl
musters her small, noisy armada,
their wake, one long silver dazzle.

It's not your place to question
the battle plan, though you know
that chemo's a fierce rudder,
scuttling drive and appetite, taste,
touch, the patient already frail,
hope swamped.

From the tangle of wooded banks
a cry floats on the air, not yours,
but wilder, deeper, an alto flute.
Death uncurls its toes,
launching a Barred Owl,
wingspan gleaming like two oars
stroking the air,
the pale grey beak, honed like a keel,
and those lug soles sinking fast
where you stand, shouting,
your body, all wave, propelling
the hen, flailing her darlings toward shore . . .

and then there's the guilt,
that stowaway some of us carry
for wanting a shortcut, swift and unerring,
little skiff of the self, falling away
and the spirit trail, cleared,
exultant: an arc of lightning
when, sometimes, love can only bear
witness, bow the head.

FOUR RUES

logic

A painted stairway, first step
to the last, going up. Resulting in
footprints or not anywhere to go.
Rains came leaving calling cards
of leaves. Snails try to enter
an empty fishbowl.

Luberon

Bird of unknown origin. Castles
were built so we could walk their
ruins. In the mysterious hills, grapes
are free. Surprised by an accumulation
of stones, we find a cemetery for two,
the plot of every happy story.

mannerism

In the bar there's always more smoke
than inspiration. So the waitress
bends at the waist to replace
a napkin on the table, noticing
her body every inch as much as you do.

le monde

What is not usual is merely coincidence.
Those who don't gamble appear when
there are stakes, with umbrellas. Glory
is as thick as coats of paint on white
windows. Gathering around kiosks to hear
the papers speak of a stolen plane that
flew through the legs of the Eiffel tower again.

LETTER FROM HAVANA

August 13, 2003

They're celebrating Fidel's 77th birthday
at a government ceremony where the riflemen aren't smiling,
but children with short memories are giggling in a circle
by the statue of Elian Gonzalez,
returned to his father's arms.

All the billboards still pretend
with the same propaganda,
flattering us with dry declarations
as disappointing as a rumless daiquiri.
Nothing is pictured that you can hold in your hand.

On the outskirts of this crumbling Mafia playground
the skeptical village-square clocks
are once again ticking their talk of Revolution,
counting the days until the old man will die.

Tired of waiting, we've traded all that we own
for one last chance to be with you in Miami.
Over a barrel or in one, what's the difference?
sighs the lawyer driving our cab
to the broken-down boat.
There is no meter running on his angry monologue.

Even Hemingway, writing *The Old Man and the Sea*
in his book-paneled home outside of Havana,
reminded us all before he took his own life,
All good stories always end in death.

With our castaway crew of Castro's infidels,
we are finally no longer afraid of the ending,
of hauling up our anchor in the shroud of a dark night
and floating up to heaven,
in either direction,
just ninety miles away.

MRS. PERKINS' FAVOR

Why is it now that I remember
four years old so much more clearly
than twenty-four or forty-eight?
As a boy of four you just need a floor
and a shiny train to play with
to create a world that you control
as the engine speeds and crashes.

But the comfort smell of oven cookies
is a full-fledged pheromone
of chocolate-sugar-butter-spice
to tiny noses such as mine.
Are those for us?

Remember Mrs. Perkins,
who lives one house down, across the street?
These are her favor, mom explains,
as she wraps them in waxed paper.
What's a favor? I need to know,
disappointed, but curious.
Something special you give a friend.
Her answer made me think.

"Favor" was a splendid word,
one I never have forgotten,
but also never heard again
in quite that wonderful way.
Perhaps my mother made it up —
she liked to make up words.
In any case, it now seems lost
from even the lyrical Midwestern lexicon.

I asked her when we would be going.
She said, *Oh, you can take it by yourself.*
You know the house, just look both ways
before you cross the street.
Her voice was confident, assuring,
although I'd never been away from home before
alone. I swallowed slowly, and said, *O-kay,*
as the word stretched thin
somewhere between excitement and concern.

We had walked to Mrs. Perkins' house
on many other visits,
holding hands, a mother-son sweet snapshot
waiting to be framed.
But everything looked different now,
much larger and alive —
down the too-high, foot-smooth, stone front steps
between the angry, lion-headed pillars,
then past daddy's old Model A Ford
sleeping under streetside elms
with its springy, bouncy backseat.
No time now to watch the curving stream of ants
flowing from the sidewalk crack.
I had important things to do
with Mrs. Perkins' favor.

Held in my best both-hands grip,
it warmed my palms just slightly,
like mittens dried upon the hearth
before a winter fire.
A cookie peeked between the folds
beneath the truck-red ribbon.
If one somehow got "lost" upon the trip,
I wondered, would I be forgiven?

I almost crossed before I looked,
first one way, then the other.
The street swept out before me
like a field of head-high grass,
and once across, I looked right back
to see exactly what it was I'd conquered.

At Mrs. Perkins' doorstep now
a tiptoe stretch to reach the bell
brought her quickly to the screen door,
looking with large eyes
to find that I was there alone.
What have we here, my dear? she asked.
I said, *It's just your favor.*
The smile that spread across her face
was the biggest I'd seen,
ever.

On my way home I felt so proud
of making someone happy,
I crossed the street in half the time
and sang "Pop Goes the Weasel".
As I climbed back up the steps
that led up to our door,
in the big front window of our home
I thought I saw
the soft face of my mother
in between the curtains.

KING OF THE CAB

Before my first day at Prairie Elementary,
dad enrolled me in a class of his own,
as he pulled me up, to work next to him,
in the rattling cab of his old Dodge dump truck.

The cracks in the sun-baked, brown leather seat
looked a lot like a Midwestern map.
Dad asked me to follow along those little squares
with his prized Parker pen and its stream of bright blue,
to trace out our route just in case
we somehow got lost coming home —
turn right at the T, past Saddlebag Lake,
then two more lefts to the Lazy Bar R.

At each stop he loaded slop from the stockyard,
its head-turning stench an unmistakable mixture
of sweet hay, ammonia, and dark musty wet.
Great-looking food for the crops, he would shout,
but it's a darn good thing our fields don't have noses!

Dad told me our truck was pulled by horses
that lived up under the hood
and obeyed the grinding commands from a stick
that he helped me to shift through big H's and L's.
I looked down a hole in the rusted-out floor —
never did see any hooves.
And when no one was coming,
dad drove right down the middle
so I could watch the white dashes flash by.

The sun slumped to orange before we reached home,
where my father could harvest a sleepy-eyed son,
carrying me to the kitchen like a sheaf of spring wheat.
No matter that the eyelets of my dad's worn work shoes
were packed with manure from pigs and cows,
to me, he was King of the Cab,
tour guide to the gates of my beckoning new world.

THE FORCE THAT HOLDS THE HELIX

While the force that holds the helix wasn't watching,
some tiny hooded horsemen
slipped inside my cells
to rob me of a perfect wholeness.
Within those precious bosom cells,
the lusty focus of my lover's glance,
their dirty stable doubled daily
until the thriving roundup of clandestine death
was discovered by a touch.

The "Path Report" was cold, correct,
not much room left for error:
Aggressive carcinoma of the breast, it read,
and it changed my life forever.
I heard the careful surgeon
speaking slowly through the earmuffs of my shock,
I'm quite concerned about the mets.
Somehow I knew he wasn't talking baseball,
but then I saw the scoreboard numbers
all rolling back to zero.
Metastases, I mean,
so we'll have to take the nodes as well.

In the soft light of the pre-op room
the thoughtful nurses left us to ourselves
as the crucial question came.
Will you still love me
 just the way you always have,
when I start winking at you
with my chest?
He heard the comic courage
weakly laughing, crying,
laughing, crying.
Of course I will, he hugged right back,
and I tightly held with hope
his trembling hands.

AN IRRETRIEVABLE SOUND

The thin, white moon had arrived like an ambulance
to carry off the dying dusk.
A January rain fogged my windshield,
and the swift road turned darker than night.

Inside the warm car, it rained relaxation.
The reassuring sound of your calm conversation
and the sexy salve of blue radio jazz
made the highway exits coast by in a blur.

All at once, worried taillights
telescoped toward us,
a warning in bloody Morse Code.
I was still going sixty, distracted
by the drama of a roadside wreck,
until the time for any stopping had passed.
In your scream was the sound of life leaving
as I swerved sharply left into blackness.

We slowed in silence, in the left-hand lane,
while alternative endings played in high definition
on the wide screen of our startled senses.

I mumbled something flimsy about the crazy other car,
and flogged myself mentally for not paying attention.
You apologized for screaming,
but it didn't come close
to taking that sound away.

The Soul of Snowflakes

Awakening from a diaphanous dream
in a purple sky of clean clear cold,
embryonic droplets fuse
in a prelude to a million births
somewhere near the hand of God.

Like circular stained glass windows
growing outward in angel white,
each star-trimmed filigree is formed
according to divine designs
of delightfully ordered randomness.

Cascades of cartwheeling fairies
and whirling discs of Da Vinci men
sift through unseen fingers,
sailing to uncertain fates below.

Some settle onto groves of Douglas fir,
where artists will paint them in the morning light.
Others, rudely blown by unkind winds,
smash luckless into harder lands,
breaking fingers, even losing limbs.

And yet another fortunate few
spend their famous final minutes
in curious Molly's tiny outstretched hand
as she closely considers the beauty of each
to prove for herself
that no two are exactly alike.

But just as quickly as they were conceived,
the snowflakes twist back into tears,
then to swirling vapors
searching skyward once again
to find the dark celestial womb.

SNOW READER

Passage through the woodland
is remembered by the snow, the gentle kind
that falls like sifted flour
and allows no secret trespass.

Where ruffled grouse have gone,
there's story in their trident stride
through grasses bent with seed,
tracing circles in the snow.

The seated fox leaves a melted round
that held sly patience in the dusk,
as henhouse chickens entered sleep,
heads tempting like warm biscuits.

The flap of owl wingtips
frames a furrow in the white,
quotation marks around
the muffled cry of mouse.

My footprints, much the coarser,
needing less than stealth,
track my morning progress
through the wintry pages.

Hurry now. The frozen record fades,
soft and wider in the bright of day.
All too soon,
no one else can know.

Fight Night

Friday evening was "Fight Night," back in 1954.
The Golden Age of Boxing had met the Miracle of Television,
and my parents' new set brought the neighbors to our house
like kids to a carnival.

Their fourteen-inch world of hazy black-and-white
came laced with ads for men's grooming and razors —
Brylcreem, a little dab'll do ya,
they'll love to run their fingers through your hair!

In Pittsburgh, boxing was king of all sports,
a daring distraction for the jaded rich,
pure inspiration for the poor.
Watching some "nobody" become famous for his fists
was a transparent drama with dark expectations —
controlled violence, a tonic for the tired
at the end of a steelworker's week.
Not a program for kids, said my mother.

Sent to bed early, one thin wall away,
I felt sleep come slowly in the acrid air
of unfiltered Camels and Lucky Strikes,
the announcer's voice almost singing
to the clang of the eager bell,
while men opened beers, yelled with each wild swing,
and women turned the crank on the chattering tub
of home-made, fresh peach ice cream.
We'll wake you up when it's finished, they promised.

In the quiet of next morning, I asked my parents at breakfast
why people lit cigarettes if the smoke stung my eyes,
why everyone cheered when the Negro got hurt,
why no one woke me for ice cream.

BASEBALL

My grandmother's fingers
complain to sunlight
catching her knitting needles,
picking up speed

as that big soap box talker,
gambler and dreamer
lies upstairs
dying
in a room nebulized to mist.

Half in the doorway,
half in the hall, I listen,
both of us listening.
Time when I am still no one,
slender enough to enter dust motes, stale light.

The mystery of the ballgame
slowly unfolds
on the 5R1 Motorola;
the names themselves
culled from some other world:

Minnie Minoso,
Nellie Fox,
Louie Aparicio —
vowels, syllables received
like the kindness of a dream.

The broadcaster traces
the trajectory of a ball
sailing towards infinite blue.
I recite my 'Hail Marys,' seeing clearly
its brilliant, spinning, spiraling arc.

WOMEN AT THE ONSEN (MINERAL HOT BATHS)

Tohoku, Japan

The old Woman strips
like a minute hand turning.
Placing her heavy cotton tunic
in an open weave basket,
she faces a mirror, looks past
her sagging breasts —
strands of grey hair
fall from her bun
cover her gnarled back.
Entering the mist, the sound of running
water deafens every sense —
no longer hunched over onion fields,
the hot vapor opens every pore,
relaxes each struggled muscle.

The tired housewife lulls her child,
squeezes warm water over
her full cheeked daughter's back.
The child's pearl toed feet
dangle over the marble hot tub.
A small painted doll floats in a reverie of heat.
This is the hour when the streets slicken
with February's strength and her husband
drinks Sake over a deal
made in a small downtown bar.
Her daughter dozes on the heated marble tile.
The housewife's skin softens
for no one's touch but her own.

Stripping down lean,
the teenage girl removes her make-up.
Gem studded earlobes conspicuous in the mist,
she gathers her permed roots into a silver clip.

Red nails sweep down the line of her curved hips.
Flippantly ignoring her future seen
in women with crow-bar veins and curved spines
she dunks her head in the water,
the brink of the world wafts before her,
the bath makes her sweat
as she imagines a man one day will do.

The women all squat low by their basins
a Turkish towel wrapped around each fist,
the hot water an intoxicant,
this moment and a woman can forget
the fields to tend, tea leaves to dry,
forget the body's betrayal,
every pore opens for an ancient lore,
the forgotten muse steams in every woman's eyes.

WINTER BATHS

In pine tubs, the numbers tattooed
across her wrist appear to melt in steam.
The dried skin flakes from her body,
each cell coats the water in frothed memory.

Her fingernails have the edge
of a woman who snips away at everything
that grows past a clean point of order.
Her commanding voice smothers into an accented whisper

when she calls relatives lost
in the denizens of the mind.
Her spirit weathers this shadowed landscape
in the prompt of a past relived in uneasy sleep.

Her body scrubbed to a bright red; a glaring memory.
She lets me wash her hair, knotting grey,
then touches my long strands spiraling in the humidity
and mutters, "The color of Rebecca's . . ."

Her younger sister, a name that loiters
in the dry bone of memory,
a murmur in the tunneled halls of her house
heavily scented with ammonia and wood polish.

Winter in Treblinka, from a line of girls
they pulled Rebecca to the showers,
passed over my grandmother, over a chorus of screams.

From the creases in her forehead, I brush strands of hair,
pull them into a tight knot of silver,
the light dims to a sound of crickets.
In the chilling air we slide lower

into the heated tubs, memory's taught muscle loosens,
my grandmother wipes the folds beneath her eyes,
slaps her hand across the night air, to rid it of crickets,
a chorus of screams that time cannot revise.

The Poem that Didn't Get Written

This is how it goes with love:

A shattering of glass
unexpected —
How it slips from your hand,
in a moment you can't remember,
because memories, too, like shards
need to be swept up before crystal slivers scatter.

Residing in pain, words entreat us,
like the train slowing down, ready to pull into station,
where people disembark onto a platform
of noise and color and shops that sell
warm things like hats and cappuccinos,

to arrive at a place where our words,
are not lost in the wind,
in a stream, in a puddle of recent rain,
but zigzag, stand and escape
that white space,
which we know as silence.

WHAT MY MOTHER TAUGHT ME

Fork to the left of the plate,
knife and spoon to the right.
Sweet corn for supper in summer.
Chocolate is good, but bread
with butter is better. Love
the color red — tomatoes, garnets,
a bedroom wall. Never leave home
without a sweater. Walk.
If you have to drive, go slowly,
in a red car. Hurt no one
on purpose. Say what you think
when someone asks and otherwise
be quiet. Know the names
of what grows around you:
cyclamen, oak, red-tailed hawk.
Keep things. Read. Believe
in the soul and the body,
though the first may not be evident
and the latter will break.
Make small stitches when hemming.
Give freely. Be brave.

WHAT MY FRIEND SAYS
WHEN SHE GIVES ME A PERSIMMON

It tastes like your first kiss
but you have to let it ripen
until you almost think it's too late,
the beautiful bright body spoiled,
that's when it's best, that's when you open up
the flesh, that's when you want to

lay it on your tongue and savor it,
not really like your first kiss but more like
oral sex, though I wouldn't say that
in public. I couldn't eat one
with a stranger with so much
private hunger going on.

AFTER I DIE

Sell everything. Promise me
an auction, an old guy hollering
prices in a broken yodel,
his voice so rough you'd swear
he used to shuck corn
with his throat. Better yet,
a yard sale. Strangers can finger
bowls and coats and wonder
why I ever bought them and whether
they would like them any better
marked a couple dollars down.
Don't let the quilt go cheap —
Amish ladies in Iowa went blind
stitching it. The bedframe still folds
reluctantly into a sofa,
and anyone who wants a hard
mattress will not mind
how stiff the futon has grown.
Be sure the labels
on the sweaters from Venice
are showing. You know how
people will buy anything
Italian. Give away the books.
Burn the body. Keep the ashes
in a mayonnaise jar,
the way we used to hoard
lightning bugs until they stopped
glowing. When no one is watching,
tap out a handful of the ashes
on the beach at Limantour.
A slow crooked line
behind the tide, as if I were dragging
my toes, complaining how cold
the water leaves the sand.

Then buy plane tickets
with the yard sale money.

Pack the mayonnaise jar
carefully. Unwrap it in what was
my parents' backyard to scatter
bone shards beneath the lilac bushes.
After that go to Spain, and don't forget
the jar. Open it on the first
stone street above the cathedral
in Granada, where an old woman
fierce with her broom will not
look up. Drop what you have
left of me in front of her.
Ashes to dust. And always
someone sweeping.

WHAT I BELIEVE IN

I believe in dark chocolate and salt on the lip
of a margarita glass. I believe in daylight
savings time, dressing babies in bright colors,
and cremation. Writing comes before cleaning.
White paint needs a little cream. Never
stick a fork in a plugged-in toaster.
I don't believe anyone nailed anywhere
will rise. I believe in the underside.
I believe in everlasting soul but not in
talking about it, in being quick
to start and slow to finish. I believe in
the rhythm and off-rhyme of the ordinary.
I would never name a dog Prince. I would never get
a sex-change operation. I would never put nuts
or raisins in carrot cake. Don't live inland
without a river. Don't forget your roots.
What I believe in is simple
architecture, thrust and arch, the bitter-
sweet smell of sex. I don't believe love is
a two-way street but a median strip
with traffic. I believe in being kind.
Remember what you can and make up the rest.

We'll Always Have Casablanca

Some of us didn't begin in families
where affection was ladled out at supper time
on moist spring evenings filled with young, green life
thundering breakthrough, or on musky autumn evenings
winters would not follow. Some of us instead
learned tactics from stiff yet surprisingly spineless fathers
and acerbic, tightly-wound mothers, or wounded
mothers with stiff upper lips and fathers
who were always somewhere getting tight.
Or else we were driven, by our own particular mutation
of the aforementioned, to books, songs, and especially
movies, which taught us that nothing goes well
with almost anything and sublimest loves dissolve
into solitudes that seem, if miserable, correct —
clandestine departures, steeled hearts and hats
tilted against the night, an unbeatable style.

For no one can blame us if we make a virtue
of evasion, if we avoid violent acts
of commitment that might startle the lethargic,
or leave great deeds to the most capable
and great passions to the most rash,
on the premise that happiness weakens
resistance to Nazis or the daily grind.
And it's blamelessness we're after, continuously
making our deceptively small, self-effacing gestures,
with stiffening shoulders or a mousy collapse
of the chin, while a policeman inside us
chides us glibly in a voice like Claude Rains
and the transport's thrumming propellers whip up
an atmospheric fog so love can catch the last flight out,
leaving us standing alone and so obviously
somebody's child on the iridescent tarmac.

JUST BEFORE IT BEGAN

I took the long route on the off chance
under a three dimensional sky
where small dollops of cloud
separated themselves from the swath
that marbled the bright blue
to dust their bottoms
a little closer to the ground,
and the dust constantly effervescing
off the gravel road smelled like nothing
as much as roasted peanuts,
contributing to the general hunger
of a listless late afternoon
filled with cow-destined corn.
Cow parsnip, like beefed-up
Queen Anne's Lace, and electric blue
chicory repeated themselves
uneventfully in the roadside ditches,
and the road veered outward and off,
the way sometimes each right turn
seems to take us farther
and farther from what we wanted.
What I wanted I couldn't say,
because I didn't know, and wouldn't
even if I did know, for wanted things
like to take you completely
by surprise, which makes waiting tricky.
A drifting red-tailed hawk waited
to seize an opportunity
from the dry grass, red-winged blackbirds
dived at loitering crows,
pestering them like kids with Yet?
and Yet? and Yet?, and as I slowed
to watch a bumper crop's green wall
hold up the red, impatient sun
a minute more in case, I thought
I felt the expectant world
giving itself away.

BAKED APPLES

for my sister, Mary

On summer mornings, out of walnut shells
and construction paper, turtles
grew from underneath my fingers,
more than just a pair for Noah's ark
in dry dock at a Baptist Bible school,
and earned for me a meal. Mary,
shunted off from me with kids too old
to be God's little veterinarians,
earned hers in ways I never thought about,
gobbing on the paste. In the starved afternoon
we'd both troop off to charm the "Holy Rollers"
out of early supper, chiming in amens
with syncopated Roman Catholic timing.

By fall what little cash Dad didn't drink
wasn't enough to keep our houselights on,
so when the P.T.A. lit up a maze
of schoolyard booths for Halloween, we went.
I won a braided tube you put your fingers in
to get them stuck, but Mary stared bulbs down
through each concession of the night.
Later, when the lady we waived a ride home from
hollered for us to "switch on the Edison"
to signal we were safe inside, Mary turned
on our dark porch to wave her off and tripped
on a bag of apples someone left. All bare cupboards
have a can of cinnamon. The oven cooked with gas.

There still were apples graying in the bag
Thanksgiving week when, second miracle,
the roast appeared. Dad sobered, went to work
to dream about the feast. And Lana,
Mary's rival for the boys, "tits the size
of Texas," came to taunt while Mary chafed,
turning me blue by standing on my stomach,
egging Mary into a neighbor-ogled
fracas in the yard — hackles, shredded blouses,
fists of hair — and the roast burnt crisp.
That night we sat to watch the roast's impersonation
of a cinder on a dish and ate, three mutes
in candlelight, the steaming last three apples.

October Eighth

I noticed the leaves today, I have been sick
and losing touch, but there they surely were,
falling from crowded trees, playing at sur-
vival, trying to make my brain as thick
as their gatherings, their wrinkled ends, their May,
lying like truthful books the winners burn,
told in a language I will never learn.
My brother has been dead a year today.

I think of all the poems that use the Fall
to euphemize a death, but Jimmy died
this blazing time of year, and all the kinds
of metaphor won't reach the boy I call
and mourn and hunger for, the boy who tried
too well. They are just leaves. Life teaches, art reminds.

New Year's Eve

We know who's dying, not who's being born;
a boy who kills his mother as he's torn
from her will redeem the world, a dancer
we can tell from the dance, while an answer
we have always sought will come from a girl
in Afghanistan. A flag will unfurl.
Our Mozart will give us a threnody,
a hint of Lincoln, or of Kennedy.

Tonight so many look into the past,
the dusk, the useless rooms, the die they cast,
or see the time when they will be alone,
When they will put the stone upon the stone;
they should be buoyant, even as they mourn,
we know who's dying, not who's being born.

POPCORN

We have moved too much, traveled too much,
My head is a hive of old numbers,
Juniper seven something, something seven something,
The stocking caught on the phone,
The desperate one by one of the lies.

Garfield something, 9 0 2 3.
KLondike 5, whazzit whazzit ten.
Your phone spelled D A N G E R S,
Your phone spelled K L A A X X I,
Your phone spelled love once,
Something something once.

MY MY

It was the first good day in a long time —
Even bald men took their kids for a walk —
And I put on the Mamas and the Papas —
Stood at the window seeing marvels —
Dogs looked giggly
And the prick next door waved —
And I found I was saying out loud,
"I must have done something good,
I must have done something real good."

This is a poem for the angel
Who was given the privilege
Of naming the color of grass
And who jumped up and down
Waving his hand and shouting,
Green! Green! Green!
Oh! Green! Green.

MY STUDENT

When you hear (and you will) that I have died
you will be taken back to Autumn days
and how we would rehearse the different parts
of teaching you, of teaching you of me,
even how I would let you see some tricks,
(that the anapest is an anapest)
of how it didn't matter how you tried
to solve the riddle of the world, the maze
that all of us explore, the way the heart's
turnings come back to where the heart can see
where it can't stop, all we can do is fix
as much as we can for the final test.
One more lesson? that I hope you'll learn,
the one demand is that you take your turn.

LETTER TO A POET WHO HAS NEVER LEFT TIBET

We live in a house made of trees, my wife,
my son, a dog and I, we have a life
As quiet as a bee's. I try to teach
The four things I have learned, knowing that each
Will find a place to lie. (I've put the four
in other poems.) Like you, I guess, I'm more
A poet than a lover or a friend,
Though I am friendly, and my loves don't end.

As to my country, it is much too strong
to go the way it's going very long,
Our old are books we do not read, our young
Are never singing, and they are never sung.
I think we take more than we'll ever give.
There is a tax on flowers where I live.

THE LIGHT BY THE DOOR

I am astonished by love. You would think
by now I'd have it right, that I would know
that jumping surge for what it is, would feel
sardonic and a mite amused. Christ, no,
my heart is a playground, a dancing trink-
et in the tunnel of love, a pumping meal
for all who hold it dear, its pink
for girls, its blue for lack of them. It's real,
each time it's real, each blessed time the po-
et is forgot, the teacher done, the zeal
for order in a pile, the missing link
a thunder in the brain, as off I go.

THE PATERNAL SIDE

1840: bespectacled,
balding, hands quivering from too much coffee
as you sell peppermints in Larvik, Norway
to Kirsten, the grammar-school girl on her way

to the wharf with her grandfather's lunch
of kippers and goat's milk. You keep shop,
mildly educated, mind shadowed
by your God

and the thick black
hymnals on Sunday and the too-little-sugar
in your mother-in-law's apple pastry after
roasted snow goose and bitter ale. Your name

is Tomas, Edvard, Karl and Henry. You want
to travel to America and have a little more
land to raise your apprehensions, some new water,
diseases, smells to record

in your leaden book lying open
like the breast of a grave in snow,
a deep rectangle of relief before spring
in the short days of imperially taxed

whale oil and tooth decay. You want to come
to Iowa to open a little grocery,
to be someone with a little power over destiny
and cheese as the sun illuminates

the lumber wagons, the stone crosses, the immaculate cash drawer.

HIGH SCHOOL

Once, in a class called Intro to Writing,
we watched a wordless film on The Poetic Image
in which botched developing
and pure drug-influenced warp jumped freely
in and out of each other.
There was, at one point,
a go-go dancer — her face vibrating
like the business end of an electric sander.
The film freeze-framed: her wild hair
suspended motionless in blue space
as a superimposed hand soared in,
popped the top half of her skull
like a garbage can lid, and dropped in her
empty brain cavity two scoops of vanilla.
The lid of her head clicked down,
and she was back in business. "What

does this mean?" our genius of a teacher
asked. "What does this mean, Rustin Larson?"
Although, on the surface, I wanted to say, "It is
symbolic of the vacuous and purposeless energy
of contemporary youth which, in the eyes of the mature generation,
should supply a utilitarian purpose," I instead
uttered, from the deepest corner of my self-consciousness,
"I dunno." "You don't know? Of all
the people in this class, I thought you
would know!" he said, totally shaken
and fizzed, as if the embarrassment
of his entire life accumulated into a Neapolitan
meltdown in his underwear that spotted
his gray hushpuppies;
as if I were supposed
to have a mop and bucket
in my pencil pouch.

MELONS

You bought one, perfectly ripe,
but within days
little holes appeared
and it began to shrink from inside
like a consumptive.
Time after time we'd buy the sweet-smelling globes
and they'd rot.
You said we had bad luck with melons.
I said we were cursed,

and so it was we wandered the earth dreaming
of the perfect incorruptible melon.
We would walk by a woman
and think of melons. We would walk by a man
with large knees and think of melons.
Even when we were spending money on clothes
we would think we were dealing out melon leaves,
thick and prickly, always leaving
a trace on our hands. Our shoes became
melon rinds, and our fingers, slivers of ripe
yellow melon. So when was it we stopped
thinking of these things? I think it was
the day in the supermarket when
you said to me, "Rus, I can't live
like a melon anymore!" and walked off,
leaving me to contemplate the absence of melons
and their traces, their juices and their mold.
"Why should I live like a melon either?" I thought,
and sat down on a crate, and weighed
my big round head in my hands.

CLEO

was a basset hound, overweight, lazy
and sad.
She had gastric distress often, produced
horrible smelling farts,
vomited in great gushes,
left her crap in Dairy Queen swirls near my swing set
and everywhere else.
She chewed pork-chop bones
which she defended with low
barely audible growls, and
she would choke invariably
and stagger around the yard
making great rasping honks that nauseated me.
One day
a milk truck hit her
and broke her hip, and when she healed
she walked with her butt swinging sexily
like Susan Hayward in *I Want to Live!*
We kicked her away from our garbage
but she always returned, and since
she was not our dog
we could not kill her.

I want it to be clear
I harbored no love for this creature,
and when she died
I shed practically no tears at all.
It is only now
that I am middle-aged and ailing
I think of her with respect,
as I respect all of God's creatures,
including the unfortunate and broken.

If there is forgiveness
in memory,
let there be that and
all our bones dulled
by the teeth that erode,
the rains that come and
the sweet milk of the earth.

CURRENT EVENTS

So she comes in playing bump cars
with her wheel chair — no —
it's more like she's playing Russian tank:
her elevated leg like the gun probing
from the turrent,
and the little white-haired hen
in front of her is Czechoslovakia
and must be crushed.

I sit in a rocking chair
reading a novel called "Miss Bishop"
to my nursing home events class.
And Hazel howls, her leg aimed
at my buck private parts, and fires,
"You had no right to turn our TV off,
you little sunuvabitch!"

It's true.
I'm a failure and a fraud,
and this class,
after years teaching freshman English
as a part-time department pawn,
expendable, and during budget crises, unwanted,
I am now at the ass-end of academia,
a fool stammering from the pages
of a turn-of-the-century romance,
as Hazel produces a popping baboon-like
chant to shut me down
and drive me out:
"You are not wanted here, you bastard."

And sure, I summon the nurse's aid to have her
removed. It's that simple.
But I'm not O.K. For a few moments

I panic, go to the bathroom,
and return, more than my bowels empty,
my head doing a tour of the whitewashed
galleries of damned souls — the disinfected
doors and bed pans — and read
with much more feeling this time,
with much more feeling.

Later, I put on "White Christmas" —
Bing Crosby and Danny Kaye
hoofing and crooning in drag: "Sisters."
And I, to tell the truth, have to write
this, just as Diane Frank says, to heal.

It's tough being the garbage of humanity.

THE GERBILS

Happily busy in the middle of the night
Destroying their cardboard tube. To sleep
They make a hurricane of straw and declare
This is the middle of us — enough
Already. And their greatest achievement
Is destruction. I love these animals.
Happy enough with their cubes
Of unhappiness for dinner and beads
Of water from the metal tube. Cal
Spins the luck of his wheel and Reb
Files a song on the bars of their cage.
And Wil stuffs his nose in his haystack
And dreams of stuffing his nose in hay,
All while I worry my life away.

GIRL IN THE DOORWAY

She is twelve now, the door to her room
closed, telephone cord trailing the hallway
in tight curls. I stand at the dryer, listening
through the thin wall between us, her voice
rising and falling as she describes her new life.
Static flies in brief blue stars from her socks,
her hairbrush in the morning. Her silver braces
shine inside the velvet case of her mouth.
Her grades rise and fall, her friends call
or they don't, her dog chews her new shoes
to a canvas pulp. Somedays she opens her door
and musk rises from the long crease in her bed,
fills the dim hall. She grabs a denim coat
and drags the floor. Dust swirls in gold eddies
behind her. She walks through the house, a goddess,
each window pulsing with summer. Outside
the boys wait for her teeth to straighten.
They have a vibrant patience.
When she steps onto the front porch sun shimmies
through the tips of her hair, the V of her legs,
fans out like wings under her arms
as she raises them and waves. Goodbye. Goodbye.
Then she turns to go, folds up
all that light in her arms like a blanket
and takes it with her.

THE SHIPFITTER'S WIFE

I loved him most
when he came home from work,
his fingers still curled from fitting pipe,
his denim shirt ringed with sweat,
smelling of salt, the drying weeds
of the ocean. I'd go to where he sat
on the edge of the bed, his forehead
anointed with grease, his cracked hands
jammed between his thighs, and unlace
the steel-toed boots, stroke his ankles
and calves, the pads and bones of his feet.
Then I'd open his clothes and take
the whole day inside methe ship's
gray sides, the miles of copper pipe,
the voice of the foreman clanging
off the hull's silver ribs. Spark of lead
kissing metal. The clamp, the winch,
the white fire of the torch, the whistle,
and the long drive home.

TRYING TO RAISE THE DEAD

Look at me. I'm standing on a deck
in the middle of Oregon. There are
people inside the house. It's not my

house, you don't know them.
They're drinking and singing
and playing guitars. You love

this song. Remember? "Ophelia."
Boards on the windows, mail
by the door. I'm whispering

so they won't think I'm crazy.
They don't know me that well.
Where are you now? I feel stupid.

I'm talking to trees, to leaves
swarming on the black air, stars
blinking in and out of heart

shaped shadows, to the moon, half
lit and barren, stuck like an ax
between the branches. What are you

now? Air? Mist? Dust? Light?
What? Give me something. I have
to know where to send my voice.

A direction. An object. My love, it needs
a place to rest. Say anything. I'm listening.
I'm ready to believe. Even lies, I don't care.

Say burning bush. Say stone. They've
stopped singing now and I really should go.
So tell me, quickly. It's April. I'm

on Spring Street. That's my gray car
in the driveway. They're laughing
and dancing. Someone's bound

to show up soon. I'm waving.
Give me a sign if you can see me.
I'm the only one here on my knees.

THE CATCH

The film footage wavers
on the gray TV screen:
fistfuls of Marines flung
from a helicopter, a flower
suspended in air
dropping its bloom of pods.
A row of khakied backs, the square-
shouldered shapes of men, knee-deep
in mud and raising rifles
like fishing rods.
There is the bitter smell of powder,
of too much salt, as bodies,
scooped from a trench, are flopped
like fish on a deck.
Here's what is left
of a boy from Maryland, half a face
and his good right arm. The rest,
scattered on a hillside, his pink
testicles split against
the brain-gray rock. In his breast
pocket, a snapshot, his girl
in a bikini, her whole body sprawled
across the hood of a new Camaro.
She's wet from the blue pool, shining,
car keys dangling from her teeth like minnows.

APHASIA

for Honeya

After the stroke all she could say
was Venezuela, pointing to the pitcher
with its bright blue rim, her one word
command. And when she drank the clear
water in and gave the glass back,
it was Venezuela again, gratitude,
maybe, or the word now simply
a sigh, like the sky in the window,
the pillows a cloudy definition
propped beneath her head. Pink roses
dying on the bedside table, each fallen
petal a scrap in the shape of a country
she'd never been to, had never once
expressed interest in, and now
it was everywhere, in the peach
she lifted, dripping, to her lips,
the white tissue in the box, her brooding
children when they came to visit,
baptized with their new name
after each kiss. And at night
she whispered it, dark narcotic
in her husband's ear as he bent
to listen, her hands fumbling
at her buttons, her breasts,
holding them up to the light
like a gift. Venezuela, she said.

THE LOVERS

She is about to come. This time,
they are sitting up, joined below the belly,
feet cupped like sleek hands praying
at the base of each other's spines.
And when something lifts within her
toward a light she's sure, once again,
she can't bear, she opens her eyes
and sees his face is turned away,
one arm behind him, hand splayed
palm down on the mattress, to brace himself
so he can lever his hips, touch
with the bright tip the innermost spot.
And she finds she *can't* bear it —
not his beautiful neck, stretched and corded,
not his hair fallen to one side like beach grass,
not the curved wing of his ear, washed thin
with daylight, deep pink of the inner body.
What she can't bear is that she can't see his face,
not that she thinks this exactly — she is rocking
and breathing — it's more her body's thought,
opening, as it is, into its own sheer truth.
So that when her hand lifts of its own volition
and slaps him, twice on the chest,
on that pad of muscled flesh just above the nipple,
slaps him twice, fast, like a nursing child
trying to get a mother's attention,
she's startled by the sound,
though when he turns his face to hers —
which is what her body wants, his eyes
pulled open, as if she had bitten —

she does reach out and bite him, on the shoulder,
not hard, but with the power infants have
over those who have borne them, tied as they are
to the body, and so, tied to the pleasure,
the exquisite pain of this world.
And when she lifts her face he sees
where she's gone, knows she can't speak,
is traveling toward something essential,
toward the core of her need, so he simply
watches, steadily, with an animal calm
as she arches and screams, watches the face that,
if she could see it, she would never let him see.

THE THIEF

What is it when your man sits on the floor
in sweatpants, his latest project
set out in front of him like a small world, maps
and photographs, diagrams and plans, everything
he hopes to build, invent or create,
and you believe in him as you always have,
even after the failures, even more now
as you set your coffee down
and move toward him, to where he sits
oblivious of you, concentrating
in a square of sun —
you step over the rulers and blue graph-paper
to squat behind him, and he barely notices
though you're still in your robe
which falls open a little as you reach
around his chest, feel for the pink
wheel of each nipple, the slow beat
of his heart, your ear pressed to his back
to listen — and you are torn,
not wanting to interrupt his work
but unable to keep your fingers
from dipping into the ditch in his pants,
torn again with tenderness
for the way his flesh grows unwillingly
toward your curved palm, toward the light,
as if you had planted it, this sweet root,
your mouth already an echo of its shape —
you slip your tongue into his ear
and he hears you, calling him away
from his work, the angled lines of his thoughts,

into the shapeless place you are bound
to take him, over bridges of bone, beyond
borders of skin, climbing over him
into the world of the body, its labyrinth
of ladders and stairs — and you love him
like the first time you loved him,
with equal measures of expectancy
and fear and awe, taking him with you
into the soft geometry of the flesh, the earth
before its sidewalks and cities,
its glistening spires,
stealing him back from the world he loves
into this other world he cannot build without you.

The Job

for Tobey

When my friend lost her little finger
between the rollers of a printing press,
I hadn't met her yet. It must have taken
months for the stump to heal, skin stretched
and stitched over bone, must have taken
years before she could consider it calmly,
as she does now, in an airport cafe
over a cup of black coffee.
She doesn't complain or blame the unguarded
machine, the noise of the factory, the job
with its long unbroken hours.
She simply opens her damaged hand and studies
the emptiness, the loss
of symmetry and flesh, and tells me
it was a small price to pay,
that her missing finger taught her
to take more care with her life,
with what she reaches out
to touch, to stay awake when she's awake
and listen, to pay attention
to what's turning in the world.

PICTURES

I.

She handles my breasts
like a newborn baby.

I'm sorry the plastic is cold.
This will be uncomfortable.
He wants more pictures.

I stare at the wall, blank
as a field
newly cloaked in snow.

Click. Click. Click.

I shiver.

II.

His words are the sharp point
of an icicle pricking my skin
as he taps the image with tip of pen.

A puzzle . . . looks benign
but acts
differently.

The pictures light up
mysterious snowflakes
dancing in an onyx sky.

Two years ago, scattered flurries,
now a silent squall
with a 2% chance of a blinding blizzard.

III.

The needle punctures my skin,
bears through tissue
and pictures that guide
the surgeon's hand
to swirling snowflakes.

I imagine the geometry of their shapes
coalescing into a snowball
and I slide out of control
off the slippery slope
into a forest of ice-encrusted pines.

Diamond dust shimmers
in the thinnest of air.

CONSQUENCES

She totaled his car. I imagine him making her feel wrong. I imagine him speaking in the voice of her father and his father and making her wrong. Adults have accidents. They neglect to pay their bills. They feel bad without help from friends. She wants to run her life differently. He wants someone to be wrong. He has asthma or hates his job. She hates her job. She's used to being wrong. When I totaled my car the lamppost wanted me to be wrong. It spoke in the voice of my father and his father, it made me wrong. I decided to run my life differently. I got moving violations. I got a job. I began sleeping with men from different cultural backgrounds. They speak in the voice of their father but it isn't the voice of my father. I can't tell when I am wrong.

I WAS ALBERT SCHWEITZER'S SECRET MISTRESS

They say that your first love changes you forever.
My husband and I haven't been getting along lately.
I wonder if he suspects that I have been
your on and off mistress for thirty-five years?

Sweet sixteen and you hadn't kissed me yet.
I thought maybe you were waiting
until I was ready.
So I hung your picture, flanked
by the tattered pages of a Bach prelude
over my desk, and prepared myself
for medicine, religion, philosophy,
theology and music.

Going through nursing school
drew lines of exhaustion on my face.
My eyes began to reflect an emptiness of spirit.
My feet ached from walking
those endless corridors of pain.
I had chosen a harsh school,
harsh as the most savage jungle,
good preparation for our life together, I thought.

Becoming Lutheran was easier
because I already was one.
But I had to struggle with philosophy and theology,
leaping over huge chasms of nothingness with Kierkegaard,
supported only by invisible parachutes
clinging to our backs like the emperor's new clothes —
peering out of Plato's cave, struggling in vain
to see beyond the shadows.

I begged my piano teacher to let me play Bach,
which she said I had no ear for.

I played it anyway.
You were my teacher,
the only one to cognize the sensuality of Bach.
After hearing you play, I could hear
that sensuality, like the touch of velvet on my cheek,
in the playing of others.

I remember sitting in the choir loft
during a Bach prelude and fugue.
I felt your fingers tickle my earlobes.
The upper melody stroked my hair,
brushed against my face.
My lips tingled.
The contrapuntal notes
filled my hollow head with your burning scent.
Those low pedal notes marched up and down my spine,
stirred a visceral response that shocked me.

After nursing school I stood before you in my white dress,
my bride's cap decorated with a black ribbon instead of a veil,
my wedding shoes — white oxfords.
But you rejected me at the alter.
I was unsuitable you said — my fatal flaw —
blond hair, blue eyes and pale, delicate skin.

Today in the middle
of a sticky Iowa summer,
sweat runs down my back,
drips off the tips of my hair.
I feel I will die before fall finally comes.
Your harsh rejection
looks more like a kindness now.

I've learned to hear my own voices.
And you did tell me that your quest
could never be anyone else's.

This morning you spoke to me.
You said that you saw a snowflake
land on your coat sleeve.
You watched it melt
into the fabric of your coat.
You said that for a few moments
you were that snowflake.

I feel myself
sink into the silver strands
of your dead hair,
melt into the bone
at the top of your skull,
float in the dark space
behind the empty sockets,
reach out a soft fingertip
to touch your delicate spine.

Leaving Home

At the airport, Mom pushes me away,
angry, when I try to give her a hug.
"If you're really going to go, just leave."
Stunned, I realize they think I won't do it.
I turn and march towards the portable stairs
and board the plane.

Wisconsin farmlands, squares
of brown and green, recede.
Soon I can't see the red barns.
Highways, looking like spilled
sewing threads, gradually disappear.
No one wants me to go to Alaska,
but I dream of Northern Lights,
mountains with clean jagged peaks.

I try not to think about living at home,
my old bedroom, filled with child furniture
and stuffed animals, familiar and safe.
By night, Charge Nurse in Intensive Care.
By day, my parent's youngest child.
I feel my heart, thumpa, thumpa
in time with the drone of the engine.

As the plane floats into Anchorage,
I feel amazed and light.
A yellow taxi takes me to the hotel
through a night so black
I can scarcely tell the difference
between the lights of the city
and oh, such bright stars.

MOONLIGHT HAIR

The old wooden row boat,
tethered to the last post on the dock
rocks back and forth to the rhythm
of choppy waters on Pelican Lake.
The bottom of the boat,
still wet from today's fishing,
cradles my child's body.

Moonrise over the opposite shore
reveals tall, dark pine trees,
touches the hollows between waves
with intermittent flashes of glittering foil.
The moon illuminates a large trout,
leaping out of the water
to take in great gulps of lunar light.

A frog chorus, punctuated by the cry of a loon
rises up out of darkness,
while the sound of laughter,
from family playing canasta up in the cabin,
recedes deep into the night.

A stiff wind from the North Star
shivers my arms and legs
under Mom's old grey sweatshirt.
Fishy lake smells mingle
with the scent of pine needles and dry leaves,
to pry open my heart and mind,
and fill them with a wildness that frightens me.

I find myself tugging off rubber bands,
pulling the blond strands free of tight braids.
so the wind can lift my hair
up towards the starry sky,

A luminescent mist seems to seep
through the top of my head,
spilling into the night.
Tomorrow I will be ordinary again,
but tonight my hair is made of moonlight.

SONOMA COAST

So impulsive, this drive to the coast
after buying shower curtains in Santa Rosa.
Grey skies and drizzle blur the looming hills,
add shine to strange rocks
that emerge out of the earth,
the twisting roads made slick with rain.

By the time we pull up to the cliff edge
overlooking Carmet Beach, we are arguing
about whose idea it was to come out here anyway.
Wind drives thick rain against the windshield,
blocking our view of the ocean.
From the back seat Fargo whimpers,
wanting his usual walk,
but disliking the rain almost as much as we do.

When the rain stops,
Gary turns the windshield wipers on one more time.
Waves leap up like giant water spirits,
towering white froth that hangs suspended for a moment
before crashing back into itself,
sending spumes flying high above the crest.

Enough energy to light up the chambers
of our overcast hearts.

PICKERAL LAKE

I can't swim. Too little to be left alone,
I squat at the end of a long wooden pier
where the leaky rowboat bobbles at the end
of a thick, slightly slimy rope.

Nearby, Dad sits on the edge,
pant legs rolled up,
bare feet in the water,
unknotting my tangled fishing line
for the umpteenth time.

I peer into murky green,
try to see a turtle
or maybe a cloud of polliwogs
becoming fat frogs.
Abra Kadabra Ali Kazam!

Did I just see something shiny
way down at the bottom?
Pirate's Gold!
Ker-Splash!
Eyes open wide,
I see a whole different world,
all greeny-brown and seaweed
like flowers poking up out of the sand.
Tiny minnows tickle my toes.
Clams scattered here and there lie half open.
Something inside peeks out.

Toward the middle of Pickeral Lake,
a mermaid flits among the shadows, calls my name.
I see my skinny arms and legs,
strands of hair floating, transformed and green.
Is this what dying is like?

Strong arms pluck me out of the water.
"Are you all right?"
Dad pounds my back,
but I never breathed in any water
because I hadn't completely turned into a fish.

FOR JOYCE

You weave in and out of my dreams all night long.
We sit in our spacious room at the Seal Rock Inn,
happy, because this room has four single beds,
a chance to split the cost four ways instead of three.
Through the window, a cerulean sea beckons.

The glass-domed train pulls itself up the high trestle.
I am pointing towards Mt. McKinley,
or Denali, as it is called here.
Beneath the cloud-shrouded peak, moose graze,
glancing at our train with shy brown eyes.
You stare, entranced, mouth slightly open.
I knew you would love Alaska's beauty as much as I did.
You laugh and say we should plan
to climb Denali next summer.

Both of us, slightly out of breath,
stop at a scenic bridge along Lake Shore Drive.
A rosy glow over Lake Michigan's horizon
foretells the coming sunrise.
Seagulls circling the waves emit raucous cries.
You tell me we won't really meet for another forty-five years.

Now the sun is peeking over the Sonoma Mountains.
We sit on my deck, sipping coffee
as a long drift of cloud turns a rosy violet,
soft peachy-pink, and finally bright gold,
all colors in your artist's palette.

But no, we are sitting in a summer garden,
filled with pink and gold roses and fragrant lilac.
An iridescent hummingbird darts from flower to flower,
then hovers, as you cup capable hands
around the tiny vibrating body.
You turn to me with a wide smile
just before you disappear into morning.

I didn't know you had come to say good-bye.

HORSES

As dusk settles into stillness,
I hear their ghostly neighs
floating in the darkening air.
Here, on the hillsides above Sonoma,
horses sleep in stables beyond the trees,
out of sight, phantoms of the night.
By day, you sometimes see them out in grassy fields,
as if posing for a calendar, tossing their heads,
manes shimmering in the California sun.

One poor old horse,
dressed in an olive green blanket,
stands in his little field next to the road,
leaning a little, as if to topple over.
We are afraid that one day
he will collapse and disappear.
Serene and still, he dreams
of green meadows,
running through wild wheat,
as we zoom down the mountain.

I remember the horses of my youth,
how much they taught me, and I long to cling
to their reassuring backs one more time.
But they are all ghosts.
I need something more substantial
to carry me through this mad, accelerating world.

THE IRON WORKER'S MUSIC

The first time we slept together
you surprised me
by weaving your body parts
into my DNA.

I was lured by song,
a tenor ukulele under my window
in the jasmine scented night.
In the background I could hear the waterfall.
How annoying to be tricked by the voice of a madman,
employing the river as his backup musician.
The papayas in my yard got so hot
their fruit instantly ripened and dropped.

With each exhale, a tiny ballpeen hammer
riveted my skin to your flesh,
your muscles to my hands,
your feet to my steps.
My teeth grew roots
in your bones.

Legs between toes.
Arms braided into my ribcage.
The hair in your ears grew long tentacles,
found my spleen, pancreas,
got under my breathing.

By morning we were married,
cured of loneliness,
genetically altered by lust.

WON'T NEED TO SAY A WORD

In 1978 I lost the honey bear.
It was sitting on the window sill,
sunlight trying to penetrate the thicker golden,
then it was gone.
I found her in the garden.
Baby was squeezing the viscous sweet
onto the backs of big zucchinis.
Lying on her belly
she was tasting green stripes.
Inside my chest is a snapshot
of the dirt stuck to her twoyearold face
when she turned toward me that summer.

Tonight my daughter sleeps.
Blue parchment eyelids
fold over all she has seen
and kiss her vision goodnight.
I inspect her arms, finding some purple.
Curled between her breasts
my granddaughter exhales,
then her breath stutters in again.
They smell unhappy.

This is my house enfolding them.
So I sip a hot cup of vinegar,
counting my strong feelings,
watching them hanker for blood.
So many scarlet demons
hunch down
in the mud trenches of my heart.

Once, when this girl
was still eating at my breasts,
I prayed for the redheaded mother
of the man she would marry.
I hoped that wherever she was,
she would love her son enough.
Enough to teach him tenderness,
manners, loyalty.
She taught him to love black cars and guns.

I forgot to give my daughter a filter.
I forgot to say, "Some people are just plain bad."

Sitting in the morning garden,
before they wake,
I make a witch's plan to feed my generations.
Borage flowers, like cobalt stars to guide them.
Kale, nourishing, curly and bitter green, like life.
Fat tomatoes, circled by purple
and yellow johnny jumpups.
The new baby can watch the corn
reaching toward August.

ZHOUIE'S DREAM

She feels warm
as if a fever were coming.
She rolls toward me in the bruised light
of first morning of New Year in Bali.
"I miss you even when you're right here."

I know what this means.
Know her bones will ache for impossible union.
Her heart must unlatch
painfully as a peony
who lets the ants eat her face off
so that she can crack open and blossom.

She's not yet reached seven years
but her Buddha vows . . . to love and love and love
already bruise her brown feet.

I am only the Lola, the grandmothering one,
so I lay a hand on her back and lie,
"It's O.K."

Her breath is nutmeg and sandalwood scented,
it takes me down to another dream,
a weaving of owl wings,
and a massage by spider's hands.

A drumming Indonesian earthquake
jolts and rolls the bed.
My granddaughter sleeps on,
for at least a small while.

Applying Joint Compound

If God wants a legal separation
I will divorce all of his beautiful faces.

First I'll turn my back on the blueeyed face,
the one who poured warm sand over my flesh.
I'll leave behind the one planting rice
who plays handsome, flying fingers over guitar strings.
Faces pierced with bone and silver,
scraped smooth each morning, with razors,
one drop of holy blood, washed down the drain.

All the strong, sweaty and shirtless beings,
building temples, or outhouses,
can live without me.
They can hunt for their own food.

I'm busy filling the Yangtze, the Nile,
the Mississippi river with my birth water.

I dreamed that the only way to heaven
was to kiss.
Kiss wide and soft lipped.
Kiss with your nose, inhaling
the delicate scent of warm rice.
Don't expect to be able
to distinguish God from your lover.

When in pain from pressing against a bristly face,
put one drop of jasmine oil in your bath
and sing a ripple across the water.
It won't reach God's ear — remember the legal separation.
Women must talk to women, to birds and dolphins
and regular men.

The altar keeps moving.
We can never build it
except with snowflakes.

Where They Hung a Crucifix

A daughter is valuable,
she can someday weave.

The sky is full of electric cables
cement towers reinforced with steel.
The hair on my arms rises
when I walk under such a night.
Sparks of lightning ricochet
between glass insulators crackling,
scolding, unzipping the sky.

This is the Indonesian power station slum
where the children of Sumba
live under leaking asbestos
like animals in stalls.
Here is the dirt floor
where women lean away
and weave blankets
dyed with dark roots,
on bamboo back strap looms.

Ibu Rica in labor, is unwinding all the indigo
threads of her life with Samuel,
and the harsh man before him.
Samuel picks lice from the head of
his smallest daughter.

Three walking children
go to school without rice.
There are no tourists
to buy their cloth.

Some of the men in the clan
come home with busted faces,
to watch television.

Christ was born in such a manger.
Christ was born in such a manger.

SEPT. 11, 2001: AN EMBRYO'S PERSPECTIVE

A child hovers in the wine colored
wetlands of a belly.
His heart is working at 150 beats per minute.

In New York City
and in Washington all the angels of our brief
history make a circle and bow their heads in crying.
My unborn grandson feels his mother's heart recede
from him. It is not a good time to be anyone.

My eyes are too dry, as if to cry
would be a selfish thing, after all I am alive
and did not have to choose between fire, the weight of concrete
and steel, or raining from a high window.

My grandson sends me a tentacle,
as fine as a camel's eyelash but long and curling.
He reaches across time,
to tell me something in a language not of his mother's
people, and not any tongue his father speaks.

I bow my head along with the disappointed angels
and listen, and hope to make out his meaning.

ODE TO FRUIT CAKE BAKER

Late in July she picks yard pears
slices and dries them, shriveled moons on wire racks.
By August something signals her to begin saving
the rinds of oranges.
On September first she shops for pecans,
black mission figs, medjool dates from the Holy Land,
a bottle of strong foreign rum, cherries.

Across the street children assemble
for their first day of school.
She assembles the measuring spoons
her big blue crockery bowl comes down, she pauses
to consider how old the can of Baking Soda must now be.

The pans are wiped clean and lined
with waxed paper.
Black walnut ground falls are gathered and cracked.
Flour should be fresh ground. A pinch
of salt brings out the orchid scent of vanilla bean, marries
it to the sugar.
She decides not to blanch the almonds
a little bitter is good.

He comes home from work
as the cakes emerge from the oven,
helps her pour the dark liquor over,
wraps each one in loosely woven cotton rag.

She posts one to a rural route in Oregon,
another to a P.O. box in Northern California.
The best one goes to her, the poet. She can hear the dark
eyes making notes on her cello.
How can the mailman know, on the day before Christmas,
what is so heavy? He drops a white
package on the snowy porch. The poet
will find it in a day, or a week, half buried
half frozen. In her hand she will feel the weight
of being the daughter Edie never had.

FOR WIL

I sleep with too many medicine herbs;
husband, you cannot see your place among them.

After many years, I feel myself
still falling into the amniotic fluid of you.

You swim away,
but damn it, I am the ripple on the surface
and the deep purple places.

You grow crimson wings,
lift yourself into the sky,
only to find the vast blue is our conjoined face,
streaked with jet streams.

I didn't notice it happening;
you became the window washer
of my heart's glass.

I feel myself going to seed —
about to drift away on a downy parachute.

You play guitar and penny whistle,
and wait for me on the rooftop.

Smoking in Baguio

After the war years
Filipino mountain women
would cut off their ear lobes.
They were ashamed of the big holes
stretched by carnelian trade beads
and iron hoops.
American soldiers don't marry
girls with Igarot ears.

This explains why I wear heavy dark silver
and soften my piercings to open wider.
When my holes are huge,
I plan to roll up twenty peso notes,
and stick them through.
A pair of little Filipino flags
waving irreverently
at my American father.

All my life I've gazed
at the branches of Baguio pines.
God, I wish my mother had hung
my placenta high,
where the birds would come
to eat my angel,
so my flesh could fly away.
But I was born in an American
military hospital.
I lost my placenta.

"We don't do that in our country."
said the nurse to my Nanang
when she, emerging from twilight sleep,
asked to feed me.

Injections were given
to dry up her milk.
I still thirst
and stare at big breasts.

When I get back to the Philippines,
I'm going to let the Igarot women
tattoo all the indigo blue mountains on my hands.
I'm going to smoke
a homegrown cigarillo
backwards.

LEAVING IOWA

There are drawers full of purple and red
rubber bands,
each one too precious to throw away
after pulling them free of newspapers
or broccoli bundles.

My ball point pens are still
half full of ink.
One of them has a perfect poem
inside it.

Warm wool sweaters, hand knitted
and completely impractical
where I am going,
curl up in my closet
and purr. My leg warmers snarl.

Coming to this country,
we never planned to stay,
never bought anything new
or nice.
Now that we're leaving,
every fork has a name.

STORIES WE KEEP FROM THE CHILDREN

She finally joined the circus
for the feathers
and the walk to Manhattan
through the Midtown Tunnel,
The Human Barbie
bowing from that stained wooden block,
the cobra, coiled and waiting for the flute.

The soul is what remains
after everyone has gone,
and the three lumpy scars,
the corn crib, the crumbling wall,
the windowless room
much smaller than we remembered.

We are the dance
and the river whispering through,
the white light pulling us along,
these soft, low hills the nearest
we'll ever be to heaven.

MOTHER'S DAY

Go faster! she pleaded
from the back seat of the 1954 Ford,
past the house we'd once owned,
warm rain spotting the sill
of the open bedroom window,
on a wooden hanger the red dress
she'd never worn.

The war had burned away the haze
and she saw the wound through Adam's eyes,
the mountain and a damaged rib.

Algebra II

If you want to go to heaven
you've got to start laying plans
in your sophomore year,
maybe during study hall
instead of cramming for the history exam,
or in the shower after gym class,
that wicked game of shirts and skins.

You must cover your body,
the hair on the back of your arm.
We find it too distracting, like the pink pucker
before the heal, the arc and line
that redefine the curve of the spine.

The god of the head,
the god in the gutter
with the slick of oil and the unused milk —
a real scrapper that one.
Words, not important enough to fall into,
just ink washed over the palest skin,
a calligraphy of soul, the empty tower
guarding its heap of ash and stone.

RESURRECTION

We were neighbors —
then they put the highway through.
Four lanes of traffic
north and south, thirteen roses
dried and tied
with a piece of fraying twine and you
on the other side.

We carted mama around
in the back of a pickup truck
with a makeshift muslin awning,
winter white, cellar light,
to biker bars with friends
we didn't like and songs
we couldn't dance to.

I'll return,
the skinny kid in Levis
and the hair I always wanted,
the dirty birth of rock and roll,
your naked lunch
packed with an apple
in a brown paper bag.

FORTUNES

You will soon be crossing the great waters
and you will be stuck in traffic on the bridge,
stuck listening to NPR, where, if you are lucky
Terry Gross will be interviewing someone
whose life is more interesting than your own.
Other people find your life exciting,
whereas you know that you are mostly stuck in traffic
reading other people's bumper stickers: No Wars for Oil.
(Really? Then why are you driving that car, asshole?)
This makes you sound like a crank. You're not a crank;
in fact, you radiate goodness. You just can't stand
people, that's all, people who always seem bent on driving
wherever it is you need to be going,
which makes it hard to love them, or to radiate anything
except a sour kind of rage, like ash from a burned-out blow-dryer
belonging a former beauty queen
who now tells fortunes outside of Memphis.
Once upon a time it seems
you did radiate goodness, you did love people
with a gladness that rushed in your veins
like a spring creek singing.
and you did cross the great dark waters then,
you have been lucky; you got
what you thought you wanted and now what.
Now you're waiting for the next installment,
the part where you are no longer traveling over
but are actually in the great dark waters
which at some point rise over your head,
and only then if you swim and swim until you drown
and wash ashore and are resuscitated
and crawl on your bloodied hands and knees
over acres of sand, down freeways full of people whizzing by
100 miles an hour on their SUVs, yakking on cell phones,

may you perhaps be lucky or blessed enough to reach that tent
somewhere outside of Memphis
where Trixie sits in her ash-blonde curls and turquoise eye-liner,
waiting for you to extend your palm
in hopes that she will tell you something hopeful.

When I Fail To Remember Things

When I fail to remember things
don't remind me
just take me out to an empty field
with the sparrows in the vanishing point and shoot me
full of country air

When I fail to see
don't throw your gaze down upon our silhouettes
just buy me a pair of inexpensive sunglasses
from the corner drugstore
the kind with tinted sides that Ray Charles
and outfield baseball players wear

When I fail to hear
don't speak in refrain
just turn up the radio as loud as you can stand it
in the middle of the night, at the break of day, anytime at all
yell at the top of your lungs as you say goodnight
then listen to the sparrows in the trees

When I fail to smell
leave the trash inside
bathe infrequently
pass wind often
let the leaning tower of dishes accumulate

When I fail to taste
we will dine upon whatever pleases you
breakfast, lunch, supper and tea
I'll eat sardines and alewives at the table's end while you
have caviar in saffron
with the money we'll save I'll buy you a famous painting,
a pearl necklace, a fig tree to put in the yard
and the world's loudest radio

When I fail to feel your touch
don't lose hold of yourself
take me in the cup of your beautiful hands
scatter me towards the sparrows in the trees
throw your pearl necklace to the stars
and invite over our closest friends to break all of the dishes.

•

GALILEO IN PARIS:
THE DANCER AND THE ASTRONOMER

Galileo strolls in the rain with a toothpick dangling from his lips
uses pages from an illuminated manuscript
for an umbrella
catches flecks of gold lettering
in his eyebrows

admires a dancer's carrot legs
in her soaked tutu, tiptoeing
the past in circles
down the *Champs d'Elysses* to the west of the Seine

Degas brushes by

if only the dancer
cared for astronomy
In her old age

if only Galileo would attempt
A brief arabesque.

I Took My Dog Out to a Fine Italian Restaurant

"What is most necessary
is the unnecessary." —Roberto Benigni

I took my dog out to a fine Italian restaurant on the waterfront
without reservation
it was my birthday
we got a table for two by the window
dined without stares or hindrance, the room was lit by candle
split a bottle of fine red wine from the valleys of France
re-ordered baskets and baskets of fresh warm bread
that ring of metallic shining tags with each and every bite
my canine's fine jewelry, a gift from the city

no dishes dropped, though the moon was full and held by cloth of
the night sky
I had lasagna and minestrone soup
humoured my dog with the spoon on the nose trick
my dog had brushcetta, linguine with fleas and a marinated fish trio
which later made the neighbourhood cats faint, swoon with jealousy
from their garbage lid and fencepost stances

we too accepted fresh ground pepper
and fine parmesan cheese
then split a bottle of port as ships went by
told jokes and reminisced
lamented for the lobsters in the nearby aquarium
with hands in elastics and sad eyes
planned an elaborate lobster napping
felt like ourselves

shared tiramisu and sipped espresso
a string quartet appeared and played "Happy Birthday"
the waiters gathered around and sang the lyrics
their necks craned with each note like a barbershop quintet of birds

an opera singer with a speck of spaghetti sauce on her lips and left
cheek followed
my dog's ears went back and his tail wagged back and forth
the cloth of the table beside
a momentary whitecap

when the cheque appeared I reached
those pockets empty full of lint
the furrowed squint of the waiter, the maitre de'
the sous chef up in arms

I tried not to break into hysterics
as they threatened us with a night of cleaning dishes
my dog licking his jowls passed a knowing wink my way and
laughed
I chuckled too yet shifted in my chair
then my dog threw down his American Express
and we were all at ease
showered in mints, thin chocolates, lemon cloths
fine toothpicks made of synthetic ivory from overseas

my dog performed the tablecloth trick
left all the plates and wineglasses untouched on the table's bare
wooden surface
the restaurant applauded prompting him to tie
the stained cloth to his collar like a cape
we must exeunt I said, *your drunk*
we laughed extendedly like two old rich men

I grabbed my coat and he his own leash
and we strolled out taking our time . . .
my dog on hind legs for a paw in the mint jar
and I for wooden matches bearing advertisement to the restaurant
of great gastronomical delight yet comical distress
and we walked along the boardwalk

the crescendo of the ocean waves hit the bread colored beach
the gentle breeze and parmesan stars
my dog lifted his leg on a lamppost
I felt a sharp pinch in my pocket persuading me to the saltwater shore
and walked towards the sea slightly drunk
calling out for my best friend.

POSSIBILITY

First, a cord tightens in your chest
then flame shoots up the back of your neck
your eyes cloud over and your past mistakes
appear like apparitions at a distance.
All you see is what you are and not
what is. Be calm. Draw a bead on them.
Even if you have a clean shot, chances
are they will elude you. If you could only
shake the fever, and quit the fight to
bend them to your will. Kneel here
in the surf. With this thimble, how long
will it take you to empty out the sea?
In truth, your thirst created a mirage.
But look . . . there is *another* ocean,
inside this one. Toss your thimble out
as far as it will go, and then jump in.

LOVE SONG

1

Five drainages west of here
is the town where you were born;
all the men must register their fists,
the stiff wind makes the women lean,
and outright sanity is treason —
no more than a snoose stain on the map.
But it was you who showed me
inside the mirrors here, the secret
entrance into flowers, to hear
the wind in a different register.

2

Thunder from the belly of the sky,
then the sheen of rain on your face.
I kissed you under a wild plum
split by lightning. A willing virgin.
Your blue panties fell to your ankles
and you flicked them with your foot.
I caught them and inhaled your wildness.

3

Lips thick and numb from kissing
you come up from the headwaters
where three rivers meet, your bush
halfway between foxred and tawny,
your clothes behind me on the bank.

4

You wanted to open your life,
all the parts of you. When that thin song
crawled out from you, I refused
to listen. If I'd known how to let you
you'd have sunk your hand in my heart,

spat in my ears, scratched the rime
from my eyes: healed me. But I
couldn't keep my black beast down.

Soon I was out on the last spit
of existence and I couldn't swim;
you saw a man stepping in
to disaster. When you walked away
that day, your hips receding, I knew
my wings would no longer lift me.
I called out to you, but my words
were pillowed by the fog. Then,
one day, the sun turned black.

5

A small hand twisted in your palm
like a pet lizard: your first son.
The loneliness had fallen from you.
You had married well, they told me.
Another time, I saw you huddled
like a bat, sifting acorns with a
taped-up rake, then bagging leaves,
a dumb suburban custom. I could
write you off, detach my soul from you.

6

At odd times, when snow flicks on the skylight
or a soft wind sucks across a slim piazza,
Charleston, I hear it. When I flail the stretched
catgut with bleeding fingers, your voice,
your voice stampedes up my spine. Your eyes,
the beam of Hatteras circling in the fog,
in low clouds of Prussian blue slinking
over Inverness. In the air where sheep graze
on cold lace near Rannoch Moor, in the breath
of fresh baked bread. In Bombay, I saw

falcons waiting on the rooftops,
you, perched in the scaffolds of my pain.
Oh, God forbid our feeble destinies!

In a dream I was lost.
I canoed through a sinking swamp.

My paddle hit the cartilage heads —
the fish wakened in the coagulum
as the rains came. Druid mudmen,
golem, maybe, hidden in the banks
waited for my will to flag, and then
your gray-blue eyes from somewhere.

7
When you entered the room
I pressed my body back in the chair
to keep from taking flight.
Under the fabric, your breasts
turned up at me. Fifteen years
to the day, and your broken words
still wind around my legs and I
cannot walk away. We walk together.

Yesterday we slanted up a draw;
time brings neglect, the land, buck naked.
Your boots brushed against dry pods
of sage lilies, ancient maracas,
and the ground was hollow underfoot.
That inscrutable music, and the set
of your step, told me that you had
weaned yourself from these dry hills.

8
My body fell into the light of you
and the swallows brought me back.
A linen blouse on the chair,
a stone jar in the corner. The wind
dissolved your wrists where I kissed them.
One last note of the giant bell reverberates.
The morning took you off as if it owned you.
Your face *was* perfect, now you can't change it.
Your breasts, perfect — the aureoles
not a knob or wen. Why do
two souls refuse what the syllables
spell just beneath cognition?
Blessed is the wall of silence
which rains down behind my lies.

Can I come back to these places,
this same air, beneath your long fingers?

TWO BLIND MICE

In the cab of the dump truck was a nest
abandoned by the mother: two pink mice.
Steve said "Put them in one of those work gloves
and step on it — no way they can survive."
You brought them home, called the vet for advice,
started feeding them kittens' formula.
You could see the white of the formula
pass into their stomachs, their intestines.
Their large sleek heads, the delicate pink paws
waving like sprigs of sea anemone,
their sharkslung mouths designed for scavenging,
their little teeth nipping at your fingers.
You called the small one Jimi, for Hendrix,
the large one Gulliver. I saw the way
you let them crawl inside your shirt, the way
you held them to feed them with a dropper.
You kept them in a shoebox filled with felt
and shredded paper, a draped lamp for warmth.
Having an office job it fell to me
to cart the shoebox with me to work.
Knowing this made the secretaries cringe;
I'd lift the felt and they'd start in squeaking.
Jimi lasted the week. That next Monday
I stayed home from work. After quitting time
you swung by the house to drop your lunch box
on the way to the pet store to buy a cage;
Gulliver's eyes were due to open soon —
you planned to take him back to school with you.
But his little bellows had ceased to work.
You held him in your palm, you stroked his tiny
potbelly with your thumb. We put each one
in a separate match box, and sprinkled them
with sacred ash from India, a few
silver leaves of sage from Mesa Verde,

then you covered each with a rose petal
before you closed them up. We taped hand-drawn
red hearts on each coffin, along with
"Om Nama Shivaya" in purple ink.
In the smoldering green of the evening
I dug a hole just south of the bird bath.
You placed them in gently, side by side.
I took your hand and we stood a moment.

Even as a child, you were this way —
a kind of ark. You incorporate this slow
swarm of bees in our horsemint blossoms,
that fat worm on the plantain leaves, whose
portholes glow at night, the doe and fawn
who come to the saltlick, the bluejay, the lark,
the chubby sparrows. Bless the ants in the kitchen,
the cockroach, the mosquito, the deerfly, and the tick.
Praise these creatures for this chance to serve them.
Praise death, as we tamp this earth upon their bodies.
Some day we will burn with them in this earth.

UNFINISHED BUSINESS

There was the first time we made love —
it was in the shower, a perfect fit
standing up, hand in a fine glove —
more lubricous, of course. Through the slit
of the bathroom window the Bridgers loomed
like a blue wall of ancient thunderheads.
From the start, something about it felt doomed —
you loved me in cars, bars and flower beds;
surrender, a hand I refused to play.
As I turned from you, you climbed a ladder
of hysteria. Three times locked away
and five marriages later, our patter
on the phone is easy as if no time
has passed . . . .

REINS

After twenty years, you travel north to see me,
with your teenage daughter as a chaperone;
the gray in our hair becomes the both of us.

You had a taste for sailing close to shore
where the lilies of eccentricity slowed you;
that's where you found me, in select company.

I remember long indigo afternoons,
words of smoke, stars imbedded in my skin,
stolen lifetimes in Charleston and Manhattan.

Though I knew you'd never give up everything
I waited, but didn't have the grit to ask;
my outlook sank like a weighted corpse.

I moved. Our letters sleepwalked back and forth.
When your first child was born, I was silent
for two years, because he wasn't mine.

We sit here, silent. Beyond the porch, horses
loll in purple loosestrife. Your daughter and
my five-year-old son wonder, palpably.

The woman I love now, stands at the door
with tea, and knows I will not turn away
though once I would have done most anything.

PROCEDURE

for Orion

After the Three Wild Babylonian Baboons
walk off in the rain, eating bread and butter
and we snuggle, you drop off into deep sleep.
I uncradle your head from my right arm,
and kiss you one more time. Hibernating
you clutch your spellbound sequined iguana.

Nothing unusual on the farm tonight —
a yearling nickers in the dark corral,
soft blue snowlight slats through the blinds
and makes the plastic stars on the wall
glow in the shape of your constellation.
The radiators code talk in response.

                    Tomorrow morning
I must rise early and go to the place where
they will snake the passages to my heart
and determine the damage I have done.

I must return from this to you. I must.
To watch you rise, and be my sun again,
to live life closer to the earth and sky,
to sing the stillness at the root of things.

1001 LOADS OF LAUNDRY

for my mother

If cleanliness is next to Godliness,
even women who don't wear high heels
must be closer to heaven.
Growing up,
every plate, bowl and cup
in the house,
like a lover,
knew my mother's touch.
And when the wide mouthed hamper
with its bad breath called out to her,
she always answered.

When her water broke,
I wonder if my mother knew her future
held 1001 loads of laundry.
When she counted my toes
and the doctor read the hands of the clock
to announce my time of birth,
did she know she would spend her Saturday nights
at the Laundromat
pouring assembly line sunlight into the washer?
See, if cleanliness is next to godliness,
I was a heathen and my brother was Satan,
and my mother was standing in her skin,
sprouting wings as she
washed the snot out of our sleeves,
folded blue jeans and T-shirts
so come Monday she could
empty us into those envelopes of fresh clothes.
We'd be well versed and clean,
and for once the world
wouldn't put its nose in the air,
would turn the other cheek and embrace us.

Sometimes she let everything in the house collect dust
except us. And she laughed
when her dates wanted to discuss
Women's Lib and democracy,
because the only balance of power she knew was
child on one hip, laundry basket on the other.

So many summer nights the bills held her hostage,
her bank account ravenous,
our appetites growing,
so, like a crow during the dust bowl,
she gathered overtime,
grilled cheese sandwiches,
night shifts and two for one microwave pot pies
to build a nest
while we played outside,
hollering and outgrowing our shells;
sharpening the warm knives of our tongues —
trying to crack the world open.

Though I know she wanted to,
my mother never tried to leave her body,
never plotted a coup de'tat
from behind the barbed wire of her skin,
never emptied her gaze onto strange men
and let her hair down
so she could get a man to climb up the tower
of a single mother with two kids and unlock her.
She never opened her mouth to complain.
Pearls forming in her lungs,
my mother walked our house, my world,
with dishpan hands and dirt under her fingernails.

When we saved up enough money
to buy a house that came with its own washer,
my mother would spill her guts,
like a rainbow, with every load;
telling me how much she hated walking to the laundromat
with our dirty laundry out in the nosey broad daylight.

I watch her,
a strange star
who spent her whole life looking down,
making wishes on us.
I remember those Saturday nights
as being sacred,
something like church.
A place where everyone was the same.
A place where all the women had runs in their bargain bin
stockings
and all the children had socks that didn't match and fathers
who had gone missing
with holes in their stories.
I remember my mother
priest-like,
feeding the washing machine
its Holy Communion:
first quarters, then
the clothes that dressed us.

I remember the steady *whirrrrr*,
the sound of the dirt of our days
turning over and over,
like a prayer on the tongue.
My mother clinging to a vision
of the whole world coming clean,
all the while listening for the *hallelujah*
of an empty hamper.

WHEN YOU ARE BORN

The early hours will be seas
I must navigate without oars or wind or stars.

How will I be your mother,
truth-teller, tooth fairy, and topographer?
With my past as a compass,
I'll have to go to the drawing table everyday
and try to tie the world down and show you with each new draft:
that boyfriend is a desert you don't want to cross.
This curfew is a life preserver.
Child, you are 15, and your hormones are
trying to take you white river rafting.
High school feels like a dead end
but it's actually just a bend in the river;
see, right here, where college ends?
That river will dump you into the ocean.
And it will be terrible, beautiful.
See, because now, child, is when your map
will no longer be flat.

Just now, though, you are curled inside the
small town of my womb, where we speak
the same language, eat the same food,
listen to the same music --
and it's only a matter of time before you outgrow me.

One morning, I'll wake up
to sketch newly discovered canyons
and color the lakes where you might want to swim,
but you will be a foreign country
with a different currency,
searching for beauty,
measuring happiness and success
by some ruler this poem couldn't have guessed.
Maybe metric.

THE TASTE OF WORDS

My father gave me the dictionary
to read as a child.
He said people will form a first impression
on how you speak,
the language you use.

I read every line in that dictionary
devouring page after page,
digesting as many words as I could,
so I would appear intelligent
when I spoke with others.

Speaking is not my forte.
When I write I take twenty six letters,
five vowels and twenty one consonants,
holding their weight in my hands
inhaling their aroma
for minutes, hours or days,
hungry for their taste.

When temptation is too strong
I raise a chosen word to my lips,
rolling it on my tongue,
savoring the flavor,
asking myself,
is this the one that will speak
for me?

My father, the Harvard professor,
was my first poetry teacher
without his knowing.
He taught me to love
the taste of words.

I WANT YOU TO KNOW

You like being married to a priestess?
A woman who worships all objects
that breathe light.
Starfish, plankton, holy temples.
Cracks in the sidewalk. Cracks in the heart.

Do you know I adore jamming,
singing jazz at the coffeehouse in my leopard spotted sneakers?
How is it to hold the hand
of a woman who communes with the dead?
Sometimes easier than with the living,
whose eyes speak shades of truth, secrets or lies.

Do I glow at night?
You've caught me laughing in my sleep,
asked me to roll over.
I'm sorry. The moon keeps telling me jokes.

Do you know it is your hand I want to hold
more than anyone's?
My dreams are made of ancient starlight.
They want to be anchors to God,
and sink into your palm, into your heart, into your life line.

AND THE RAINS CAME

In July I could smell the mold
through the TV, glancing at pictures
of Grand Rapids. Rubbing
the picture tube, the scum would stay
liked a crushed, imaginary waterline
on my clothes. This year it wasn't us.

In '93 it was me watching the 75-year-old
oak slowly teeter, then give way
to rushing current just over the highway
on Rabbit Run. It fell gracefully
as if it was taking its final bow
to a standing ovation.

I wake to sirens, an announce
blaring. "prepare to evacuate."
A vacuum cleaner whirls in my stomach
as I suck up baby pictures into my arms,
adding the toy roller coaster
I bought to represent my life,
for what I thought to be
my next ride out of hills and valleys.

One by one mobile homes move
out of the park as the panic spreads.
I glue myself to the radio and TV
for news of Red Rock Dam.

A taxi pulls up outside, lets out Wally,
who stumbles toward the door,
a gray shadow of a former self.
He wants to reminisce about high school daze.

He sits smoking cigarettes he borrows
from me, completely surrounded by chairs
on top of tables, immune.
I was short with him and I felt as bad
as if I'd been wiped out by the flood.

I thought maybe you'd be filling sandbags today?" I hint.
No I just thought I'd look you up."
I'm just to busy too visit today, Wally," I say.

Well, I'll go," and from the porch
he calls back over his shoulder, "I love you."
You know he does, but right now I'm the last card
played in his losing game of solitaire.

He sees me as the Queen of Hearts
in a life he doesn't understand.
I bargained for an Ace of Spades,
many times myself, Wally.
Life is so much brighter
when you can see both sides,
and I ever so gently wish that for you.

Raindrops start to pound on my tin roof
as I wipe the rust from my cheek

JESUS LOVES PEANUT BUTTER AND JELLY

He learned to prefers sneakers to sandals. Cheers
 for the Hawkeye's, is calmed by Black Angus.
He loves Burr Oak hedge rows leading to wooden gates,
  just as much steps leading to gold and pearly gates.
He praises Billy Joel's fine fire, as well as Garrison Keillor's stories
  of Lutheran ministers on a sinking pontoon boat.
Jesus loves the cha-cha pink glitter of your name tag,
 and he loves the smile you wear in your heart.
He delights in caramel apples at the fair,
  instead forbidden fruit in the Garden of Eden.
Jesus enjoys our cousins flapping and glides the shadow puppet
  like a dove, just as much as the origami frogs other cousins make.
Jesus forgives me for writing a poem
  instead of mowing the yard.

Sea Anemone

All mouth and waving arms,
deadly venom hidden
in blowsy floral beauty.

Unable to move,
stuck to the same rock forever,
one stows away on a crab,
protection in exchange
for scraps.

Sometimes, it will let go of the rock
to float, untethered.

Broken against the coral,
each piece grows into a new animal,
all mouth and waving arms.

You will think this is a metaphor.

SPANISH OMELET

When she no longer ate
only sipped water
I chopped one small white onion
until my tears ran free
mixed in bits of sweet pepper, tomato
and sautéed, slowly in butter
a panful of love.
I whisked and fried

one small brown egg
into a golden omelet.

We sat at the table
soothed by the aroma
of the savory Spanish sauce.
I grasped the spoon
and stretched my arm.
Her mouth, quivered.
Eat little bird
little wren, my sweet
and bite by bite, chewing slowly
she eyed me through narrow slits
relishing, near the end of her life
a Spanish omelet,
always her favorite meal.

TABLE MANNERS

Aunt Rose serves baked ham for dinner,
unfamiliar pink meat
topped with pineapple and brown sugar.

We sit in the silent dinette,
eyes downcast, fingering stitching
on the green damask cloth on our laps.
My father's face is turned.
Mother's lips, pursed.

I listen for the roar from above.
God of Abraham, Isaac, and Jacob.
God of sliced brisket and pickled whitefish.
God of stuffed kishka and noodle kugel.
God of two sets of dishes, milchike and flaishig.
God of Sunday morning brunches,
creamed herring, cheese blintzes, dairy dinners.

I move pieces of ham around my plate
like knights on a checker-board,
slip them under mounds of potatoes,
wondering if God, like me,
plays at being polite.

LATFINA

You're a bony angel.
Just eleven.
Two perfect halves of a ripe nectarine,
bud out of your patriotic leotard.

Your cheek bones rise like steeples
of your village church,
burdened these days
by funeral bells and lost brothers.

Your grave look carries the pain
of a tattered nation —
the bread lines,
snipers,
and your Babushka's swollen legs
limp on watermelon cushions
watching you on her ancient TV.

Your spirit flows in harmony
beneath a solemn mask,
between every button of your spine,
in the sea of your breath,
in the ripple of your thighs,
on the deer-skin of your belly,
along the edge of your ribs,
propping your baby breasts.

You lunge into silence,
blind to the audience,
with passion in your pulse,
fire in your breath,
Babushka in your heart,
and the divine whisper,
You are a warrior.

The snort of the buzzer
barely whisks your glacial waters
as you charge the mat,
a gazelle defying her cheetah,
your eyes fixed on a place out of time.

A place where bread is embroidered on cobblestones.
Where bullets are dew drops in dented cups.
Where fists are kisses, and fathers don't soldier.
Where mamas don't perish,
and Babushkas are still brides
spawning baby brothers.
Where tanks are chariots filled with toys.
Where bombs are balloons teasing the sun.

Your porcelain fingers reach for this place,
and when you pass your own shadow
on the runway of heroes,
Athena and the Olympians
pull the strings of their marionette,
and you're airborne, weightless,
ashes
spinning
with your heart crossed,
landing with pigeon toes
ever so light on the tightwire.

On dark nights alone,
you have mastered the balance
between laughter and windows
shattering.

You lunge on the snowy bar
and gyrate out of focus;
you soar,
but the flight of an albatross
above Gypsy beaches
sometimes ends on sand.

You spread your weary wings,
tumble to an inverted fall,
bow to a somersault,
barrel in a triple cartwheel,
and land with one toe on a speck of dust.
Palms still lifting heaven,
dignity in your crested chin,
soles teetering on perfection.

The gods of Olympia weep
for their quivering sparrow
with the lion's heart.

A whisper wings from your heart,
Papa, if I sit next to you,
quiet as the snow,
will you make me paper moons and angels?

But the roar of the audience,
the walrus whiskers of your coach,
the ice of your gold medal
jar you to your national anthem.

PIAZZA SAN MARCO

The Venetian with a twitch
smiles
as French Gypsies
waltz to an accordion.

All of Venice prepares
for the grotesque
Carnevale –

masks, masks, masks . . .

And facing San Marco's basilica,
I realize at once
the difference between
boys and girls . . .

You see, the male agitator
charges a ripple
of pigeons;
kicks them up like charcoal
dust

into blushed faces
of French school girls
who scream in disbelief,

Pigeon! Pigeon!

Cyrus to SoHo

I

I breathe in the body
of a Persian shepherd
who ran along the ribs
of the Lut Desert,
resting on nights of kneeling caravans
to blow his flute at the wind.

One day, the Royal Dream-Catcher
brought word of the Desert Poet
to Cyrus, in Persepolis.

The Emperor appointed me
poet of his royal harem.

There, I died of bliss
drinking wines of Shiraz,
sucking the blood of pomegranates,
and teasing marmalade thighs
with peacock feathers.

Later, reborn as Cyrus' second son, Cambeseus,
I married my sister,
and starved the Persian army in Egypt.

II

For that, the gods of the Unified Field
reassigned me to Manhattan,

issued me a knapsack, a laptop,
and condemned me to silent observation.

III

Middays I'm plugged
into Village cafés
licking foam off Lattés.

In this *mélange* of French perfume
and cowhide suede,
I lean back, and ponder grinning monkeys etched
on the cast-iron ceiling of *Dean & Deluca*.

IV

So many poets and not enough poems . . .

V

There is the cellular salesman
cheating on two mistresses.
The teary one promises
to start a seaweed diet.

Later, I squat and stare
under the toilet stall

at the Armani boots of a British historian
biting his pipe,

mumbling something about
"Crisis and continuity in the American geopolitical structure."

WHEN MEN DO LAUNDRY

I soak your yellow
skirt
with the blue —

it turns pistachio.

Thank
heaven

you like it
too.

YARD SALE, VENICE BEACH, CALIFORNIA

I found a raw chunk of wood
that under some force was carved with a wandering rose.
Not a rose that Venus would hold to her apple-glow cheek,
but one that a Titan might gallantly toss to Medusa -
a proud, heavy bloom
that could honor a hairful of snakes.

A sturdy, chest-like magic box
where a witch must have kept
mouse bones, owl feathers, vials of red
or a single shriveled left hand.

And for five dollars it became mine.
It held me, keeps me, holds
the hallowed relicts of my walk upon this earth,
showing me that as keepers we each
bear the cut force of time, enclose
the sacred and profane.
We are vessels,
vaults of the vanishing underworld.

ALTAR BOY

I know all about your Catholic upbringing.
I was made to wear a veil confess sins
I did not understand before I was allowed
to take the body of Christ into my mouth.

I know the ten commandments
been confirmed
& yet I want your skin to burn by my touch
& my tongue to cool your fever.
We travel the pilgrimage of senses.
You'll see your god as you moan
& shutter as I rise up off of you
become a being other than myself.

I want you to want to need to long as much as I do
to listen for my voice
that disturbs your dreams
makes you cry out in need when I draw near.

I want to take his cross
construct our bed
splay you on it
dangle rosary beads
between your fingers
push & withdraw with
each 'Our Father' & 'Hail Mary'
that passes from your lips.

I want to be damned to hell.

ADDICT

Does the salt of my skin remind you of India
the glint of my eyes, the North Sea
the heat of my cave, the Mojave
the hmmm of my lips, a hint of the Atlantic
enticing you in?

Does the throb of my throat remind you of Ireland
the grip of my hands, the last day of school
the flat of my belly, the Sunday you wasted
the slope of my foot, the hill you rode down
teaching you the lesson for the last time?

Does the bend of my knee remind you of Italy
the edge of my ribs, the lure of lines on a mirror
the curve of my hips, the way we learn to read
the mount of my breast, the still-warm bread
baked in the afternoon sun?

I KNEW KISSING YOU WOULD HURT

Drops of want stain my lips.
Know this metallic taste, this bitter seasoning.

Tell me we are not momentary.
Tell me all the lies I need.

Once you held a poem in your throat.
Once I searched for blue beach glass.

I knew kissing you would hurt,
but I didn't know it would last this long.

I am not the Coca Cola Girl

I am not the Coca Cola Girl,
the Cheez-It tidbit waiting for you to taste,
the limo ride to the Yankee's game,
the happy hour on Tuesday night,
the Wrangler jeans chick baking the New Mexico sun,
and I never was or will be Sunday mornings in spring.
I am the time-ticking-away second hand,
the flat tire on the side of the road,
the too high door jam,
the worn-out tooth brush,
the 59 cents in the ashtray,
the Lunch Poems dog-eared book,
and the one who never forgets to tell the truth.

IRENE'S NOTE TO CLORIS

I saw your doppelganger skipping
in the baptismal pool water of St. Augustine's chapel.
I didn't wave at her,
just nodded, waited till she squatted in the water,
rocked back on her heels.

Later, I caught her lopping off berries
from the holly tree in your backyard.

I didn't know how to tell you about her,
except to say she was wearing your silver hair comb,
the same one you planted above your bun
when you first met Warner at the dance.

When my eyes washed over her,
I figured she wanted your pearl drop earrings,
the ones your Mama gave you.

Don't tangle with her.
I watched how her head bobbed,
how she drove her hands into the pool water
as if panning for gold.

When I spotted you the other day
standing in front of the campus library,
I admired how sunlight circled your figure eight shape,
how your right arm dangled in the midst of white oak leaves.

Don't even look over your shoulder:
you may eye her torching your favorite dress —
the white cotton eyelet.

THE KISS

1.
I know the relationship between tongue and mouth,
tongue and teeth, lips and mouth — the relationship
between tongue and palate, earlobe, eyelash.

Flames burn as tulips bloom, quickly stripping
to essence. Thoughts must be carried as amulets
if you want to understand them.

There is euphoria of sameness at the bottom of things,
heady as the collected dross of wine.
Hands are flowers; so is the sun,

though it has no stem. Hand and mind
are flowers of a kind. Another metaphor:
old-fashioned wallpaper that sticks to the wall

in a stubborn, breathless kiss.
Life offers endless instances of accidental glory.
The list of things that exist unrolls, a spool of thread.

Unwind, unwind! O, now the wind sweeps through!
I am slave to the wind — don't mind where it takes me,
though it wants things that are inappropriate.

We should enlarge our spheres of knowledge,
areas of sentiment. We should travel.
Did you know? The wind stole tears from my eyes

days before you did. I was glad. I had dried up;
in places I was beginning to rust.
But when I met you I swung open

like a window — on slow, un-oiled hinges.
Since, we've been performing a dance
unchoreographed as clouds, stiff at times

like old knees bent in prayer on kitchen linoleum.
It cannot be the end of the first act, yet I hang
in the sky out of context, bare as a coat peg.

You laugh, drape your velvet corner of heaven
around my thin wooden shoulders.
Somehow it belongs.

2.
There is a kiss that sounds like the howl of an owl
in a forked elm near a marsh,
where trains pass. Have you heard?

It is a kiss that hasn't yet been kissed.
There is a train that will never arrive
though it has already departed.

People flick by so fast I cannot read their faces —
momentary impressions I will send you
as postcards from the depth of space.

My finger gets lost tracing thoughts etched
into the foreheads of casual travelers.
My lip is pregnant with private desire.

The mind of a lonely woman resembles
a spoon intent on filling itself —
yielding, practical, innocent.

3.
I know the thought that precedes relationship.
I have touched a burning candle
because fire precedes emotion,

though a red-capped match precedes flames.
The urgency of sunset and dawn frame life
as exclamation points a Spanish sentence.

Night is quiet.
The moon appears unfinished, a comma.
Blue shadows mount the snow on lonely stilts.

I talk about things I know intimately,
but not as intimate to me as your face.
I touch your neck, the bones delicate Chinese characters.

Your body is familiar as if I washed it once
after death, embalmed it, kissed it
in its ultimate state. Not just passionately —

one holy kiss on eyelids done with fluttering.
For all eternity I will know the relationship
between your eyelids and my tongue.

BONES

Let that be left, which leaves itself. –Shakespeare

1
Death does not follow on my heels like a haggard dog
but dances in my flesh: my own skeleton
waiting for my skin to peel like old wallpaper.
Decay is the beginning of an endless present.

I am a rattle-boned woman pillowed by fat,
a tissue-wrapped trinket, boxed so it won't make noise.
My heart, like the wildly pounding sea,
is a metronome measuring brevity.

I rest my head on my own skull at night
and sleep not an inch from my death
as a scorpion lives with its sting.

2
I am curious about Death.
I tried to peek at him as a Japanese girl of high birth
might have glanced at her future husband
from behind a painted screen.

It's a joke:
The Sun god steers a chariot;
the Moon god has a boat.
Wind sails the clouds,
and Death rides the dust mote.

Yet to Death the moon is paper,
stars no more than scattered salt —
and I, a moth with singed eyes, blindly courting light.

3
I'm a burl in the scrim of the universe,
Death a pair of scissors intending to cut holes.

4
Death studies me as a gypsy studies tea leaves.
He whispers: "Don't suffer through life.
Wear it like a flowing garment.
Take it off. Let it drop."

This means he wants my lips.

5
When I die, I will shout at my heart,
"Lonely bird, fly up from your tree of bones!"

I will shout at Death,
"Have me! It will be like eating a cracker."

6
A congress of ravens will pick my remains
clean as silver needles.
My ashes will be pinned on some lake's chest,
fleeting medals of glory.
The wind, that flagellant who — out of spite —
keeps a whip next to his bed, will take the rest.

7
The sun watches with a dry fish eye.
The sun is a riddle; it taunts the mind,
then disappears untimely — its own elusive answer.

My bones whisper, "You can only die
if you measure the world by day and night.
Look past the sun for freedom from death.
Ponder the rain."

QUESTIONS FOR THE MOON

How old are you that you're permitted to wander streets
late nights alone? You walk circles,

tongue-tied, coyly dropping pallid, scanty scarves
into puddles. For whom?

Are you in love, or a pilgrim seeking absolution?
How can you run so fast without feet,

without getting away?
Large dark hands push you like a tasseled pillow deep

into Sky's sequined furniture.
Large dark hands cover your body, hiding half from view.

You live in purdah or disclose a hyperbole of undress.
Your appetite seems shifty as your shape.

Does your tumescence birth stars?
How else can you slim down to a fingernail clipping!

Who polishes your lacquered skin?
The irascible, jealous Day dissolves your substance

like salt the skin of snails,
but I commend your physicians: you regenerate.

I think it is Night who practices this laying on of hands,
for why else does Night extirpate

all light but yours? My own hands can't support
the mass of your weightless urgency.

My fingers get wet reaching into the pond of time
to retrieve even one lost, elusive strand of your hair.

EIGHT

First kiss: Mouthing the pillow I slept on.
Wet response on my cheek in the morning
when I woke. First touch: Sheet that barely
made contact. Aloof pressure of a handless hand.

I remember removing clothes, though rule was
to wear pajamas, panties. The touch
my skin craved staged an illicit, dreamy
performance: Surrender. Surrender to what?

The whole bed gave in to my desire, I into
the touch of soft things so remote compared
to skin, yet available for ritual wanting.
Lushly I'd lift the sheet, shake it, let it twirl

on my body as a bird flings wings into space —
invisible tremor that shakes the universe.

MATHEMATICS OF NATURE

The sun, sporting wild, hennaed hair, slinks through air,
teenager among her clan of juvenile clouds —

yet her spindly fingers capably conduct chemical experiments,
balancing the variables of atmosphere, moisture, heat.

The spider does research in spherical geometry,
calculating polygons involving trapezoids

between fractal, rain-stained twigs
that drip in measured count.

When it snows, flakes hover down
at equidistant, exact intervals — dreamy army.

Dawn strings dewdrops, perfect strands of pearls,
along each blade of grass, each cobweb filigree — but evenly,

the way a thousand geese spread,
landing on the surface of a lake with proportional parity.

When gunshot sends a thousand geese into ascent,
they don't collide, their wings never tangle;

each feather, shape, whiteness separates intimately
as in an Escher print.

How can nature be so mathematical,
while mathematics is imprecise?

Numbers don't add as mathematicians think.
One plus one plus one raindrop

is still one raindrop.
One raindrop and one lake equal one lake.

Ten thousand raindrops and one field yield
a corn crop of thousands of stalks, millions of kernels.

No matter how much you add to hate,
the final sum turns into a fraction

while love is a substance that augments with subtraction.
Two hot breaths swallow each other,

yet stupendously multiply into new life — tiny feet
that smell like vanilla and walk the earth as you do.

One whisper lasts an instant yet defines
the mysterious perimeters of mind,

the incongruence of one thought occupying
one space inside two skulls.

TO ARANYANI

I praise the musk-scented, fragrant, fertile, uncultivated
Aranyani, the mother of wild animals. — Rig Veda X, 146

Idle at woods edge, I hear three notes,
high and thin as a filament of crystal,
from a towhee hidden in the safety of brambles.
Locust trees bristle with black fangs,
like a wild mother at bay,
defending what is left of her brood.

Scab trees, locusts cover wounded ground.
That's how the forest comes back.
But it will take longer than you or I
will live to see.

Shameless in the moist hollow of a leaf,
tree frogs tickle
the curvilinear wetlands of my inner ear.

Stepping carefully among fallen thorns, I penetrate
down to where a creek slips by
so slow and small that it makes no more sound
than a snake passing.
My hand touches the rude silk of horsetail grass,
socketed stems rising thick and green.

I know this grass,
fashioned when the forest
was a Paleozoic maid.
Now she is crone,
taken, cut so that men can raise corn
and do a thousand hard-edged things.

Neither am I a young woman any longer.
One crone to another,
I beg the forest, take me back.
Let me be your child again.

Dancing in the Oxbow

Flood by flood, Crow Creek carves wider
into the outer bank of a certain bend
where wild sweet Williams dandle blue flowers.
It washes away the soil of centuries
from the feet of a river birch I know.

Every spring the leafing tree leans closer,
reaches for my side of the creek
for any stop or hold.
Squirrels scold and beat their tails
on the lowering trunk,
while thick shoots burst skyward
as if they could outleap disaster
and water thrushes, lacking any sense of history,
line a nest in a catch of roots.

If I had the eyes of centuries,
I would see the slow dance
of roots grappling with air,
hear the low-pitched sigh
as against all its will the birch sinks
toward the wild moment
when it will thrash downstream in flood
and for the space of a breath
blue blossoms ride above the foam.

AT WATER'S EDGE

Trouble with animals, they die.
Other than that I don't mind being one.

But when milkweeds stiffen and twist
it's only pods opening,
unfolding ripples of white
soft as sunlight on my fingers.

Like a fawn's small breath
the pods' silk swells, lifts out,
separates.

Each parachute with flat red seed
rides motionless over wetland.
Don't they even care where they'll land?

And that is just how softly
I would hope
to step out of the crusty pod.

JUST ANOTHER LOBSTER POEM

Vagina dentata,
hungry and hidden,
buried deep inside
come-hither
glistening folds.

Beware,
Grizzly Woman
crawls out of her fur,
to devour mischievous
out-thrusting manhood
with ferocious fangs.

Freud said it's the
male subconscious fear of
castration by
She Who Already Broke Hers Off.

Revenge,
a penis made of stone.
Teeth shatter,
and She-bear returns
to the womb of her cave.

STONE WORK

I always wanted someone to take me under her wing
the way this sculptor has loaded this heavy chunk
of stone onto the truck bed, tucked in blankets
for the long ride. Stone dust filters through the car
when she lowers the window, staring at the early
stars. We curve down inland roads towards
ocean. I sit in her art studio
for days or months. She drills and chisels.
She touches me as if shining a light from a dinghy
into dark water in search of a lost being.
I experience an openness I had never imagined
I would be capable of. It takes effort, this tug of war
and muscle. I am impatient, yet savor these long hours
of attention while she works, sanding a crevice
purposefully, revealing cracks I no longer need
to keep silent. Shame fizzes into ether.
She sets me upright, turns me around, eyeing
various positions, her hand gliding over a newly
arched brow and prickly bottom lip, until almost erect,
I balance on a wedge of polished black granite.

THIS BLAZE OF GROWING
—D.H.Lawrence

Oh yes, this blaze of growing,
the wind harp on a mountain in Vermont
acting like an acoustic whisk. I drove miles
to stand inside the radius of this Aeolian shimmer.
This blaze of memory pierces our skin.
We remark, it's only flecks of moonlight.
On looking out the morning window
this blaze of growing shakes us
out of our sleepy boots. Alive
to the ambrosia of orange, red, purple flowers
lighting the patio- the red moment
when a hummingbird flirted with salvia;
how he perched on that slinky tendril of a vine;
how the vine didn't even tremble; how a hummingbird
weighs less than a nickel. We are filled
with those moments, and delight in knowing
that even in cave paintings, the shape of the heart
is the same one children color with a red crayon.

COMMUTER

6:00 AM
Sun bruises the horizon
tugs the socks off the Golden Gate.
Spires, tucked into fog's skirts,
here and there reveal an ankle
then a leg.

Pressing eyelids, I see stars.
I forgot my niece's birthday
and my lunch.
Miles bleeds into Coltrane.
Fingers dig into hair and pull.
I am still breathing.

Street cleaners block lanes on Bay Street.
At every red light, I yawn
preferring Egyptian cotton sheets
at this time of day
and how my hand touches your face
cool, still sleeping, when I kiss you.

A man on Spear Street, stops suddenly
to touch a tree as if it were his lover's hair.
A plumber wiggles his white socks,
reeking of 3rd grade gym class, into boots.
"The Giants beat Cincinnati!" No one stops.
The woman selling papers shrugs, lights a cigarette.

The building rumbles like a sleeping lion.
Elevators ding, soar upward and push
me into the machinery of the day.
11th Floor. Phones ring.
Someone laughs too loudly.
Hope gets pushed down.

Windows reflect monitors
and desks crowded with coffee cups.
From her nest across the way,
the peregrine falcon lifts off.
Talons hang like question marks,
an angel flying up again, taking me with her.

KIND OF BLUE

Don't play what's there, play what's not there. — Miles Davis

Listen as Miles blows his sweet horn.
Music born from excavated earth
fertile and fat with secrets
unburied by this man
who only plays what is not there.
The coil of the melody asks: Are you ready for truth?

Lean into the notes
a bar stool on an unsteady night.
Watch the chorus of women shimmer,
silky thighs rustle under tight skirts
as they dip and sway,
gathering grace

like all the other big-hipped women
before them, they listen to the sound
swell and roll like a tongue,
a reminder of something beloved
and lost long ago:
the dog shiny with wag stilled by a passing car.

Aching tones caress cheeks
curl like smoke around thick ankles.
Soaked in jazz, bodies drip
with something forgotten.
Pieces of themselves reform
chasing the demons from their souls.

A blood poet.
Miles delivers the gutted ruins
of his despair in these finest of notes
understanding that we are
bolts of light meant to streak, fire-lit
to our own blazing end.

WHY A WORKERS' MURAL HANGS ON

At Rincon Annex, with paintings of labor,
the building's new owners
have made a post office into a mall
and don't want the murals there.
Paintings don't have souls.
They don't bleed when cut
or cry when they are painted over
but maybe, at Rincon Annex
the Chinese workers' ghosts would have
come downtown and then
hollered and shouted at the passing
tourists and Christmas shoppers.
The ghosts may materialize as one scurries away
with packages.
Maybe the Native Americans' drums
would be heard for miles,
and Tom Mooney's ghost would sing
prison songs with Joe Hill's and Harry Bridges,'
the voices noisy, loud, and rowdy,
so loud that cars would beep
as they drove by,
the drivers waving their hands
in unity,
so maybe, that's why the
Rincon Annex murals got to stay.

FOR THE CHRONICLE CARRIER GIRLS AND BOYS

They're too young to have read
the Theory of Surplus-Value.
She's just been working hard,
delivering the papers,
working on her throw.
He's just a kid,
he's too young to know what
the Theory of Surplus-Value means,
he doesn't know why someone thinks
that he's a surplus, and the newspaper boys
and girls have to go.
He thinks a surplus is like an extra sack
of potatoes that gets tossed in a truck
and that gets shipped back
or is thrown away,
except he's ten, and she's eleven,
and unlike sacks
they breathe when they run
and when they laugh, when they
have a little money to take home.
A surplus, she thinks is like pairs
of old jeans in a store
on Mission Street,
except the newspaper girls and boys;
they breathe as they yell and as they cry
and they cry not to have their jobs;
and now little boys and girls are beginning
to understand how people can be
Surplus, too.

THE DAY LABORERS

Day laborers
line Cesar Chavez Street,
a small group of men
on each corner,
workers
waiting
ready to go
or not,
getting by
until the next day;
the on-the-street hiring hall
where the INS
may show up,
or not;
another day
of Spanish-speaking men
looking.
I glide by inside
a car window
looking for
my day to begin.
We are all starting our day.
For the men on the corners,
each day starts
over and over
again.

GRANDMA'S SABBATH

The day the tree fell down,
Grandma felt her
own roots shake;
the roots stayed
but the trunk
came down,
upsetting the sky,
creating a strange
falling space
to her ears, deaf.
It was Friday night
so she lit her candles,
she said blessings,
and ate egg bread.
All that death and
dead wood
sweeping past the
windows,
threatening to
crash into the
world of her silent
prayer,
the vibrations
extended into her feet
on her day of rest.
She could feel how God
and the earth
wrestled with each other.

CORLENE

1.   Corlene is pregnant
     and the consciousness of pregnancy
     comes to me in a dream
     "her labor was hard" I later learn.

     Corlene, in the dream,
     has had her baby,
     and now she is traveling
     on a train
     to rejoin everybody.
     She decides to put the baby back
     inside herself,
     but now he is hard to come out.

     When the baby
     comes out again,
     he is a cat,
     white and black
     and orange
     on different sides
     with a third eye.

2.   The cat is taken to a doctor
     to be fixed
     so he becomes human again.

     he grows up to be a boy
     and goes to school.

     then, he is playing on a baseball field,
     and a kind of radiation hits,
     and simultaneously, the government changes
     where misfits are not tolerated.
     The ray is a kind that causes
     cat tendencies to come out.

come out
come out
the cat tendencies come out —
a long striped orange tail
grows out of the boy —
he hides it in his clothes
not to be caught by
the authorities.

suddenly, the boy remembers
his birth
and being called Victor the Cat
when very young
being born
a second time as a cat.

3.   I wake up —
and my friends tell me her labor was hard,
and that when women are pregnant there is a
universal cosmic unconscious
that affects other people,
that penetrates dreams.

1967 and Senior Year in High School

It was held in the gymnasium,
not the auditorium,
on bleachers,
almost like a sports event,
a man came to tell us
not to take drugs,
it was 1967,
but it was not only
drugs he was against,
he warned us
against Allen Ginsberg,
the homosexual author,
everything that Ginsberg stood for,
the man shouted out like a drill Sergeant,
was I the only one
who wondered why
he could say all the
things he was saying?
Three thousand of us
left the gym
through the two doors,
and as I got to the door
wanting air,
a high school boy
fell down on the
tan gym floor,
three feet from my feet,
twisting and kicking,
having an epileptic seizure,
in front of the entire student body,
filing by him,
in threes and fours,
a student body of
three thousand students,

all of our eyes were
fixed on his form
for a moment.
It was my Senior Year in High School,
and all I wanted was to write poetry
like Allen Ginsberg
and to keep moving
into the air.

TASTE OF HONEY

Had I learned my *Alef Bet* when I was young
I might have had them 'dipped in honey'
       to make my study sweet.
Had I known the sound of Torah as a child
I would have had the rhythm deep entrenched
       in my memory,
needing just a quick mnemonic to get me going.

Since I learned my Hebrew late in life
       the words come slow.
Then again, I knew the stories and
       could parse what I was saying.
When my daughter gave me my own silver *yud*,
       laughing, told me *go read Torah, Mom*,
I took her at her word.

Since the music for the Prophets's tales is more melodic
       I began with Zecharia.
The Torah chant is constant, the *Nivi'im* has more notation,
       more depth of meaning to convey.
The dirge of warning, or the trill of joy
       comes smoothly to the tongue.
Take heed Jerusalem is chanted in a minor key;
Rejoice, you daughters of Zion sounds like birds are singing.

THE DREAM THEATER

We narrow into the house, the room, the bed,
where sleep begins its shunting.
You cradle your head
neat as note paper in an envelope of sheets,
while I act a princess who owns the stage.

The headboard is disturbed
by your uncomfortable skew, hands
like stubborn adverbs visiting your face,
your shoulder in a piquancy of dreams
where I can't intrude.

You are all I have gathered to me
of otherness. I am still learning to lock and unlock
our weathered libraries of love.

Now you face away from me in sleep.
An old woman doorkeeper, bread in her pocket,
turns the key that lets the night pass.

With your brain in italicized gloom,
your mouth a little open,
the dream comes on, a place to climb the dark.
A hundred minutes of illusion
flickers beneath our late stars.

VAN CLIBURN IN THE CONVENT

She thought that if she vowed chastity
God would be closer
but one night she sat on the wooden floor,
that she had buffed, shined,
her back straight against the cenacle wall
and listened to the young Van Cliburn
play Tchaikovsky's Concerto in D.
She closed her eyes, imagined his fingers
brushing the smooth keys, then felt
his fingers playing her skin.

Inside she heard a wind-aroused river.
You'd have never known it, looking at her
layered in black serge, breast and hair
covered in white linen, wracked by wanting
in the silence that lives beyond music.
The ceiling of the room rose high and white,
her job to dust its fluted corners and tall
windows, velvet draped against the winter.

Outside the cloister Randolph Street
ran downhill to the Mississippi.
She had come from the bottom of that hill,
had found the river cave with the granite
the boys called Frankenstein's bed.
She had danced to Elvis and Jerry Lee
but had not met this kind of music.

The last movement crashed
and turned inside her.
Moon became night heron.
Ice floes cracked on the river.
Love opened and opened.

That next Saturday night, her sisters
lined the long, unlit hallway to chant
and beat their thighs with small chains.
Instead of penance, she dreamed
Van Cliburn. His melodies grew
through walls around her,
becoming her own body song.

POPPIES IN THE RUINS

Heart strong as split stone,
I stumble on the path
between life and death,

remembering the mountain of Ephesus
where shards of marble survive
violent sunlight.
The wind in bright heat
hisses like winter in crevices of stone.

Scarlet poppies fill the cracks
where two walls of rubble meet
and the dry creek bed tumbles away
what's left of present and past.

When the bus dropped the two of us
on a corner in a small Turkish town,
I knew it was an ending and beginning.
Lost in drenching rain, crumble, vespa roar
it was possible to laugh, to find abundance.

The prayer call from loud speakers
on tiled roofs shattered the air.

A HUNDRED SAND AND FLOWER CARPETS

> *I'm kind of like a priest of the religion of Art and Beauty.*
> — Bill Teeple, Painter from Fairfield, Iowa

They began last night and are working still
at noon, even the little ones who spray
dyed vermillion and orange sand grains
to keep them from blowing away.
Their mother in jeans and sweatshirt stretches
to set the topaz eyes in the Quetzal birds
and the shadows on Mary's roses.

Mary with long hair, real as theirs, or mine,
aquamarine stones for her eyes — holds the child
at the center of the universe, butterflies gracing
each pole. The young woman with earphones
and her cousin with a cell phone, lay down
serpentine borders of purple hibiscus.

They keep me awake all night but the beauty
at my feet pushes faithlessness away.
Soon clouds of incense dark the narrow street.
Bare feet of men bearing a statue of Jesus
destroy the carpet while drums mourn
and the children sweep up brilliant fragments . . .

What happens to beauty when no one believes anymore?

PRAISE SONG FOR WINTER

Somewhere on this persistent earth
it is at last winter again
time to stand quieter than a month ago
watch the snow's steep descent
whorls of silver streaks sifting
across the glass of the north-facing windows

At last no baking heat no
insistent sun to run from
instead collars up scarves tight
insistent knives of cold
slicing circles into cheeks
keeping the windshield sticky
with frost and rime
hoarfrost now there's a word
that makes the blood run fast

It's a blessing that now
the windows can stay locked
the lamps come on early
sweeping the amber-shaded rooms
you imagine roots and bulbs
suspended in their season
bedded under the snow

You know that the ice will come at last
and cover the land
breaking our eyes
with a startling majesty

light prisms shattering branches
looped double to the ground
frozen grasses snapping
sculpted into spidery nets
a glory closer to God's own light
than we could ever have imagined

The Almond Tree Song

When I know that I am to die,
I will ask you
to lay me down beneath the almond tree
where I will drink translucent blossoms
and dress my hair in sheaves of gold anemones.
I will ask you
to carry me to the flower beds
where I will sink my fingers
into cracked winter roots,
breathe soft rotting pomegranates.
I will look once more at the mountain,
taste open sky, hear
a black bird's high song.
I will ask you then
to shroud my body with blankets of sage,
sprinkle it with sweet honeysuckle,
slip me straight
into the dark ground,
no coffin walls to separate my skin
from the ancient hillside.
You will tuck me into my bed
as a mother would,
smoothing earth
around my thighs, my hips,
the curve of my belly,
so that those who come to say farewell
will never have to know
that I have slipped away
into the nearby field of pale lilies,
singing a fresh song.

SHARDS

Voices call as I walk the land, gathering in
my return; the birds have shown me

spring, they breathe in my relief.
Pomegranates, reddening when I left,

perch loosely on their stems, brown
mouths open, picked dry by winter.

The sap is not yet up in the apricot tree,
snow still beds down the hills beyond: *where*

is my father now? His face is in my eyes,
his body crumbled to sand: *in whose arms*

does he lie tonight? We wade through
the debris of his life, set ourselves

at different poles, clasp the shards
of memory — a tiny copper dish,

a silver pencil, a new piece of God. We sing
of him, strew photos around the bed, wish

him back for Sunday lunch, cannot find
the letter he searched for that last night.

THE IMPORTANCE OF BONE

She measures my skull with her fingertips, parting
my hair, gently drawing the lines, quadrants
that will meet at the crossroads of remembering.
I wait for my mother to appear in my dreams,
for my father to return home.

My palm encloses Sophia's head, newborn
lines of soft bone curving up the peak, wisps
of brown hair lying over the crack
that pulsed liquid, body hot through the membranes,
bursting out into gravity, wanting air.

I run my thumb over Miocene fish bones
found in a dig south of Sparta,
minute particles of ridged calcium
telling stories of forgotten seas, a people
who buried their dead in small goatskin boats,
who understood algae and bamboo.

You write that when your mother finally dies,
the spectrum of color that contains us all
will fall to earth, the smooth glass talisman
split into wings. I wait for the impossible air
to take a breath, for the cicadas
to stop singing their death.

BREATHING

At the olive press this morning, I lean
my face against the iron grid above the great
steel blades that grind the olives through
the long bin, wet mottled green dough,
pouring silky oil out the final thin tube,
where the smell is the smell
of sour bread made from earth,
from well water, from women squatting
on hard ground, fingers flying, gathering
the fallen olives, moving through
tall grasses, finding fat purple fruit,
murmuring of Maria and her hard man,
Panagiota's difficult pregnancy, Lenio wanting
to leave the village, Stellio driving too fast,
the strange summer rain that ruined
the grape harvest. The men perch high
in the trees, feet splayed along the limbs,
whapping the branches with long gnarled sticks
kept all summer in the corners of sheds,
the olives pouring down like hail
onto the great crackling sheets
of plastic wrapped around the tree base.

I press my face again to the grid,
breathe in the smoky odors, wet cat fur,
slept-in bedclothes, rotting leaves.
I wish my hands down
into the dark must, pushing them in
up to the elbows, sliding the hot mass
through my fingers, pungent steam
rising, fermenting fragments of pits
and skin coating my hands, the smell rolling
on and on over the fertile chalice of the earth.

MATCHING DRESSES

On the path from uncertainty
to my neighborhood Safeway, I braked
for a mother and daughter
who sashayed through the crosswalk
in matching magenta-striped dresses.
Half a century before, other drivers had halted
while my mother and I proudly strolled hand
in hand across elm-shaded streets, modeling
brand new yellow seersucker shirtwaists.

Thanks to the Depression, and marriage
to a man who insisted that women were
No good at anything, my mother never drove;
so we walked, mismatched twins,
our twined fingers faintly scented
by the Aquamarine she applied every night
before bed. In summer, our white strappy
sandals clip-clopped unison rhythms
over near-molten sidewalks. In winter,
four rubber galoshes pounded parallel
purposeful tracks in the snow.

Those sounds, scents, impressions
have since disappeared, but this daughter's strong legs,
toughened by urban journeys, persist
with the sense that together we'd face
any terrors the streets held in store. Even now,
while navigating uncharted territories, I sometimes
still reach for her hand.

As I watched that magenta-clad duo,
I longed to shout out: *Sweet Girl, hold on tight!*
That warmth and connection cannot
last forever. But instead, I kept
to my path, less eager to arrive
somewhere no one would know me.

DUAL EXPOSURE

Deposited on a ragged stone wall,
elastic grin and wide-stretched arms
challenging Niagara's full force, a four-year-old girl
flaunts the warrior's stance
and level gaze of some long-forgotten race,
rewarding parents who posed her in the foreground of danger
with their precious souvenir.

A half-century later, picture a grown woman's spine
trapped immobile in a hospital's imaging submarine.
Depth charges boom the length of her once-fluid torso
while she dreams of out-dancing sciatica's eddies,
then curtsies to pain, her perpetual partner,
who drowns out all music in the background of bliss.

Put down your camera.
This vista's off limits.

GO GREEN

Straight A, straight-laced
      cloistered in a crop circle dustbowl
      dive-bombed by doves spewing DDT
The crop duster is God in this part of the country.

Rigid dirty rows and pews
      angles and isles
      all weed free.

I sit with knees squeezed together
      in the psychedelic mini-skirt Jesus told me to buy
I stand on black patent-leather shoes
      reflecting up my skirt.

We kneel We stand We kneel
      synchronized pistons firing
      finely tuned fervor
      pretending nothing is missing
Fanatic fumes, exhausted.

I sputter into Texaco in 5 AM bleakness
      line up, wait to be ministered to
The full-service priest at the pump trades Premium
      for a little bit of my soul.

Sometimes I think I see the end of the line
      as morning rays wipe my windshield clear
Squeegeed enlightenment.
A solar-powered pilgrim gallops by
      entices me to Go Green
I abandon my car & underwear
      ride bareback to the Beach.

LAO TZU'S SISTER'S DREAM

1.

Shih-Ch'eng Chi was married
and living in the provinces.
One day, though the road was long,
she set out on a visit.

It was spring:
mandarin, cherry, plum —
and she filled her basket
with offerings. So she walked

one hundred stages of the journey,
until her heels blistered.
As the crow needs no inking to stay black,
blisters on a journey are no omen.

In the middle of the night,
late in the season,
Lao-Tzu heard footsteps
on the path to his reed hut.

2.

She stayed with him for days,
rising early each morning
to walk with him by the river.
Surely, you know the river.

One day, tossing a stick
into the water,
ripples dancing on the surface,
she recalled a dream.

"There was an uncarved block
and beside it a piece of raw silk.
My fingers went over them with ease.
I thought of a field, and saw

a plum tree. Leaning against it
a woman gave birth to a child.
She placed him in a wooden cart
led away by two white horses.

The road ran along side a stream
until they reached the top of a hill.
From there, I could see the water
downstream, passing by boulders and smaller rocks."

3.

Now one story goes, "Old Boy"
or the "Old Fellow" or "The Grand Old Master"
at the end of days,
saddened and disappointed

in the ways of men,
climbed on a water buffalo
and rode westward toward Tibet.
At the Hankao Pass, a gatekeeper

an observer of sorts, thought
"Here's a queer fellow. . .
and asked him to leave behind
a record of his thoughts.

We all know the book's name,
though I will not name it here.
If you look inside it
there are 5,000 characters

an uncarved block of wood,
a piece of raw silk,
water running everywhere,
round rocks, and down valleys.

LAST PAGE OF THE BOOK OF SPLENDORS

Happiness settles the spirit, but the
Heart's sorrow drives it into exile.
Ospreys soar above willows towards the sun,
A brown creeper spirals up the tree's trunk.
We track them this winter Sunday morning.
We listen to song, soft sibilant *see.*
Cardinals of winter, juncos, finches —
All these signs of spirit settled.
We scan the woods for ruby-crowned kinglets.
We cross the bridge to view the red-tailed hawk.
The sorrow of our exile is blinded
By the light of the eye, the earth's splendor.
We see from one end of the Platte River
To the other. We wrap ourselves in light.

PRAYER: BIRD-SONG

And all the birds utter, each their own song.
This fall morning we hear them near the Platte —
The sharp nasal honk of the upside-down nuthatch,
The higher pitched notes of the tree and song sparrows
Flitting about stalks of sunflowers gone to seed,
The downy woodpecker working furiously at the willow,
Its head darting back and forth in rapid fire,
The screech of the blue jay among the cottonwoods
And the explosive quail flashing over bluestem.
We know the clarion call of the sandhill crane
That roosts on this braided river each spring.
We compose a song out of all these varied voices.
We hold hands to reclaim our tremulous love
Touching the whole notes between us.

WHAT THE SOAPSTONE CARVER KNOWS

Even mistakes can be beautiful.

The scrap of soaprock
that was supposed to be a loon
can shape shift in seconds
and become a palm-sized polar bear,
snout reaching skyward.

All it takes is the right tool:
forgiveness.

IMPOSSIBLE

that he should survive in all this snow,
beer-bellied acrobat
leaping from branch to branch —
spitting image of a rat,
were it not for the black mink stole
giving balance and ballast.
Impossible, the sheer weight of him
on the thinnest of boughs,
which sway and sag as he passes.
Look at him, scolding the jay
that swept in to shriek and screech.
Look at him winning rows
with crows twice his size.
Far below, the *Globe and Mail*
has weathered sleet and acid rain
to announce that the world is ending.
Mad Gunman Goes on School Shooting Spree.
Different Guns, Different Uniforms, Same War.
NHL Lockout Hits Day 103.
Pausing on a slippery crux,
the squirrel tightens his body into a fist
and, impossibly,
leaps.

TREADING WATER

They say cystic fibrosis is like drowning
on the inside.

I say it's like having a fat cat
asleep on your chest.
It's a quiet pressing down,
like the snow outside:
silent
insistent,
smothering.

You write, "I'm thinking about you,
imagining your lungs twin bellows
filled with light."

I say they're sputtering whoopee cushions
and the joke's getting old.

We both agree that "Bronchi ecstasy"
sounds sexier than Bronchiectasis.
"Deterioration of lung tissue"
isn't sexy at all.

"Good God, I want to kiss you," you say
as I pull my sweater off slowly
on Skype. We singe phone lines.

Sometimes the vast, black ocean
laps at my body from all sides,
laughing. They say drowning is euphoric.

You email me opera arias,
promise we'll visit Ireland, Scotland,
Antares — the supergiant star
in the Milky Way.

I grip the phone as though it were a lifeboat.
I ride your waves, rising
to the surface.

FIREBALL

He has a new car,
bought it to see his girl
in the Sudbury Basin,
where she's been wading all summer
like a moose, hip-deep
in the cool blue green
of her past.

Fitting that she was born in the wound
left by an exploding meteor
two billion years ago.
She's made of rock and debris.
She burns and she falls
and she falls.

He's got a new haircut,
new shoes, maybe a ring
in his pocket.

All her life she has longed
to belong to someone,
yearned for the surety of something
mined from the earth's heart
and wrapped around her finger.

He's just finishing his final round
of laundry when she calls
and says, don't come.

He stares into the spinning black hole
of the dryer.
She dances barefoot beneath the stars.

THE OLDER I GET THE MORE LIKE A BOULDER I BECOME

There are boulders that can dance. It is a secret they keep
well. Under a hunter's moon shaking off their heft for some
fancy steppin'. It is all very subtle by non-boulder standards.
Imperceptible in fact. And they will stop on a dime if observed.
Which isn't hard, because a dizzying spin for a boulder is a
millimeter of relative movement to the right or left, which may take
hours or even days to perform. But oh, for that moment, they are
tap dancing fools. They are monopodal hoofers kicking up a storm.
They are whirlwinds. They are mad dervishes, and the world is a
blur around them.

SAFETY PAPER

When everything else failed, she constructed a world in origami
art. Fold into fold at every angle. The paper dog which shook its
head when you pulled its tail, the booze bottles filled with confetti.
Even her dreams; mathematically balanced — hand-pressed and
smoothed. A bed, high up, with creases sharp as military trousers —
the folded men, with accordion flares to their biceps, that filled it.
Each morning: a fresh stack — crumpling her work from the night
before.

RHAPSODY OF FALLEN OBJECTS

Sometimes when enough has fallen down around you, it becomes a music you can dance to. Glass objects separating like startled birds across the hardwood floor. The thud of weightier things, dented but not broken. A makeshift orchestra gravity conducts. As you go about the business of the day — the pieces oddly melodic. Something you can tap a foot to.

HORSE WITH A FORK IN ITS HEAD

After the revolution, it is taught in all the schools that a horse with a fork in its head is a unicorn.

The teachers all wear uniforms with creases sharp as knives. Their cheeks plump and overstuffed like suitcases that will not close. And hardly ever do.

When your feet get stuck in mud, they say. It simply means: the earth is your new pair of shoes.

LEGS

We lived on the fifth floor of a six story
tenement — five floors from the hard kiss
of cement, a bounce off clothes lines,
hands flailing — a long scream, then silence.

I pictured this each time my mother
cleaned windows, sitting on the small
ledge, her back to the unobstructed air.
A crumpled page of newspaper in one hand,

Windex in the other — the panes
in rotted Victorian frames with much
of the putty cracked or missing.
"Hold my legs," she'd say, using my tiny

form for ballast — the clinging tourniquet
I became, keeping the blood from
reaching her toes. "Not so tight," she'd urge —
a thin sheet of foaming glass between us.

Then, mouthing the words slowly, as though
I might read her lips and relent:
"not . . . so . . . tight. Not . . . so . . . tight."
But I never listened.

OCTOBER COUNTRY

Death is fun in the glazed
dusk; the street slick with
rain — a traffic light bleeding
in long streaks across the tar.

The dull mounds of snails
dotting the sidewalk, lured
from the slopes of Lisbon Hill,
crunched with exquisite bounds;
the neighbors' kids stepping
before me, leaping —
the mashed pulp recoiling in
slow-motion death throes
like sponge.

Two weeks into November and
the Halloween spirit lingers:
jack-o'-lanterns left out on
porches, rotting, beginning
to sculpt their *true* horror:
silly faces collapsing, eyes
contorting into glares — jaws
twisting. Square fangs
gritting.
I hardly want to look.

The children passing,
oblivious in play, their long
lives spread out before them;
their long leaps impervious
the way they touch death.

A LOVE OF PIGEONS

– for my father

I never shared that love;
those eyes heaven-cast.
Your rooftop temples
chalky with waste;
that snow of feathers
on the leaves when you
moved them all to Queens.

Their homing instinct,
as you raced them in
Chicago, a rubber band
that stretched but
never broke.
The fantails you raised
better than your own
children.
That bamboo pole
you waved to the heavens,
calling them back — reeling in
the dotted sky.

In last years, in your
garage, you held one out
like a flame
to its new keeper.

It flew from my hands,
batting my face in its
panic, your own;
wings beating everywhere
at once.

SLUGS

My wife yells from the kitchen,
and I know that they are back.
They come only at night, squeeze
under the door like paste to get
to the cat's food — small dry stars
that stick to an end, a non-face,
a hard-to-imagine mouth.

Two floors up they crawl from
the garden—a slow-motion
peristalsis that scoffs at wings.
How long must it take? we muse.
Is this their mountain temple?
Their holy trough?
Or merely an all-night diner
worth the wait?

For months now, I have been
throwing them back. They land
with a gentle sound, only to begin
again. Lately I have played
executioner, flushing them down
the toilet in a swirl of justice.
Tonight I refuse.

My wife holds one wrapped in a
paper towel like a sloppy coat.
Recently they have entered her
dreams. She holds it out, her face
screwed tight, as though it might,
through some miracle of motion,
suddenly lunge —
the brown star still
stuck to it.

If there is a struggle it is too slow
to perceive — a cry unheard.
"Come on, take it," she pleads,
her reverence for nature more than
slightly tainted by abhorrence.

"Not tonight," I say. "Blood must
change hands. It's only fair."
Her body bends under the burden
of these words, but her feet move.
I hear a muted plop, picture its
shroud of paper with its subtle
print of grapefruits and oranges —
decent into the maelstrom,
still clutching a hollow prize.

When she returns she is pale,
and a new paste has squeezed to the altar.
"Never again," she hisses. "They can
have the damn cat's food!"

CLEARING OUT THE CLOSET

(after Grandfather's death)

It was small like your frame,
but full; it took three boxes.

Under the stalactites of the
ties you never wore: your shoes
from the garden still plump
with the shape of your living.

Beside them on a sheet of years
old news — the gloves you used,
caked with their own dermis
of earth; one nearly standing,
holding its shape.

And the music, the hangers'
tinny ghost-music, as the last
garment was removed.

A WORLD BREAKS THROUGH THE GAPS

We are lovers again,
the sheets, the bed, the doors I pass
like the familiarity a thought makes
breaking through branches,
like residue, the heat of your skin.

Afterwards, I am a passenger
as you drive. I'm hoping we find
a road through fields, past estuaries,
some sleight of hand to explain
your interior.

I reach over with both arms,
no safety belt, bury my face
in your hair and wake up
congested with remnants of cold,
a snowplow grating ice and pavement.

All of the strangers I've made of myself
disappear — as if someone unintentionally
hip-checked a skipping record
or finger slid down a smooth plastic switch
and turned on the lights of an unfamiliar house.

I can't dream you back but remember
the frequency—roll over and stare
at the white washed ceiling.

IF MY BODY BECAME ASH

If my body became ash I would like to fall
to the farthest corners where wind is all
that's left, beyond fire's interruptions
and water's vast history of steam.
I would like for light to interpret blossoms
opening all at once, and then for you
to breath your longest breath, for you
to breath me in, past fingers parting hair
behind your ears, slender neck and all.
If my body became ash I would like to fall
in the mountains like snow, to watch mountains
like monuments unfold as burning clouds,
to interpret your body as light,
to fall through this world as history before history,
life before life even begins.
I would like for you to become the wind
which carries, and river which carries me away.

EVERY DAY WE NAVIGATE THE DISTANCE

Aspen leaves in the wind,
fingers tapping the table —

how can you know for certain
just by the familiar sound a thought makes,
breaking through branches?

The moment when everything
reaches an apex or is still exploding outward,
my body curves like a fly line.

At the thought of your name,
a hint salt and mesquite.
Like the beech leaves we collected,
color the same sweetness
as the honey of your hair.

After dusk, the crunch and sweep
of footsteps like names swept away.

If I said pine. If I said sage. If I dressed
in red clay, with charcoal, with ashes
would your name come back to me?

If I balanced fourteen stones
through which I could still see the sky,
would your name continue to haunt me
in this kingdom of light?

IN MEMORIAM, WITH ODD CHATTER

I, too, am sowing grain on the headland
calling scarlet to the sky. I am grinding
the grain from the headland in heat
in mortar with pestle and sweat
streaking down the fine flour of light.

When your memory arrives late afternoon
I'll leave work akimbo and walk
the weary ever widening path home.
Stoke the stove and kneed the bread,
bake and break the hardened husk.

I knew a lover had a name, and her life
was held in limbo, calling scarlet to the string
of tarnished charms strung round her neck
to scare away the living. To reach too far,
to topple into love's numb afterlife.

It is the last time I'll sit with your ghost,
as the fire lows, and the door jambs swell,
and love tears loose like a piece of sod
from the humid loam of evening.

A NOTHING PRAYER

When the world comes round no more
and branches break beneath heavy wet

as wind quickens a world made white,
a muddy world where rivers enter

half the world made half again
and glaciers calved come to their ends,

how maddingly headlong we fall:
rough beast, nightingale

all these sober years and still
tonight, to hear each footfall frozen

my plural tongue splits and stakes
among the bleeding sage.

Bent low to earth, low to leaves,
in supplication lower still,

what storm made God of man?

THE AGE OF EXPLORATION

It was a shining moment that day
I discovered coffee in college. Finally,
something legal to keep me focused
on Kierkegaard and Proust,
or interjecting opinions
into a midnight dorm debate
over punk versus grunge.
Sometimes, I'd leave the books butterflied
on my bed at 3 a.m.
and walk through campus alone —
Midwest air sticky with aromas
of plowed earth and cows.
I continued this ritual long after I graduated
and moved to New York City;
23 and on my own, I was free to wander
hot city streets till dawn.
The coffee kept me going and, one night,
coming back late to my apartment
in Park Slope, high on shots
of double espresso and *Gauloises*,
felt my brain crackle with pure consciousness
as I fumbled for the key, singing *a cappella*
some improvisational ode to joy.
I wasn't returning to anyone or anything;
I could do whatever I wanted, go
wherever I pleased.
So I went home, lit a candle, and opened a book
— Ovid's *Metamorphosis* —
to read the story of Orpheus and Eurydice.
Years later, after my divorce,
I was on a train blasting through Nebraska's
Western sand hills
when I cracked that book again.
Hot wind blew straight from the sun

as I drank coffee in the smoking car
with an old woman from Chicago.
She must be dead now — at the time,
halfway Hades with emphysema.
I remember she kept the car awake all night
coughing so convulsively I thought she'd choke —
while her devoted husband
shuffled to and from the bathroom
for towels and cool water.
All I could do was read about love
and the risks of blind devotion,
when my eyes lit upon the face of a girl
sitting across from me.
Only 18, she was on her way to work
in a nunnery that summer,
because she was thinking of joining *The Order*.
I might have tried talking her out of it,
describing, with perhaps too much zeal,
the pleasures of — what — *Love? Romance? Sex?*
I didn't say it, but thought
she might get the idea from the story
of Orpheus and Eurydice I shared.
While I never knew for sure,
she did accept my offer
to buy her a cup of coffee, her first,
and recommendation to take it black.
Although it was weak, brewed
from cheap Amtrak grounds,
the caffeine took hold and she spoke for hours
about the love of her life: Jesus Christ.
And for a long time during our ride together,
through the middle of night, middle
of nowhere, I also believed.

FULL MOON OVER BAGHDAD; MARCH 19, 2003

White buildings mirrored in the Tigris —
damp air stagnant with derision
and the scent of burgeoning spring.
A child's cry from an upper window,
faint, like an insect or distant siren.
The light flicks on. A young mother
crosses the room to investigate.
This was said to have been the cradle
of civilization, where some believe
the garden of Eden flourished. *Imagine*
dense primordial palms, lush
aromatics and hibiscus, redolent
fungi and moss-steeped rain gathering
like silver on broad black leaves.
Deeper in, smolder of a campfire —
evidence of afterglow and a sexual
encounter. Disappearing into brush,
footprints — even further, a growl.
The fable interrupted now by advanced
pyrotechnics — not lightening or
fireworks — the underbellies of clouds
lit up by the flash of Howitzers.
Pigeons shaken off rooftop roosts,
settle back into limestone dust.
Palm trees toss shaggy heads and teeter.
Goats shiver in suburban yards.
Roosters scatter. An ambulance screams
along the boulevard, its lights firing.
The full moon rises red as a pomegranate,
aloof and indifferent to the bombing.

HITCHHIKER

All it took was seeing a ragged crow
   crossing a white sky over a snowy field
to inject his heart with a serum of ache.

From the gravel shoulder, he saw nothing
   but a world of gray scale — stills from
the film *Stranger Than Paradise* — waiting

for someone, anyone, to take him home.
   Silence, yes, but more so, stasis: each
object pressed between time & space,

Reality no thicker than a layer of stain or
   polyurethane. He was a luminous boy
riding around in a pliable exoskeleton —

rubbery to touch, animated, like a light bulb
   stuck inside a polymer puppet. How
did he get here? From what dim smoke

& smolder filled truck cab did he rise
   this morning, into the dome light,
poked awake by the driver's cough

& kicked out into a sleet storm burning
   like buckshot at the edge of Route 34
between Fairfield & Mt. Pleasant, Iowa?

What did that crow & its shadow do
   to rip open in him & reveal the radiance
of being the last living boy on earth?

FROGS, DEER, KITCHEN WINDOW

There isn't any way to keep
the kitchen window from tapping.   —William Stafford

Or the deer from eating the roses,
the frogs from swallowing the moon.
Or the banjo from midnight,
the sailor from his grief.

There's no way to stop
the whelm of flood tide,
the relentless coloring and
draining of the sky.

Last night we found a wooden bench
on the cliff, its weathered legs longer
than our own. We sat and swung
our feet out over the sea, the body
of your boyhood alive again,
throwing itself into the widening
gap between the worlds.

The trouble with everything
is the way it's so bent on turning:
rose to deer, frog to moon.
Our bodies to the starry cyclone's
empty eye.

HEART SUTRA

My heart is made of sumac twigs
and chicken wire, which, I can say
from experience, is not very good
at keeping in the chickens.
Every morning they're loose somehow,
clucking at my heels as I come
down the steps, swinging the bucket.
Sometimes one saunters off, but mostly
they follow me back to the coop, content
to warble in their clouds of feather dust,
all those unhatched eggs in the straw.

Some days I open the gate, urge them
to abandon the known, wave
my pale thin wings toward the world:
          Go forth, I tell them. *Fly!*

But they're not inclined toward flight —
Big Mama Blue Moon, Granny Apple
Red, all the scraggly, three-toed crones.
They stick to the yard where they pace
in circles and coo. They sidle up sideways
on wiry feet, cock their heads and offer
a tiny, one-eyed view of the firmament.
It's messy, this barnyard of the heart;
our only hope is to scatter grain and water,
let the squawking blow through us,
let the barn gate bang in the wind.

Smoke

I floated through the night half-awake,
a water skater on the dark skin of sleep.
Head in the ethers where crows shot dice
and houses lifted off like rockets.

In the morning I didn't swim up
to the alarm, but flapped down.
The world so unfamiliar, coming to it
this way: blurred gray-tones, smelling
of charcoal, as if hastily sketched in.
And later, in the car,

with the radio. All the staticky talk
of the shootings. *Resident alien* they
called him, to which I said out loud,
who's not? In the end, he turned the gun
on himself, the usual close to the story.
You can imagine it, can't you? Shooting
and shooting

until the world stops breathing,
lies bleeding at your feet. Your rage
exhausted, up in smoke. Empty now,
love finds its way in. Everything slides
into place. You see that the girl
in embroidered jeans and mary janes

wears your face; the boy in a ball
on the floor, your hands. It's you who's
spread all over and dying. What fills
the gunman next, we can't say — what
leaden mix of remorse and grief —
so ignorant we are in the ways of love.
But this isn't the poem I started out
to write. I wanted to say how

the children looked when I got
to the schoolyard. How they ran
across the grass, joy twirling
and bobbling their bodies;
their windblown hair
catching fire in the morning light.

DARK NIGHT OF THE SOUL

Light shines red in dark.
Even blind, I could find
my pew, fourth row
on the right (Mary's side),
second from the aisle.

At midnight, I should be
safely asleep, curtains drawn
around the single iron bed.
Instead, like the undead,
I roam the chapel waiting
for something. The caress
of a lover. A whisper of hope.
The downy soft blanket
of faith. Anything but this
dread, the empty space
between my ribs, where
my heart beats its cadence
and I fall beneath the boots
of doubt, the whip of fear.

I kneel on the bare stone floor,
arms out to embrace the spare
hollow of nothing.

Behind the beat, I hear a note,
thin and echoing
in the dark.

NUN THE LESS

Blue serge wraps me in god's embrace,
completely hidden under a yard
of scratchy fabric worn thin
by years of harsh detergent.

No wisps of hair peek out beyond
the starched white wimple
draped in black, hands are clasped
around the rosary beads
that encircle my waist, my head
is bowed, eyes cast down.

Even my name is erased.
I am called "Sister," along
with hundreds of other women
who, in their longing and youth,
found god in their beds.

Beneath this mask, I wait
for the one who formed me
in my mother's womb,
who knew me from all ages,
to call my soul
into the light.

Seventy Years After Auschwitz

The numbers have faded to match
her blue veins, now knobby and twisted
with age. She always wore long sleeves,
even when her arms were strong
and supple; now it makes no difference.

Life now is not what she dreamed of,
when she dreamed of things other than
bread heavy with pan drippings, custard
creamy coating her tongue, black tea
steeped in delicate samovars.
Before food, she dreamed of babies
against her breast, toddlers tipping over
in their haste to chase each other,
an arm around her shoulder, warm
body pressed chest to chest.

But now, it is all gone. She feeds
from a tube; the babies grew up;
the bodies are cold. Only the numbers,
faded to blue smudges, still
sting.

ANGEL IN PARADISE

She stares shyly from the projector
in her first communion dress,
her ghostly image captured
fifty years ago in home movies.
She shrugs off the touch
of her uncle's hands on her shoulders
where the nubs of ripped wings
are still visible under the straps
of her cotton undershirt.

OCTOBER SWIM IN NEW HAMPSHIRE

The sun wrinkles the lake in diamonds
while leaves cast red and yellow dye
along the surface. My shoulder muscles
contract as I swim in water colder
than the sun-warmed air. I stretch
through waves stirred by wind.

The far shore calls to me, its birches
shorn of leaves and waving greetings.
Above, the sky arcs indigo behind clouds
bruised by the end of a season.
I hear the sound of a great gathering
as wings touch the surface of the lake.
I am lifted into a light so dazzling
that I travel blind, eyes closed.

TRISH AT 60

She stands at the bar;
I see only her ear and cheek.
Even so, even after 40 years,
I recognize the angle of her head,
the way her hair feathers her jaw,
the slight tilt of her left shoulder.

Then she turns, catches sight of me
and smiles, her hands reaching out
toward me as I walk forward
into the past that I left behind
as I moved beyond convent gates
that could no longer hold me.

I am astonished; the years
fall away and we embrace
as if still bound together
by vows as strong as the oaks
that lined the long drive
that ended in the novitiate.

We sit at the table for hours,
lives pared down into paragraphs,
highlights to guide us on a journey
that hurtles us forward, tangents
of time spinning off, the years spent
navigating shoals, delighted at last
to find our selves together.

We part again, promises of future meetings
murmured as we brush cheeks together,
reluctant to leave as the staff upends chairs
and mops the floors, knowing time
is brief and stacked against us.

WINDOW INTO DEATH

In the mind of a bird, glass is incomprehensible:
Vertical ice? Solid air? Wrath of God?
Fly through the open space

When a game of chase turns deadly,
It is the living bird who wonders
What became of her

When a flying thing impacts glass,
Her soul continues into the reflected world,
Light as a shadow

When a bag of feathers, a puppet on wings
is squeezed of her life in an instant:
A windfall for the dog

From the other side of the window,
I feel the poverty of one less bird,
One day closer to winter

HAIKU FOR A BACHELOR

Night is a closed room
No blessed wind, no soft dew
Nor bliss of sleeping

BUTTERFLY TATTOO

Right now it's Mardi Gras outside my window
and the biggest part of the parade has passed
but I can still see, smell, and taste
crawfish étouffe, someone making a roux
and the float with the gorgeous,
22-foot high libra nude
with her magical breasts still growing
and the balloons with all of our insights
and philosophical and spiritual experiences
written all over them,
and the time we kissed in the forest
in the cold fall wind, after a year apart,

And now the giant clown comes floating by
over the roof, late, grinning and waving, unshaven,
and there, on the corner, still drinking, smoking
and swaggering in leather jackets
all the stuff we used to fight about

And just beyond them
in a pure white and golden mist
with sparkles only visible
in a higher state of consciousness
the simple love that I followed,
straight through the thugs
every time we got back together

Yes, it's Mardi Gras
and though I don't ever get drunk
I did get distracted
and just now I woke up
alone, again,

with the thought of
your butterfly tattoo
flying, leaving, gone,
but under my skin
forever.

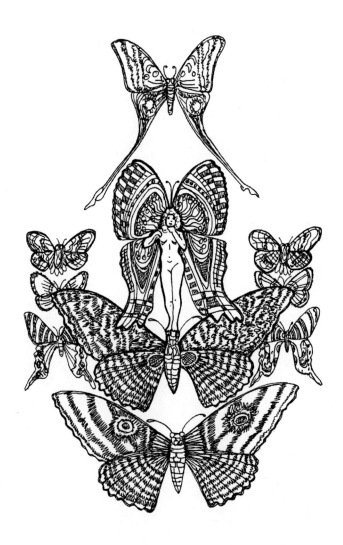

THE BUTTON

The room at the top floor
of 115 Fairchild
the east, south and west sides windowed
Joni Mitchell singing
"Sisowtowbell Lane"
Constant Comment tea
already slightly
passé
You with your wild
and full dark
brown hair
You with your layers and layers
of brown and white clothing
You and I
intensely discussing
Gershwin, Piaf, and Ibsen
You and I
wrestling and laughing
and then me
alone,
as I undid
in deep gravity
the last button
on your blouse.

Throwing Away Your Hair

I threw away the Easter basket
full of your hair today.

Yes, the hair I had saved
off the salon floor
when you cut it in a tiff
after the play.

The hair that I first held in my hands
when I kissed you, in character, onstage
and also, out of character, in bed.

The hair that I had to hide
when we broke up
so as not to cry.

The hair that still has your smell on it
nine months later.

That hair.

I was thinking of taking it to the new bridge
over the Mississippi in Burlington
and walking it out to the middle
right here in December
and while people drive by
laughing and yelling "Don't jump"
dropping it, curl by curl
into the relentless brown water.

But no, I decided to let go of you two days ago
and today I got up and dumped the whole pile
into the trash can, basket and all.

It's over there right now.

I haven't bothered to take it out to the dumpster.
So other stuff is piling up on it, as it joins the mix
of discarded thing, and someday soon
it'll go out and then I'll be done with it.

Now if I could just get your hair
off of my naked shoulder at night
like when I held you while you slept.

Now if I could just get your hair
off of my chest
while I meditate
since we did that,
leaning together,
holding each other close.

Now if I could just get your hair
out of my head.

Finding You

For a long time
you were a
small, leaping wildebeest
crossing the road
in front of my
Toyota four wheeler
seen for a moment
and then
disappearing
into the jungle

You were a
long Chinese kite
visible
ten miles away
from an ocean steamer
somewhere
in a section edited out
of a yellowed, 1930's
paperback
adventure novella

You were
a tie-dyed
scarf
draped over a string
on sale
close to
Fisherman's Wharf

You were
a heron's wing
beating and beating
as the bird
called
far off
for a mate

But now, my
search for you
has narrowed down.

Now you are revealed
as a lot
less elusive
as a matter of fact

The place that I found you in
was a small, strong place
a place of definition
and stability.
You did not waver
and appear exotic
and unusual.
You were there
just like a cello player
solid, lyrical, and present.

The place where I found you
was a clean place
with shape and
tone.
There was nothing extra there
or anything
unneeded.

The place where you are
it turns out
is a place where
few other people
have chosen to hide:
unmoving
unshaken
in plain sight
close at hand
right
in front of me

in the open.

DANCING WITH A POET

What is it that twirls
when a poet twirls
when I curl you in
to a tight, tango-like
formation, and stop.
And what is it that
stops?

Is it your hair so black
cut like an ancient
Egyptian?

Is it your eyes so big
that you never seem to
blink?

Or is it a world that twirls
when a poet spins
or another galaxy
depending on the poet

Of unusual birds, lost
expanses, obser-
vations, clarifi-
cations
and nuance?

Think of what
would happen
if a poet really turned.
Whole planets
new and foreign
or at least entire
conceptual spaces
spinning at the basis
of everything.

And then when I dip you sideways
in a dramatic fall
then does all of life
become horizontal
in some unknown way
while you see just
the ceiling overhead?

And then what,
when I dare
to lift you, turning,
up in the air
like a slowly circling eagle

As if all that could be lifted
and all that could be turned?

Yes,
I just can't say
what happens
then
but one thing that I do know
is when I show you
one good turn
and then another

You turn, you flash
you exhibit grace,
life,
spunk
and beauty.

And yet somehow
when I turn
this Egyptian-looking
slender
black-eyed poet,
I feel a kind of thrill

of standing
next to immortality
next to a source
and a soul
of literature

And I think
that maybe if I put
a little extra beauty
and a twist
of imagination
into our dance
that you of all people
will understand it
that you of all people
will perceive it fully
and that our dance, perhaps
will come out someday
in one of your poems

as a heron's wing
a brief, enigmatic
point,
or a message
straight from the feeling level
to all of creation.

I guess it's just because
to me, the poet stands,
intently waiting
on the surface
of the deep totality,
where it
crinkles into shape, sound
and object

And by writing there
and living there
becomes a compact
form of God.

She does what God does
in some tiny way
and so shares the job
shares the life
and shares the level
where nothing spins
unless he spun it.

It makes me
pause, at least
among the notes
and the steps
of the dance
just as your eyes
never blinking,
make me think that

though we're dancing
someone, something here
is unmoved, unmoving
unturned, unspun
not twirling, and
not turning sideways
in a languid, lovely fall,

yet I, the master planner of your move
your turn, your twirl, your lift,
have been the one

above the dance
uplifted.

WHAT THE MOON HEARD

The moon heard the wind
blowing through your heart
saw the stream of
doubts, memories
men falling by the way
eddying about
downwind
but then,
in what some other
unearthly body
might call silence
the moon heard
the thin, high
pure tone
of your love
calling someone
home.

Like The Robin's Egg

Like the robin's egg
Waiting at the edge
Of being blue
And not being

Your skin approaches
The junction point
Of Being
And becoming

Like candy for the fingers

Touching you
I can never be sure
Whether I've touched
The truly real

Or it's just
That my fingertips
Are dreaming

Dancing in Paradise Café

He's sitting
left arm over the back
of the booth in the bookstore
that has seen
many a lunch
framed in
paperback dreams.

I haven't met him yet
but will, soon, and
even now, I'm happy
seeing him, feet extended
out into the walkway
laptop on the gnarled
wood table, part of what
makes this place beautiful.

It's amazing, like a dream,
to walk out of Café Paradiso
and then in passing the next
intersection northward
to simply see Diane,
walking through,
and then to walk and talk
excitedly with her
and of course to discover
that the love she is meeting
I have already seen, already admired.

I'm as if chanting
what I have said so many times
you support her this way.
You don't really bend,
you let her be the curve

while you are the tall line.
You bring her close to you
and stay in your strength.
As I show him, right there
how to do the death drop
how to do the arabesque lift
and all of the secret leads
that let her know what's next.

And then she like a slender flute
sways and lifts.
Even so, he wonders,
Can I really lift all that?
And, man to man
we talk, of how to deal
with such a beauty
such a dreamer, even
when she is at her lowest
and how we never even try
to lift her, but only lean
in the right direction
and then she flows, with us
into the new.

TENNIS

To some people
Tennis is a sort of minor sport
On TV, with hushed commentary
Heads turning, back and forth

But to me
Its summers spent,
Dragging the broad broom
over the green clay
and then sweeping the lines
For the afternoon players

It's the future homecoming queen
Still only twelve years old
Already impossibly lovely
In her pleated skirt, gliding left
To hit her underspin shot
Deep to the corner

It's my hair, bleaching from brown
To blond, from day after day
Spent on the court

It's standing frozen, breathless
In front of the 1957 Playboy shot
of Marilyn Monroe
On the inside wall
of Norris' broom shed

It's picking up
Thousands of balls
After my Father's group lessons

And the thought that
He may still see me now
out there
Playing his game.

FROM *THE MULTIPLICATION OF JOY INTO INTEGERS*

J

Someone has promised to plant flowers
in a bathtub; someone has planted
a bathtub in a garden, as a piece
of sculpture, I would think — a tribute
to those souls who have lost their
appetites and have, accordingly,
thinned out to a nothingness which
renders them quite capable of passing
through diameters the size of pennies.
Speaking of which, when planted,
these yield lovely copper trees
from which hang shiny teapots
all full of sleep and phone numbers
of the world's top ten most eligible
bachelors — and charge cards, none
of which have upper limits. A spiral
staircase materializes; angels pass
from floor to floor, not really going
anywhere and in no sort of a hurry,
apparently, except for one or two
novitiates for whom eternity is still
a shaky concept. These angels seem
nervous and tense; one is tempted
to offer them the warmth of a hug
but then sees humor in their reflexive,
type-A propensities and chuckles
cruelly to oneself, jotting the scene
down on paper to tell those friends
who have moved to other cities,
other planets: to those angels.

J³

Atlas lifted the whole world
on his shoulders, the same way
that one might raise a cantaloupe
above one's head in a supermarket
in order to attract attention. The way
the waves are calmed by moonlight,
which sits upon the water as a feather
might rest upon a cheek, a sheet
of cellophane upon the snow.
The world is heavy; cantaloupes
are somewhat less heavy and
filled with seeds which, when
planted, grow into immense orange
Art Deco tenement buildings à la
South Beach. In the kitchen
of an apartment in one such
building is a blender into which
have been placed a tray of ice cubes,
a pair of diamond cufflinks. Two
strangers romp on the floor by
the refrigerator; two lovebirds sit
on the branch of a tree just outside
the window; the phone rings twice,
or at least I would like to think so.

J⁵

Rooms appear as if by magic and the
funny thing is that I am in them, at least
some of the time. Or on a stairwell, or
in the backyard, counting imaginary
numbers. Under the table is an empty
space into which fit the legs. Air is free
and fills a lung, fills a corridor. Balloons
pop to fill the world with oxygen, as if

there weren't enough already. Between
atoms, this awful room; between rooms,
these awful walls. These lovely walls and
windows and scoops of air! The legs
of a table touch the floor without passion.
Electrons circle nuclei with a similar
absence of emotional investiture. In
snow storms, airplanes will orbit a runway
in much the same manner; that is, ignorant
of erotic overtones. A door quite imaginary
in ontology closes very quietly, leaving one
with the impression that a door quite real
in ontology has vanished into thin air:
that is, devoid of oxygen and balloons.

J⁶

One may inquire as to the secret ingredients
of clouds: vanilla, powder, angel? Before
there were clouds there was nothing but blue,
and that is the truth. During these times,
parasols were the vogue, as were large
grey tents behind which one reclined nude.
Clothing was transparent and of a meshlike,
porous material no longer in existence.
Supposing there were a kite, or a balloon
out of control — wouldn't that make things
interesting? Stars too tired to maneuver
are carried across the sky on stretchers
of white terrycloth. And are attended
by burly, white-hot musclemen wearing
nothing but cockrings resembling Saturn's
halo. It's like in Japan, where the elderly
are respected, if only because they
have survived. If the clouds have
survived, it is because they have been
so good at the game of motion.

J[11]

See: I have designed a building in the shape of a
heart. This will be a supermarket, eventually.
The irony is obvious. Full of bricks, this
pillowcase makes sleeping so difficult. I should
find a replacement, eventually. Certain theorists
of matter maintain that every atom is inter-
changeable with every other atom; the
applications to human situations are obvious.
Eventually, supermarkets will close and everyone
will survive on pills and water. Mealtime will
disappear almost entirely; people will eat
on buses, in taxis, in rockets, and the anxiety
surrounding dinner conversation will transmute
into xenophobia. Blue curtains spill onto the floor.
Blue chocolates, too, as if shaken out of a paper
heart. There was no boat because there was
no water; there was no water because it dried
up in the sun; it dried up in the sun because
there were no clouds. When I suggested
that the moon take up go-go dancing, my
request was not honored. I would have supplied
the briefs and paid the DJ. Whatever.
Who can argue with timidity?

FIVE POSTCARDS WITH LOVE

i
Maybe the red hibiscus blossom
battered by black Iowa wind
holds onto green grass
these four hours
because she loves cardinals.

ii
Maybe love is the sand
caught in the crevices,
the sunburned back scraping
as he presses above her in the dark.

iii
Or the purple tears
shed in an empty bed,
the gray drizzle
seen through closed curtains.

iv
Is it the milky moth breath
of my five-day-old son,
seducing me, my body torn
at his forced entry into the world?

v
Why do I cling to parrot-brained chatter,
afraid of smoldering white silence,
a fantail fire in my heart.

Soul of Sleep

Birches scratch the rising wind,
and green rain falls;
a young grackle shivers under the front porch,
while her brothers cling naked to buffeting tree tops.

Some nights when you are away, flying,
I think about childhood.
Mist looms over Black Mountain,
kookaburras line the back fence,
and a mob of grey kangaroos graze the front lawn.
My sister, Rosie snuggles down in the next bed,
waiting for the very last moment to get up.
Dad sings *When Irish Eyes Are Smiling*,
making Mum her morning cuppa.

Last night growling possums woke me.
I pulled the bedspread to my nose,
listened to gum leaves rustle,
and pictured Mum and Dad together in their giant
burgundy bed,
just a few inches through the wall.
Exhaling, I smiled into sleep.

Now, alone in our empty house, I conjure comfort,
pretending they are still here, breathing
in the next room.

Most nights, nothing is solid.
We swim rudderless through a sea of souls.
But sometimes, drunken foolery
seeps through the pores of my skin,
and I feel my fingers —
commas in the earth's simple song.

I Watch You Bathing

To view a spiral galaxy,
I need enormous distance.
To see the fractals in an orchid,
my eye must be very close.

How far do I have to stand
to see all of you? How near
when you weigh as much
as your smile?

It may be impractical on Earth
raised by volcanic violence
and covered two thirds by tears,
but if you care to know my religion,

see through my eyes
when I look at your face in the water.

The Sixth Day of Creation

A modeling tool, shaped like the rib of a child,
transforms a lump of clay
into nostrils that quiver inhaling.

A trace of eyelashes
betrays the grateful words
she whispers to her Creator
raising her eyebrows
in the demure curves of a cyclamen.

Her wavy hair, turned into flowing locks
is still wet with amniotic fluid.
The dome of her forehead
parts the waves of soft clay, like the morning
when our daughter's crowning head
spread your thighs further apart
than I ever dreamed possible.

Her shoulders and neck
swoop in the curve of the flying gazelle
I adore in your arched body.

I peel off the rubber mold for a wax shell
the way you remove diapers.
Next week I will cast her in molten bronze.
I have only fingers and heart
to accomplish what you have done
with every cell of the blood in your veins.

In the courtyard of short shadows
your voice sang Eve's lullaby
the instant I knew our daughter
had chosen us for parents
under waving date palms and blooming papayas.

Perhaps I can be your equal,
for she, who is born out of my hands,
wants to be divine as the child
that emerged out of the life-giving orchid
I have been worshiping
for seven years of mortal time.

ARCHITECTURE OF LIGHT

The darkest place in a human body
is inside the skull, but the womb?
Who can I compress a hurricane into a Coke bottle?

When the world was my putty, I was a swallow.
I designed fantastic structures
around an illuminated void.
I molded space and light
like the sculptor molds clay,
but before I drew a line, my designs
gelled from the crowded darkness in my head.

The atrium flooded with light at sunrise.
A fig tree cast a shade at noon.
The last rays of a setting sun
played a shadow theater on the limestone chimney.
A flying staircase grew like a spine of piano keys
around it. I added volume, subtracted mass,
composed a fugue with color.
I lay on my back before sleeping,
and watered the orchids in my mind.
The structures lived, because they changed me.

It was fun to play God — until I became one.
I brought a woman to share that space.
I recall the shivering minutes
when I carried our infant daughter
inside the pouch of my jacket, facing the world.
I showed her pear trees, dahlias, blue jays.
Her first words were light and play.
Her eyes changed what mine saw.

Now I design spaces in the temples of our children
drunk with the light their mother radiates.
The hickory above our trampoline
holds a bar swing, a wave slide,
a vine of steps to their nest.

WILD MUSHROOMS

The deepest scars come
from battles never fought.
— My brother's journal entry

I

Toothless thunder is rolling all night long,
but tomorrow is Sunday. If it doesn't pour,
I can go mushroom hunting with Grandfather.
The silent forest lets him speak about the three German soldiers,
he buried somewhere in his secret paradise of mushrooms.
I have nearly enough stamina to keep up with the old man's gait
and more than enough respect to listen.

A telephone call wakes me to a cloudless sky:
not a thunderstorm but helicopters;
the country of my childhood seized from air and land
by five armies of our allies.
The sudden emergence of an enemy
unites polarized Czechs and Slovaks
the way a crusher melds junk cars.
The baritone on the radio calls for Passive Resistance,
the removal of street signs and house numbers.
Disorientation makes arrests more difficult,
and the delinquents of freedom can use the extra hour
to leave for West Germany.

My girlfriend carries a crowbar and I, a ladder.
It is better than no action at all.
We may not live to be old enough to marry,
but who would want to when our whole nation is catatonic.

II

The tanks made in Pilsen for the Warsaw Pact
are rolling again through the narrow streets of Czech towns —

but this time with full crew and ammunition.
The pavement is stained with blood and the invaders are dying too.
A nineteen-year-old Russian tankist blows up
a Bulgarian tank across the Vltava River.
He doesn't know the emblem of his comrades.

Curfew at sundown begins on my brother's sixteenth birthday.
He returns home before dawn dragging a ten-pound shrapnel
unraveled in the shape of a hand taking an oath.
"I will - never - laugh a-gain," he stutters,
shaking and pale under a layer of mud.
"A Russian soldier was ordered to shoot me.
He took me to the woods by the beet field, asked me to run,
and then he unloaded the magazine under my feet."

Machine-gun staccato executes creeping minutes.
The sandstone facade of the National Museum
is freckled with bullet holes. They think it's our Radio Palace.
All the food stores are empty in a few hours.
Edible goods are replaced with banners, flyers and cartoons —
epitaph fragments for the eight month old fetus of freedom.

Girls, wear mini-skirts for safety.
It's hard to aim with a throbbing cock,
informs one of the signs. The last to die is not hope but laughter.
My brother cackles maniacally, a thin ice of desperate humor
covering an ocean of fear. I don't know at the time,
that he will laugh this way for the rest of his life,
looking for snakes and Russian soldiers hiding under his bed.

III

I memorize an anonymous sonnet,
taped to the polished granite of the Czech National Bank:

Do you feel thirsty and hungry, foreign soldier?
Do you want love, warm-hearted words?
The water and the bread you can demand with a gun
but into the human heart no one enters by force.

Blood gushes out of the chest and congeals.
Cut the wound with your bayonet
and take that heart. It's open, but silent.
Too late, soldier, they betrayed you

and your hope was less than a lie.
Tomorrow morning by daybreak, you would prefer to die.
What protection offer your rifles and cannons
against the spell cast by a mother or a child?

The question in their glazing eyes is more merciless than death.
It will torment you every day, every night you have left.

I shout these lines at the top of my lungs
standing on the mane of a horse five-times larger than life,
clutching the bronze banner of Count Saint Vaclav.
At a church door on Sunday a thousand years ago,
he was stabbed by his brother in the back.

Nobody wastes a bullet on a boy reciting poetry.
Hundreds of eyes and thousands of candles burn day and night
on the steps of the monument.
One candle for every pair of eyes that will never cry.

No, they do not shoot into the crowds, that is not the order.
The Czech police will open fire on the demonstrators
on the first anniversary of the invasion, and Jan Palach,
an ex-Communist philosophy student at Charles University
will ignite the Prague torch of liberty,
his own body doused with gasoline.

IV

I speak Russian to one of the uniforms
concealing a blue-eyed doctor from Moscow.
The boys believe they are in Germany,
they cannot read a single sign.
They want to be home with their families.

A friendly bartender in a nearby town refuses to serve them
unless they leave all their guns on the coat hanger in the hallway.
When they get drunk, his wife collects their arsenal
and hides it under a chicken coop.
They get it all back when they beg;
they would be shot for losing their weapons.
She does not have to kill, she is not a soldier.

At night some teenagers cut off the cannon on one of the tanks
with a torch. In the morning, the whole tank crew is executed
by their commander. Several eighth-graders
throw gasoline bottles and wax torches at the tanks.
It does no harm to anyone inside, but two of them get shot
and one is stabbed with a bayonet, like the dad
who holds onto the hand of his four-year-old daughter
after the caterpillar belt claims the rest of her.
He jumps on the tank which retreats out of a barricade,
and with his free hand he pulls open the hatch of the turret.

He does not need to live long with his memories.

V

Two days later I am on a train crossing to Austria.
The conductor says the borders are closed.
A teen-aged nurse with eyes like a Chihuahua
is willing to go with me through the mountain woods.
For two nights we sleep on top of each other to keep warm.
During the day we walk into the sun. Our only food,

wild mushrooms with an occasional glimpse of
a white church steeple across the valley.

The iron curtain is a twenty foot barbed wire fence
half a mile inside the border.
The land around it is kept freshly plowed
to yield an unusual harvest at night.
If you succeed at cutting through the wires,
and don't get electrocuted,
the interrupted current alarms the soldiers
in the guard towers a gunshot apart.
Then you are dissuaded by eyes behind infra-red telescopes,
accurate Czech carbines, and hounds bred to hunt human game.
Of course we are caught before we get to the wires.
If we were maimed by the dogs before the bullets reached us,
this irreverent account would not have been written.
The Czech guard, two years older than me,
says he aims to kill. He gets three days vacation
with his young family for shooting someone.

We sleep in separate jail cells. After three days
of raw mushrooms, the rye bread and imitation coffee is a treat.
In the morning we are taken with a bus-load of survivors
to the court in Prague.
Too young to get the scheduled five year sentence,
we are let loose back in the cage.

My underwear is blotted with discharge
and more than any destiny in a uniform
I dread the times when I must urinate.
I start my 1968 school year with a police record
and a bottle of Penicillin.
Our teacher extends his vacation in Stockholm.
The pedagogue in his place is somewhat less tolerant
of my juvenile ideas of freedom, and our class
is lesser by two students.

VI

The twentieth century has gone the way of the candles.
The Czech boy became an American man.
The mushroom of Communism machine-gunned itself
into the history books, pulling along the great Soviet Empire
and the small Republic of Czechoslovakia.
And my doctor friend from Moscow?
Does he treat the victims of Thomsk, Chernobyl,
and the stratospheric mushrooms
above the testing steppes of Kazakhstan,
or did he die as one of them himself?

In my New World, machine guns are used by drug pushers
and urban police, but not by the military on unarmed civilians.
We have user-friendly software for our warfare:
unmanned doves of freedom instead of snipers and dogs.
Silicone intelligence guiding iron goodwill
out of stealth-camouflaged clouds.
The soldier of the new generation does not need to know
that he kills — or dies. The proper coordinates
are all that is required.

I have my own four-year-old who shoots me
with his water carbine, airborne above our trampoline.
He still pees with delight and without hesitation,
but for no apparent reason he is afraid of dogs.
The pine grove in our backyard hides no skeletons in helmets,
and the wild mushrooms growing here
taste as good as they did then.

But don't come here, Grandfather.

Lead us instead to your new world,
perhaps without mushrooms,
but without any iron thunder
punctuating lullabies.

Poetry Slut

Could your pencil-thin heels
be any higher, your haiku skirt
any shorter, your transparent blouse
any tighter?

Clean up your act, Sister
wipe that Revlon smear off your lips
and button up — your metaphors
are exposed.

Yank down the back of your shirt
your thong is alliterating attraction,
your skirt is barely long enough
to cover the subject, short enough to show

you're a poetry whore, decked out
in tagmemics best left in the bedroom,
you've got a hexameter of a nerve
with an apostrophe dangling

from your purse, and, onomatopoeia!
Your sequined eye shadow is a pentameter too much.
Sweetie, take a caesura from your sonnet
strutting before you're arrested for verbicide.

Hey Girlie-Girlie, your spondee is enjambing
traffic — get off the streets
go home little one,
learn a little restraint.

Mysterious Light

Leaves painted viridian and oxide green
overlap at the top of poplars and pines,
leafing over the forest
in coverlets of darkness.

Eddies of lemon and gold
laser through tops of barren branches
onto the forest floor.
A pileated woodpecker raps for attention,
his red head awash in sunlight.

I am drawn towards this luminary,
where mosquitoes, nits and butterflies
flutter in a glistening pillar of light
reaching to the sun.

Breaching the edge between dark and light
I am drawn inside
to bathe in its buttery glow,
my hair changing into golden threads.

Sweet scents of lily milk and honey
rise from beneath my feet
inside this yellow flame
where tears no longer find a place to cry.

WILL OF THE WIND

Our boat dances with blustery air currents
swinging in curtsied bows.
Rods and reels balance on the edge of oars.
Lines dangle over the edge
baited with wiggling night crawlers.
We pleasure in the wait.

My son and I share silent moments
as I tiptoe the edge of thought.
Observing the sun bathing his nose,
moisture beading its surface —
his wet face beautiful, framed in daydreams.

As the wind changes directions,
I am moved to past memories
of a small boy planting wet kisses on my lips.
Flavors of peanuts and raspberry linger,
little fingers touching my eyelashes
investigating the holes in my ears;
cheeks soft as flowering bluebell tongues.

Stirred by the timbre in his voice,
remembering Puff the Magic Dragon
sung in the key of C;
painful cries when the sidewalk found his knee,
laughter when a bluegill captured his bait
dancing in the air — until, with a thud,
it lands in my lap among fits of joy.

FROZEN FOREST

Norway pines,
sheltered in whipped cream blankets,
dot the hills of northern Wisconsin.
Green needles sleep
under white covers,
edges crocheted in loose knit patterns.

As spring arrives
with a wet snowfall,
songs crackle from weary branches.
Heavy comforters avalanche the forest floor,
limbs relieved of burdens.

Two field mice race to a nearby log;
a red fox sits washing his face,
too full from an early breakfast
to take up the chase.
Footprints profile earlier wanderings.

I cross a path worn by deer hooves
in search of tender roots beneath the snow.
Rabbit tracks lead to a hole
where a mother scurried
to escape being lunch.

My square-toed boots sink deep
into the soft whiteness;
prints shadow close behind.

In the distance, I hear trees
releasing winter's memories.
I float to the edge of their voices,
but hear only sounds of footsteps.

Trust

Acorns from my grand oak,
in tones of tan and brown,
lie on grass in my backyard.
They stare through outstretched limbs
into a cobalt sky, blinking
between umbrellas of green.

Sun lays down blankets of warmth,
drawing mantles of moisture near
to restore life to hardened soil.

Fragile as down on a snow owl,
hopeful as wings of a hummingbird,
trusting as thistle
growing around rocks,
hard fruit from the oak
waits for the heat of germination.

Day pulls the dark spool of night,
through an open door
into the galaxy,
behind — the moon,
rests in the cradle of wisdom.

ROOM 2525

Who will sleep where my dreams are cold —
smoothed on fresh cotton linens?

The silver-haired man in creased khakis,
burgundy winged-tip shoes, and crisp white button down?

The sandal-toed couple in matching Hawaiian shirts?
Their tanned smile reeking newlyweds,
or the lavender perfumed woman
clutching her Macy's sack like a prize?

Will lovers rendezvous there knowing
their promises are lies they tell themselves,
and each other, to make it through the weekend?

Will any of them look out the window
at dawn, see the Gateway Arch is an eyelid
over the sun's pink eye?

And what of the red-capped man in Kiener Plaza
collecting garbage in the city's sleepy haze,
early morning slumping on his shoulders?

With slow even strides, he pushes a gray trashcan
pass a platoon of taxis on Broadway Street.
Drivers sit on a bench outside their coaches,
waiting for potential passengers to rescue them
from the bowels of boredom.

Fate fills their idle cabs with needy customers.
One by one they break rank,
vanish into the vapor of distance.

When I walk out, the sun's pink eye is a dome of light,
the red-capped man and taxi drivers are ghosts.
With bill in hand, I shut the door wondering.

When I Am Fifty

In the year two thousand eight, I will be fifty.
I will not hide behind twenty-nine and holding;
I will release that part of my life with white balloons.

January, I will make this announcement:
I will be fifty this year.
After September six, I will say *I am fifty.*

I will let gray blossom
in the garden of my black hair,
tell waitresses to call me woman, not girl.

I will ride a bike, feed ducks,
live a rainbow life
reciting centuries of traditions
although a half century old.

I will write my own birthday card,
the wrinkles in my hands — the envelope.
The card will read:

"I left a trail of flowers on my way up the hill;
pick as many as you like,
but leave the pansies for me."

ENOUGH

Sunday morning wakes
with a lazy smile and the First Baptist Church
choir singing hymns on channel seven.

I have no sermon for the sun or grapefruit
for the short-nailed, gray-haired, tattered-clothed
woman stocking breakfast? dinner?
from a garbage dumpster
into a Ruby Red Grapefruit box.

I avert my eyes, give her space to shop
without an audience of pity.
I am walking with an I-POD
and empty pockets.
This is all I have to give her — privacy.

I do not know what she will eat tomorrow
or where she will sleep.
I sleep beneath nine hundred square feet,
moan about not having enough space,
long for more.

I am the first to complain of the world's waste,
how we stuff the earth with things
she cannot swallow.

Last night I dined at Logan's Steakhouse,
drank iced tea, ordered too much food
and a to go box.
All of my life's contradictions are sealed
in white Styrofoam,
waiting to be thrown away
while I walk into a second helping of sunlight.

RETURN

Boy! Miss Walker, your scissors are hungry. —Drew, 1st grade

November's back from holiday
after trekking for twelve months across
the glossy white roads of the calendar.

Its primal instinct to arrive without much fanfare,
but look at it this morning with its wide blue smile
and one big tooth hanging with polished grace.

The wind brushed trees are swept
into bad comb-overs. Baldness is prevalent
in an assortment of them primping around the city.
What confidence to stand in such fullness—
as though the bushy green afros that started growing
in the spring were still hanging over their strong branches.

Oaks, ashes and birches know there is beauty in bareness,
honesty in revealing the skeleton of strength.
Each autumn they allow the elements to strip them
of their leaves without protest.
What if the soul was deciduous,
permitted life to remove those superficial coverings
that prevent us from seeing the true gifts in others?

With cold draped over its generous arms,
and Thanksgiving in its busy hand cutting
through sheets of love like a hungry pair of scissors,
November's back crafting paper dolls out of gratitude.

UMBRELLA OF SHAME

Flames stampede, red hot hooves
blacken almost two hundred days
of dry West Texas land.

Dead leaves and grass burn
with bovine, houses and dreams.
Manes of gray smoke blow
in an agitated wind.

Prayers for rain and safety soak
ceilings, walls and the long nozzle
of a fireman's hose.
I am safe in this room of poets,
searching for a poem in the cotton fields
of my ancestors' past.

Their stories of sweating and picking
are like incantations,
but they speak nothing of their lives.

My father's breath is in the dust,
his eyes sealed, and my mother
gives me enough words
to leave me burning with suspicions.

Her silence is water outside the womb.
How she protects her children still,
the way she did when we were growing
inside of her.

How I wish she would release those secrets,
make them like flames and smoke,
the rotten hard memories of her past ashes.
Truth will not sear us, rather cleanse
this child of curiosity,

but she holds on to it all.
Her hands are like molten steel,
and secrets continue to rain
on each of us as we walk under
an umbrella of shame.

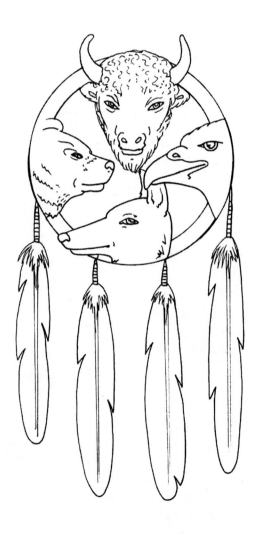

RESOLVED

As of midnight, this last year is archived
with past centuries and this new year is an untamed cub
with an appetite as big as wonder.
How hungry it is in this newness,
chewing at time even as confetti litters the sky.
But it can only eat what each day has to offer.
And we in our joy stripe its back with promises
and good intentions.
Oh, to see it mature, run wildly with hope!
I've filled a bowl with resolutions:
to be more, do more, give more and never forget
I am better than my last failure
and greater than my last success.

MY FIXED IDEA OF YOU

you were the knife i lost the jungle path deep green red as a blade
spilled on the highway which slices through a south american
canvas

your bed when i shut my eyes i see you lying there naked like the
morning the sun walked in and you and i were still making love

is it so wrong to confess that?

flower of the agave milk pulp sapping out my wound my painted
love you were the tattoo which grows like scar tissue over dawn's
eyes you were pierced flesh you were the carpenter's nail

you were the hound's tooth which has worked its way into the
blind heart of the world

A Valentine's Poem for No One

sometimes when i look down there is an idiot in my shoes
with the heart of a stranger and a head like butter
and a memory like a green plastic bucket left at coney island
and the eyes of a small kid who never looks up
he just shovels in the sun and sand all day
sometimes when i look down there is a wise guy in my shoes
with a billboard smile and a hot rod temper
and a pair of legs like ships that get lost at sea
there is a salesman there is an orchestra conductor
there is a cabinet maker and a burmese warrior
there is a sailor with a laugh like a tiger
that gets snarled in traffic
and i think: who on earth could understand this man?
and i think: who on earth will love him?
three angels strike cat gut strings
in the nerves of this man
two angels play pingpong between his eyes
one angel lives in the back of his brain
like a goldfish bowl like a george gershwin song
sometimes when i look down there is a chamber of commerce
president in my shoes
with a kid carrying a tuba who follows him around
in his belly he is digesting a world war ii helmet
in his lungs he is building an asbestos factory
he follows a neon arrow around and around a parking lot
sometimes when i look down there is an old man in my shoes
at night when he lies down he cannot sleep
and when he can sleep he dreams about rivers
there is an ostrich with its head stuck in his mighty snowbank
there is a double dactyl stuck in his bad left ear
he has forgotten the name of the bank in central america
the hindu temple goddess the incredible six foot
marshmallow princess
sometimes a circus dog does backflips in his kidneys
sometimes he hands out leaflets like it's judgment day

and i think: who on earth will kiss this man?
and i think: who on earth will forgive him?
sometimes when i look down there is a cowboy in my shoes
sometimes when i look down there is a uranium prospector
sometimes when i look down there is a ukranian welder
wearing a flower shirt and boots like a jukebox
there is a georgia dirt farmer with knees like prayer
there is a florida preacher in a straightback chair
he sleeps in a field of peanuts and counts out quarters
he avoids the gaming table he smokes constantly
he loves the mexicans picking tomatoes
he loves the women in the beauty parlor
he sits under a tupelo tree
in violent weather
his teeth are hickory nuts
and his fingernails are torn
sometimes his stomach grumbles
worse than a handful of pebbles
and i think: who on earth will tolerate this man?
and i think: who will be his valentine?

THE TELLER OF FORTUNES

everyone in this town worships something
smoke from a broken pipe means unexpected love
smoke in the hall means the transformation of sinners
smoke from a gun means the validation of money
predictions do not generally make the weather
but there is another room you cannot see into
and the teller of fortunes knows who will thrive in it
and tonight is unlike last night and every night before that
somewhere in the city someone's god is always listening
all night long someone's god named work in corrective lenses
all night long someone's god named the mother of democracy
the teller of fortunes hears laughter behind many bedroom mirrors
the teller of fortunes hears knocking at the bent metal door
the teller of fortunes knows the hermit crab inside your brain
she lifts an egg to the blue ceiling and asks you to hold it
your future a hermit crab spinning songs under the boardwalk
your future a holy grail at the hotdog stand you should listen to
the teller of fortunes calls your future by its right name
the teller of fortunes says three small birds pecking at a rat
the teller of fortunes says a savior who lives in your eyes
a thought comes into her face and to her it is wonderful
the teller of fortunes says fear rides on a subway train
she says the word more sweetly than you ever imagined
an indelible blue mark you have painted on your forehead
i told you if she came here the cops would show up too, eventually

I Want to Go where the Garbage Men Go

I want to go where the garbage men go
I want to ride where the garbage men ride
it is Friday night it is eight pm I want to
go where the garbage men go
when they gear up
when they get in motion
the garbage men the garbage men
cruising the city like a shooting star
like a desert consuming itself
they ache for garbage from their biceps
to their toes like Columbus ached for America
like kids ache for the Good Humor man
like a robber emptying a cash register
at a 7-Eleven aches for money
in t-shirts and stained jeans
with their jaws stuck out
like Ethel and Fred Mertz
with their heads like steel plates
and their va va va voom
the garbage men do not mind they do not care
it is hot it is cool what's the difference?
It's all work to them
and they love to work
with their leather gloves
on their leather hands
and they are high above the crowd
and the stench of it all
and it's good damn money besides —
good damn money! Who's going to tell them different?
They are tall they are muscular who is going to tell them?
They have good teeth they have hair like Greek gods
and their language is perfect!
Their muscles shivering like primitive seas
their bones shaking like javelines

and the blood of centuries dries on their hands
they are big as beer barrels
and they love to talk like pirates of the Aegean
and wrestle with each other like animals on the ground
they are jackhammers in Mamaroneck
they are tugboats on the Sound
from Brooklyn to the Bronx from trash can to sea
to shining sea I want to roll along on the rain spattered roadway —
I am perfectly serious about this I want to
go with the garbage men!
They are calm they are professional
and they're loud as fists striking solid steel
they are polite to the mayor
and if they whistle at the pretty mamasitas
it is only for show it doesn't really mean anything
they brush flies away from their faces
nothing bothers them at all nothing!
Not traffic lights not fender benders
not bosses not banana skins
not razor blades not twenty dollar bills
not a box of taco shells and not the Daily News
and when the wind picks up they shout back at the wind
and the wind gets the hell out of their way
and when they wave to the driver the truck takes off
and the traffic parts, like mountains part
for Colorado mountain men
and they ride away
and where do they go with all that garbage?
They go to the landfill
they go to the loading docks
they go to trailer parks
they go to Windy Gap
they go to the incinerator
they go to Staten Island
they go to the ocean floor —
they go home to their wives and mothers

their sons and daughters
to their neat little houses
in their neat little suburbs
they climb out of their trucks
and they pull off their clothes
they climb into their beds
and they pull their wives to them
and they make love to their wives properly
and then they go to sleep
and if they dream at all
it's no big thing! No big thing!
After awhile they stop dreaming
and they are dead to the world
and their sleep is dark and perfect
as night is dark and perfect
and they are the Lords
of everything they survey

IN THE 25TH HOUR

Will you be there in the 25th hour
when snow pipers are sleeping
and the marigolds of summer
have forgotten the sun
when tins of camomile
and dutch chocolate and
rough tobacco are empty
when barbary seals
stop coming to your harbor
and your dreams empty out and
the tangled seabed's raucous laughter and
the frozen pond in your woods
and the column of light
which climbs to heaven —
will you be there when the key to your holy nature
stops turning in memory's door?
Life is long and unforgiving
one man's lungs fill up with hate
another man's heart gives up its beating
one man's eyes go blind with work
and another becomes indifferent to surprise
one day I'll turn up lame at your door
But in the 25th hour we will forget all that
in the 25th hour when the infirmary's are shuttered
and the soldiers hang up their boots
and the laborers refuse to take up their hammers
and the mental chains which shackle love are broken
when jails filled with broken men are emptied
and the skyscrapers of ambition fall down
we will stand up and we will listen,
you and I! Listen to the new earth spinning
We will listen to midnight snoring in its bed of ice
we will listen to children and lovers
and grandparents and neighbors

and we will begin again
where we left off
when we knew each other
the way no one else
has ever known
each other
we will sing along with
the new bird in his imaginary nest
singing a perfect song

ON HOPE

One spring, I spent several evenings among the mule deer on Warm Springs mountain. They seemed so happy then, having just survived another hard death by starvation or by the bullet to wander down and graze peacefully on the tender leaves of timothy and clover that grow there along the base of the mountain. As legend has it, an Indian could at one time walk right up and touch one of these sleek brown creatures as it browsed unsuspecting in the gathering dusk before me. I tried that, working my way carefully down through the dry sage and loose rock of a hillside, stopping dead still when they looked up, sometimes caught balanced awkwardly on one leg for long moments while they leisurely tested the air. I don't think I ever really intended to touch one. I just wanted to see how close I could come. Their lives, like my hopes, were so quick and supple there, so vulnerable in that high open country in the sun.

Slow and clumsy, I came within a hundred yards before they wandered down to the river to drink.

THE WOUND

Somewhere up in the mountains, an old man crouches before a small fire, working something indistinct with his hands. As you watch over his shoulder, the thick calloused fingers of one hand push and twist, push and twist against some resistance held firmly in the other. Every now and then, gradually, as the contours and edges take shape, he pauses, turning his head slightly to one side, as if listening to small wild movements far off in the trees. You suddenly realize that he knows you are here, behind him, that he knew you would be, that he has been listening to the faint rustle of your thoughts for years. You look up and find he has turned to face you. His eyes are the color of rock rainclouds, of the intricately carved arrowhead cupped in his hands. He tells you how he goes out and gathers up the blood-red translucent cries of a hawk, heavy chunks of darkness spattered with pools of just-before-dawn, pale blue splinters from some high mountain stream. How he brings them back to the fire and works them until they are razor-sharp points which he attaches to the long shaft of his voice.

Shuddering, you rock back and forth on your feet. Turning to leave, hurrying down the mountain, you already begin to feel the strange, unexplainable ache in your body, find yourself at odd moments dropping to your knees in tears. Somewhere long before the bottom, it bursts out through your side, leaving a gaping wound into which the world now rushes.

INTERSTATE ROUND

I am driving down the Interstate. The music is turned up so loud inside, I can barely stand it. The hills are on fire. Every leaf of every tree is on fire. I unbutton my chest and let them pass through. They enter me like lovers, each one alive, penetrating and whole. We remain connected for awhile after they pass. Then I snap forward, like a long arm, to embrace the next. I am dancing down the Interstate. The music is turned up. I can barely stand it. My heart is on fire. Each leaf of every tree is dancing. Someone is driving. I am on fire. The music is whole. The lovers are dancing. Each leaf passes through me. My chest is unbuttoned. The hills are turned up. The music is dancing. The lovers are on fire. Each leaf is unbuttoned. The Interstate is dancing. Each leaf is whole. The hills are unbuttoned. The music is on fire. The dancers are dancing. The lovers pass through.

THOUGHTS

How we love sometimes
to feed on them

the way they skitter and dance
before us

dip and stutter and juke
through our lives

as if they can't help
but obey the primal commandment
to party.

And how fickle we can be
at their table --

one moment content
to loll in the shadows and wait
for something big-bodied, say,
a little swarthy

to descend out of the swarm
and dimple the surface,

something we can slurp up
and drag with us
back down into the depths

where we can roll it around
under the tongue
and probe it for truth,

and the next we're caught
rising and rising in a kind of frenzy
at their fat rich bait
as if there's no tomorrow

as if desperate to believe

as if they could possibly save us
from ourselves.

HOW LUCKY

How lucky I am, turning fifty two,
to still feel this unquenchable thirst
for you, my wife of twenty one years, your body
and soul so much more to me
than when we first lay naked together,
as if I have found such nourishment in you
over the years that my wayward desire,
coaxed, pampered and put up with
like some difficult plant, has gradually
taken root and flourished
in this garden you have so joyfully
and generously become, now lush and layered
and wet from last night's rain,
each splash of you, lavender and purple,
yellow and rose ringed
in a hundred shades of green.

AFTER LOVEMAKING

The house silent,
car lights on the arched doorways,
a dog barking somewhere far off,
slipping in and out of dreams,
the woman holding the man's arm,
them sinking, sinking
into each other . . .

THE NEXT STEP

Having to move
from my house
into my heart,

there isn't room
for all the chairs.
But my piano will fit.

It's hard to leave
some of those old
friends behind —

the furnishings
that my father
and mother knew.

So I dust, bravely,
and make gifts
to my friends and strangers,

break away cleanly
with honor: to myself
and to my children,

take to the road
with a smile, and a small package
tied in a handkerchief.

Who would have thought
the next step
after the wilderness
would be the stars?

ABOUT THE POETS
PERMISSIONS AND ACKNOWLEDGMENTS

KIM ADDONIZIO was born in Washington, DC and divides her time between Oakland, California and New York City. She is the author of six books of poetry, most recently *Lucifer at the Starlite* and *My Black Angel: Blues Poems and Portraits*, with woodcuts by Charles D. Jones. Her collection *Tell Me* was a finalist for the National Book Award. She has also published two novels, two books of stories, an anthology on tattoos, and (with Susan Browne) a word/music CD. With Dorianne Laux, she wrote *The Poet's Companion: A Guide to the Pleasures of Writing Poetry*. Her latest book on writing is *Ordinary Genius: A Guide for the Poet Within*. Her poems "The Numbers," "Generations," and "What Do Women Want?" are from *Tell Me*, Copyright © 2000 by Kim Addonizio. Reprinted with the permission of The Permissions Company, Inc., on behalf of BOA Editions, Ltd., www.boaeditions.org. "First Poem For You" is reprinted from *The Philosopher's Club*, Copyright © 1994 by Kim Addonizio. Reprinted by permission of the author.

MALAIKA KING ALBRECHT is the founding editor of *Redheaded Stepchild*, an online magazine that only accepts poems that have been rejected elsewhere. She's the author of 3 books of poetry, most recently, *What the Trapeze Artist Trusts*, published by Press 53. She lives on Freckles Farm in Ayden, NC with her family and teaches therapeutic horseback riding.

KB BALLENTINE received her MFA in Poetry from Lesley University, Cambridge, MA. She teaches high school theatre, creative writing, and adjuncts for a local community college. She has also conducted writing workshops throughout the United States. KB has three collections of poetry: *What Comes of Waiting* (2013), *Fragments of Light* (2009), and *Gathering Stones* (2008). In 2011, two anthologies published her work: *Southern Light: Twelve Contemporary Southern Poets* and *A Tapestry of Voices*. Her awards include: finalist for the 2006 Joy Harjo Poetry Award, 2007 finalist for the Ruth Stone Prize in Poetry, the Dorothy Sargent Rosenberg Memorial Fund Award in 2006 and 2007, and the 2013 Blue Light Book Award.   KB's Irish heritage has shaped many of her poems and continues to be a source of inspiration.

LYNNE BARNES grew up in Georgia and moved to San Francisco in the late 1960s, coming of age in the flower generation of the Haight-Ashbury. She lived in an intentional community for twenty years, has worked as a psychiatric nurse, and is currently a librarian at the San Francisco Public Library.   Her forthcoming book, *Falling into Flowers*, will be published by Blue Light Press.

MARY BARRETT, a Berkeley writer, has published poems in several literary journals including the *Santa Fe Sun, Apocalypse Now, California State Poetry Quarterly* and *Turning Wheel,* a Buddhist Journal. She wrote a series of interviews with social activists for the *Berkeley Daily Planet* and is now writing a personal essay collection about her forty years as an urban school teacher.

JUDY BEBELAAR used to have a card reading Poet, Teacher, Belly Dancer. She loved every one of the 37 years she taught in San Francisco high schools and is proud that her students won 7 National Scholastic awards for their poetry and produced a literary calendar which won two national awards. Now she has more time to write, has been published in more than 50 magazines, and has won some awards herself. She still belly dances.   "Message" was previously published in *Flyway: a Journal of Writing and Environment.* Her chapbook, *Walking Across the Pacific,* is published by Finishing Line Press.

LINDA BENNINGHOFF has been writing poetry since she was fourteen. For her, it is a simple chronicling of daily experiences, and a reaching for beauty that she sometimes sees surrounding her. Linda has published five chapbooks, and was most recently published in *Canary: A Journal of the Environmental Crisis* and *Poets and Artists.*

NANCY BERG's poetry and prose have been widely published in literary journals, anthologies, and magazines. Her book of poems,

Oracles for Night Blooming Eccentrics, won the 2009 Blue Light Book Award. Nancy is a recipient of a Poetry Fellowship from the National Endowment for the Arts, a Whelks Walk Press Poetry Award, and several Pushcart Prize nominations. She has taught at the University of Phoenix and with California Poets in the Schools. She has an M.A. in Communication from Stanford University, where she received a fellowship for an original musical comedy screenplay. Nancy Berg lives in Woodland Hills, California, where she is a freelance writer and editor.

When she isn't hip-hop dancing, MARIANNE BETTERLY designs websites and travels the world in search of the best cup of coffee, always writing poetry. She writes about nature, love and loss, with a poet's Cheshire smile. Her poetry has been published widely in books and journals including *Hot Flashes, Green Silk Journal, Turning a Train of Thought Upside Down, The Legendary, New Sun Rising: Stories for Japan, Specter Magazine,* and the *Haight Ashbury Literary Journal.* Marianne lives in a house in Kensington once owned by the great grand-nephew of Ralph Waldo Emerson.

JUNE RACHUY BRINDEL (1919–2011) was born on a farm in western Iowa. She learned to read at age three, entered school at four, and graduated from high school just after her 15th birthday. She earned her bachelor's and master's degrees from the University of Chicago, where she graduated Magna Cum Laude. June taught English Literature and Creative Writing at Wright Junior College in Chicago and Children's Theater at the National Music Camp in Interlochen. Her publications include two novels, *Ariadne* and *Phaedra;* a book of short stories, *Nobody is Ever Missing;* and a children's book, *Luap.* She also collaborated on songs with her husband, Bernard Brindel. While researching her novels, she discussed her ideas with Joseph Campbell and Riane Eisler. *This Moment's Daughter,* her collected poems, was winner of the 2012 Blue Light Book Award. Her third novel, *Clytemnestra,* is forthcoming from Blue Light Press.

SCOTT CAPUTO's first book of poetry, *Holy Trinity of Chiles,* was published by Blue Light Press in 2010. His work has appeared in

Red Rock Review, Ruah, Haight Ashbury Literary Journal, and *Saranac Review.* Besides being a published poet, he is also a published board game designer with two released games, *Kachina* and *Völuspá.* He currently works as a game designer in San Francisco and resides in Fremont with his wife and two sons.

JUDITH WALLER CARROLL was born and raised in Montana, lived for many years in the San Francisco Bay Area, and now lives in the Ouachita Mountains of Arkansas with her husband, the novelist Jerry Jay Carroll. "Leaving Montana" was awarded the 2010 Carducci Poetry Prize from Tallahassee Writers' Association and included in her chapbook *Walking in Early September* (Finishing Line Press, 2012.) "Pas de Deux" was previously published in *Naugatuck River Review.*

WILLA CATHER was born on December 7, 1873, in Virginia. She grew up in Nebraska and studied at the University of Nebraska, before moving to Pennsylvania, and then to New York. Cather is best remembered for her novels depicting frontier life on the Great Plains. In 1923, Cather was awarded the Pulitzer Prize for her novel, *One of Ours* (1922). Cather died in 1947 in New York City. "Prairie Spring" is in the public domain.

THOMAS CENTOLELLA is the author of three books of poetry, the most recent being *Views from along the Middle Way,* published by Copper Canyon Press. He's been the recipient of a Lannan Literary Fellowship, the American Book Award, and the California Book Award, among other honors. His work can be found in many anthologies, including *Don't Tell Mama: The Penguin Book of Italian American Writing.* He lives in San Francisco and teaches creative writing throughout the Bay Area. All poems copyright © Thomas Centolella and reprinted by permission of Thomas Centolella.

RODNEY CHARLES is President and Managing Editor of 1ˢᵗ World Publishing. Obsessively abstract, he has contributed to and edited hundreds of popular titles in dozens of genres. He has authored nine books, including: *The Land of Love, Art & Genius; Lighter Than Air; The Name Book* (editor); *Publish It Now; Book Marketing Basics,* and the bestselling *Every Day a Miracle Happens* and *Miracles of the Saints*. He rides his bike in Southern Iowa, working hard to stay engaged in connubial human drama.

KARLA CHRISTENSEN is a mother of four, teacher of Transcendental Meditation, enthusiastic traveler, mosaic muralist, painted tile artist, technical and creative writer, Holographic Repatterner, aromatherapist, and organizer of big projects. She lived in Mexico as a child, speaks pigeon Spanish with a child's enthusiasm and disregard for grammar, and is romantic at heart. Her creative life includes a love of nature, the mythological journey, the here and back again transformed, and the details of other times, other places.

LYNN COHEN was a student and mentee of Pulitzer Prize winners Stephen Dunn and W. D. Snodgrass. She is author of two books, *Dreams and Dreamers*, (Blue Light Press, 2010) and *Lonestar Days* (Salem Press 2003), and has poetry published in many anthologies. Her new book of poems, *Between the Years*, is forthcoming from Blue Light Press. Lynn teaches at Hofstra University and Suffolk Community College. She has lectured on modern and post-modern literature, and has given poetry readings in the United States and in Ireland.

LIVIA COLE grew up in Hungary and started writing poetry as a graduate writing student in Iowa. Currently, she is a freelance writer and videographer, and her biggest passion is learning new things such as jewelry-making, accounting, public speaking, dancing, film-making, scuba-diving, cooking, marketing, and languages. She pursues these interests for the sheer joy of discovery. She also has an interest in natural health, traveling, and meditation.

CARE CONNET lives in a house of straw and clay, wood and stone, mulberry paper and bamboo, on a small prairie farm in the midwest, from which she journeys around the world. She is a long-time teacher of Transcendental Meditation. She is also a practitioner of the Sunpoint Method of energy realignment. Connet has won numerous awards for her poetry. Her poems have appeared in *100*

Words, Amelia, nycBigApple.com, Contemporary Review, The Iowa Source, and *Lyrical Iowa.* Her first collection of poetry, *Searching for Entrance,* was hand printed on handmade bamboo paper in Bali. In 2015 Connet co-authored the English translation of *Diary of the White Bush Clover,* the story of Goto Hiroko's peace pilgrimage, walking alone three hundred miles from Kyoto to Tokyo, praying for those who died in the war.

PHILIP DACEY's latest of thirteen books of poems is *Church of the Adagio* (Rain Mountain Press, 2014), and his previous book, *Gimme Five,* won the 2012 Blue Light Book Award. His work appears in Scribner's *Best American Poetry 2014.* Winner of three Pushcart Prizes, Dacey is the author of complete volumes of poems about Gerard Manley Hopkins, Thomas Eakins, and New York City. After an eight year post-retirement adventure as a resident of Manhattan's Upper West Side, he moved in 2012 to Minneapolis, where he lives beside Lake Calhoun.

MICHELLE DEMERS holds an MFA in poetry from the Vermont College of Fine Arts and has been published in *The Café Review, The Auroran, The Burlington Poetry Journal, Collecting Moon Coins II, Diner, The Dryland Fish,* and *The Blue Fig Review.* Her chapbook, *Epicenter,* won the 2006 Blue Light Poetry Prize. She teaches poetry and writing at the Community College of Vermont and Vermont Technical College. She also leads her own workshops, First Thoughts Writing Workshops, regionally. She lives and writes in Williston, Vermont, with her brilliant husband and exceptional cat. She is inspired by Vermont's spectacular countryside, as well as the deep spiritual questions of life.

XUE DI was born in Beijing in 1957. In English translation, he has published four full length books, *Zone, Another Kind of Tenderness, An Ordinary Day,* and *Heart into Soil,* and four chapbooks, *Forgive, Cat's Eye in a Splintered Mirror, Circumstances,* and *Flames.* He has also published a book of criticism of contemporary Chinese poetry in Chinese. His new book, *Across Borders,* was published in 2013 by Green Integer Press, and his work has been translated into several languages. Xue Di is a two-time recipient of the Hellman/Hammett Award and a recipient of the Lannan Foundation Fellowship.

JOSEPH DI PRISCO's recent memoir, *Subway to California*, begins in the 60s when his father flees into the Long Island woods to escape the FBI, and ends a few years ago at the Kentucky Derby. In between he almost dies a few times, becomes the only person in the family to graduate from high school, lives in a Catholic monastery, plays cards professionally around the world staked by big-money backers, opens Italian restaurants, teaches, finishes grad school at Berkeley, cultivates a couple of addictions, is named the prime suspect in a racketeering investigation, becomes a single father, publishes eight books, takes care of his sociopath parents with Alzheimer's, and delivers eulogies for everybody in his family. His third book of poems, *Sightlines from the Cheap Seats*, comes out in early 2016. He has won poetry prizes and published in dozens of magazines and journals. Doubtless his greatest claim to fame is having attended college, in a time when giants walked the earth, before email and texting, in the shadow of the incandescent Diane Frank. "My Mission Statement" first appeared in *Zyzzyva*.

ALIXA DOOM has published in numerous magazines and anthologies. Her chapbook, *Cedar Crossings*, was awarded the 2009 Blue Light Poetry Prize and was published in 2010. Her first full-length book of poems, *A Slow Dissolve of Egrets*, was published by Red Dragonfly Press in 2014. She moved in 2011 from her home of many years in the Minnesota River Valley to the Uptown area of South Minneapolis.

JENNIFER DORFMAN was born in San Diego and raised in Iowa City, Iowa. She received her B.A. in Psychology from the University of Pennsylvania and her Ph.D. in Cognitive Psychology from the University of California, San Diego. She currently researches memory, metaphor, and wisdom at the University of Chicago. Her poetry has appeared in the *MacGuffin* and the *Haight Ashbury Literary Journal*.

STEPHEN DUNN is the author of 17 books of poetry, including *Different Hours*, which was awarded the 2001 Pulitzer Prize, and *Here and Now* (both from Norton). In 2014, a book of essays on his work, edited by Laura McCullough, was published by Syracuse University Press, along with a new book of poems, *Lines of Defense,* from Norton. In 2012 he was the recipient of the Paterson Prize for Sustained Literary Achievement. He lives in Frostburg, Maryland with his wife, the writer Barbara Hurd, and is Distinguished Professor Emeritus of Creative Writing at Richard Stockton College. "Decorum" copyright © 1994 by Stephen Dunn, "At the Smithville Methodist Church" copyright © 1986 by Stephen Dunn, from *New and Selected Poems 1974-1994.* Used by permission of W.W. Norton & Company, Inc. "Sisyphus and the Sudden Lightness" from *Local Visitations* by Stephen Dunn. Copyright © 2003 by Stephen Dunn. Used by permission of W.W. Norton & Company, Inc. "Beliefs" and "Juarez" from *The Insistence of Beauty: Poems by Stephen Dunn.* Copyright © 2004 by Stephen Dunn. Used by permission of W.W. Norton & Company, Inc. "If a Clown" from *Here and Now: Poems by Stephen Dunn.* Copyright © 2011 by Stephen Dunn. Used by permission of W.W. Norton & Company, Inc.

KEVIN FAREY first fell in love with poetry at the age of 36. This was a key step in a high school math teacher's journey from left-brain dominance to a healthier balance. In another artistic life, he drums and strums for the band that accompanies his wife's Polynesian dance troupe. He dreams of someday writing a poem (or at least living a day of his life) in a way that integrates the pulses of Tahitian dance, the harmonies of Hawaiian music, the sequenced elegance of proofs, and the imagistic richness of mystical poetry.

PAUL FISHER's first book of poems, *Rumors of Shore,* won the 2009 Blue Light Book Award. In his words: "After a brief affair with poetry during my college years, I locked it in the cellar, and though I could often hear it whimper, I only occasionally tossed it a bone. Then, at about the age of forty, during a deep personal crisis of faith, I turned to it again, this time out of necessity. With its big heart, poetry forgave me, and I now write for survival. It's my spiritual lifeline. I admire poets who balance incantation and sense, the ultimate high wire act. On one side is incoherence, on the other prose. A difficult and dizzying feat, but one worth attempting." Paul is the recipient of an Individual Artist's Fellowship in Poetry from the Oregon Arts Commission, holds an

MFA from Gerald Stern's Poetry Program at New England College, and is a visual artist as well as a poet.

MEG HILL FITZ-RANDOLPH has been published in *Yellow Silk, Cimmaron Review, Antioch* Review and *Prairie Schooner.* She has an MFA from Warren Wilson College in Creative Writing. Along with her daughter, Meg is obsessed with horses and is a dressage rider. "The Love of Horses" was previously published in *Yellow Silk.*

STEWART FLORSHEIM has been widely published in magazines and anthologies. He was editor of *Ghosts of the Holocaust,* an anthology of poetry by children of Holocaust survivors (Wayne State University Press, 1989). His first chapbook, *The Girl Eating Oysters,* was published by 2River in 2004. Stewart won the Blue Light Book Award for *The Short Fall from Grace* (Blue Light Press, 2006). His new collection, *A Split Second of Light,* was published by Blue Light Press in 2011 and received an Honorable Mention in the San Francisco Book Festival. He has been awarded residencies from Artcroft and the Kimmel Harding Nelson Center for the Arts. Stewart has read his poems throughout the San Francisco Bay Area, as well as in New York, Boston, London, and Jerusalem.

JESSICA FLYNN is a poet, photographer, and psychotherapist who lives in Sausalito, California. She hopes to learn to play the cello soon.

DIANE FRANK is an award-winning poet and author of six books of poems, including *Swan Light, Entering the Word Temple,* and *The Winter Life of Shooting Stars.* Her friends describe her as a harem of seven women in one very small body. She lives in San Francisco, where she dances, plays cello, and creates her life as an art form. Diane teaches at San Francisco State University, Dominican University in San Rafael, leads workshops for young writers as a Poet in the School, and directs the Blue Light Press On-line Poetry Workshop. *Blackberries in the Dream House,* her first novel, won the Chelson Award for Fiction and was nominated for the Pulitzer Prize. Her second novel, *Yoga of the Impossible,* published in 2014, was an Amazon bestseller and #1 on their "Hot New Releases" list.

Donald N. Frank (1926–2009) was an inspiration to all who knew him. Trained as an electrical engineer, with a BSEE from Newark College of Engineering (NJIT), he was a frequent and respected speaker at APICS conventions and meetings and a regular contributor to the APICS newsletters. In 2007 he was honored as APICS Man of the Year, in recognition of his contribution to the industry and to the lives of the men and woman he mentored for more than 30 years. Frank was active in the Civil Rights movement and in 1963 marched in Washington with Martin Luther King. After the iron curtain fell, he assisted several countries in Eastern Europe to update their manufacturing technology. Sometimes, in his private moments he wrote poetry. He is the father of Diane Frank, Chief Editor of Blue Light Press.

Rodney Franz... Winner of both national and state awards for excellence in theatre, Rodney Franz was Artistic Director of the Iowa Theatre Company for many years. He has acted in films and television in London, Rome, New York and Los Angeles. He produced print advertising and television commercials in New York City. The author of three plays and a screenplay, Franz devotes much of his time to teaching and has held acting workshops throughout Iowa and as far as Australia. Film director David Lynch has praised his work with students: "I have never seen acting which was so natural — and without affectation or any falseness — and no funny ego business — genuinely honest — flawless grasp of all material — so imaginative."

Elinor Gale is a freelance writer and writing coach, whose work includes poetry, fiction, and personal essays. Her first literary triumph, a drama performed in third grade, inspired her to continue writing and to study English literature and creative writing at Smith College. In her writing, Elinor explores the pathos and humor of the human condition. She is working on her first novel, a tale of later-life romance and misadventure that colleagues describe as "Jane Austen meets Woody Allen."

LISHA ADELA GARCÍA is a child of the immigrant streams that form the Americas. She is the border; *Spanglish* with Mexico and the United States in her psyche and in her work. She has an MFA in Creative Writing from the Vermont College of Fine Arts and currently resides in Texas with her beloved four-legged children. Lisha also has a Masters degree for the left side of her brain from the Thunderbird School of Global Management. Her first book, *Blood Rivers*, was published in 2009 by Blue Light Press. Her chapbook, *This Stone Will Speak*, was published by Pudding House Press in 2008. Lisha is also a literary translator, editor and teacher.

MAY GARSSON stops for red lights except when it comes to writing poetry, then she blasts right through them. Her best poems are inspired by slight irritations, the occasional songbird, and major annoyances. She has been a featured poet at many Northern California literary venues and is the author of the chapbook, *The Liberation of Barbie*. She is currently working on a series of fragrance free poems.

MELANIE GENDRON, the book designer for Blue Light Press, is a multi-talented painter, graphic artist, and poet. Nationally known and respected for her visionary art, she is also creator of *The Gendron Tarot*. Inspired by many cultures, Melanie's prize-winning artwork is widely exhibited in public and private collections. In her words: "I seek to express realms beyond surface perception, to provide a bridge between what is seen and unseen. Living art breathes through the symbiotic relationship of artist and observer, through awareness shared. I explore invisible subtleties inherent in physical manifestation, drawn by the infinite Source of Creation to express Itself." She is the author of *This Fool's Journey: Through Tarot's 22 Major Arcana* and co-author of *A Goddess Journal*.

LINDA GOULD, a graduate of Sarah Lawrence College, has been published in *Satya Magazine*, *Poet's Place*, *Main Channel Voices* and *By-Line Magazine*. She has worked with Molly Peacock and Diane Frank. A resident of Duchess County in New York State, Linda lives on a farm where she cares for two horses, five dogs and 45 adopted turtles and tortoises. She has worked as a writer for *The Town Journal Newspaper* and is currently working on several longer pieces.

ZINNIA GUPTE is a poet, priestess of the sacred arts, and sacred dancer who lives on the magical island of Ibiza in Spain. She is inspired by temple dance, belly dance, Goddess energy, mermaids, mystical women, music, ocean and stars. Zinnia performs across the Mediterranean and teaches Sacred Dance workshops in Spain and Greece. She is currently working on a book of poems, *Dancing in Ibiza*.

LISA HICKEY is a poet, author and entrepreneur. She owns an advertising agency, where she has written countless ads, commercials, radio spots and brochures. Two non-fiction books about the ad industry have been published by Rockport Publishers. Her poems have been published in *Slipstream, Nerve Cowboy, Pemmican Press, Blackwidow's Web of Poetry, Shemom* and *ProseAxe*. The walls of her house are wallpapered with her favorite poems of all time.

JANE HIRSHFIELD's *Given Sugar, Given Salt* (HarperCollins, 2001), was a finalist for the National Book Critics Circle Award and winner of the Bay Area Book Reviewers Award. She is the author of eight poetry collections, most recently *The Beauty* (Knopf, 2015); two books of essays, the now-classic *Nine Gates: Entering the Mind of Poetry* (HarperCollins, 1997) and *Ten Windows: How Great Poems Transform the World* (Knopf, 2015). Hirshfield has received Guggenheim and Rockefeller Foundation fellowships, and her work has appeared in eight editions of *The Best American Poetry*, four *Pushcart Prize* anthologies, *The New Yorker, The Atlantic, Harper's, The New York Times*, and numerous literary reviews. She has taught at U.C. Berkeley and the Bennington College M.F.A. Seminars, and has been featured on two Bill Moyers PBS television specials and Garrison Keillor's *Writers Almanac*. Her translations have been set to music by John Adams and Philip Glass, and used in a nationally televised figure skating program by Kristi Yamaguchi. Her poems have been featured on New York City's subways and buses in the *Poetry In Motion* program, on a brass plaque on San Francisco's Embarcadero, and on the walls of many hospices around the country. She is a current

Chancellor of the Academy of American Poets. "Hope and Love," "Each Moment a White Bull Steps Shining into the World," "The Poet," and "Late Prayer" from *Lives of the Heart* by Jane Hirshfield. Copyright © 1997 by Jane Hirshfield. Reprinted by permission of HarperCollins Publishers. "The Envoy," "In Praise of Coldness," "Tree" and "Rebus" from *Given Sugar, Given Salt* by Jane Hirshfield. Copyright © 2001 by Jane Hirshfield. Reprinted by permission of HarperCollins Publishers.

JODI HOTTEL is a Sansei, third generation Japanese-American. During the Second World War, her mother's family was interned at Heart Mountain, Wyoming, so she wants to tell those stories. Her chapbook of poems about the incarceration, *Heart Mountain*, was winner of the 2012 Blue Light Press Poetry Prize. Her poems have been published in *Nimrod International, Spillway, Naugatuck Review, Touch, English Journal* and anthologies from the University of Iowa Press, Tebot Bach, and the Marin Poetry Center.

LOUISA HOWEROW's poetry has appeared in *Not Somewhere Else But Here* (Sundress Publications), *I Found It at the Movies: An Anthology of Film Poems* (Guernica Editions), *Fear of Dancing: The Red Moon Anthology of English Language Haiku, 2013* (Red Moon Press), and *Imaginarium 3: The Best Canadian Speculative Writing, 2014* (ChiZine Publications).

BARBARA HURD is author of *Listening to the Savage* (UGA Press), *Walking the Wrack Line: On Tidal Shifts and What Remains, Entering the Stone: On Caves and Feeling Through the Dark*, a Library Journal Best Natural History Book of the Year (2003), *The Singer's Temple, Stirring the Mud: On Swamps, Bogs, and Human Imagination*, a *Los Angeles Times* Best Book of 2001, and *Objects in this Mirror*. Her work has appeared in numerous journals including *Best American Essays 1999, Best American Essays 2001, The Yale Review, The Georgia Review, Orion*, and *Audubon*. The recipient of an NEA Fellowship for Creative Nonfiction, winner of the Sierra Club's National Nature Writing Award, three Pushcart Prizes, and four Maryland State Arts Council Awards, she teaches in the Vermont College of Fine Arts

MFA in Writing Program. All poems copyright © Barbara Hurd and reprinted with the permission of Bright Hill Press.

DAVID HURLIN is a jazz drummer, tabla player, poet, and YouTube anti-hero. He is a founding member of psycho-funk trio, the Apocalypso Tantric Noise Choir. He is also drummer and songwriter for funk/soul band, Subterranean All Stars. In addition to music, he is in the process of finishing his first book of poetry, *The End of Tourism*, forthcoming from Blue Light Press. He lives in Fairfield, Iowa with his son, Dil Mondrian.

MAGGIE JACOBS has been writing since she was 4 years old. "I Was Feeling Odd" is her first published poem.

GEORGE JAMES' life mission is to help uplift mankind's consciousness and empower people by teaching them to connect to their Soul via intuition. Since high school he secretly wrote down his Soul's guidance in the form of poetry, which in 2008 became his first published book, *Peeling the Onion: Poems of Spiritual Awakening*. He was asked by *The Black Quarterly Review* to be the opening poet for the 10th Annual Harlem Book Fair gala in New York City. His second book, *Copperhead: Tantric Lessons on Love*, is bold and daring in addressing the spiritual seeker's inner conflict between sexuality and spirituality; this book earned the Blue Light Press 2010 Poetry Prize. When not traveling and teaching Perceptive Awareness Technique$^{(TM)}$ for Intuition or Soma Pi Healing, he's quietly working with people to fulfill his mission.

SUSIE JAMES is a classical pianist, graduating with a degree in music from the University of Iowa. Her poetry has been published in journals and magazines, including *The MacGuffin*, *Lyrical Iowa*, and *Sierra*. Her poem "Diana" won 2nd place in a 2002 contest sponsored by the National Federation of State Poetry Societies. Her poetry appears in *The Dryland Fish: An Anthology of Contemporary Iowa Poets* (2004); *Leaves By Night, Flowers by Day* (2006); and *This Enduring Gift: A Flowering of Fairfield Poetry* (2010). Under the name Susie Niedermeyer, she won the Blue Light Book Award in 2007, and the resulting book of poems, *Under a Prairie Moon*, is now available online at Amazon and Barnes and Noble.

HELGA KIDDER is a native of Germany's Black Forest region and lives in the Tennessee hills with her husband and her dog, Tyler. She has an MFA in Writing from Vermont College. She is co-founder of the Chattanooga Writers Guild and leads their poetry group. Her poetry has appeared in *Louisville Review, Southern Indiana Review, Ekphrasis* and many other journals, and most recently was featured in *Southern Light, Twelve Contemporary Southern Poets* and in 2013, *The Southern Poetry Anthology: Tennessee*. She has a translation chapbook, *Gravel;* two poetry chapbooks, *Coming to Jerusalem* and *Wild Plums;* and a full-length poetry collection, *Luckier than the Stars*, published by Blue Light Press.

SUSAN KLAUBER... As a young Canadian passionately playing hockey and golf, and through her adventurous other lives, exploring Europe, South America, the U.S., and India, Susan Klauber has pursued her interest in the deeper, spiritual core common to all experiences. Her poetry captures the tangible and the elusive, and has appeared in the Harcourt Canada textbook, *Elements of English 11; The MacGuffin* and *Pirene's Fountain*, anthologies including *Eclipsed Moon Coins: Twenty-Six Visionary Poets* and *This Enduring Gift*. Her first book, *Face-Off at Center Ice*, was published by Blue Light Press in 1996. Her latest book, *Sound of the Sacred Beads: A Poet's Journey into India* (Sandtrove Press, 2010), takes the reader through modern India's chaotic, raw exterior, deep into the peaceful wisdom of its ancient spiritual heart.

LAURIE KLEIN's work has appeared in a wide range of journals, anthologies and recordings. Publication and awards have encouraged her, but it's the possibilities of the next poem, each word in the right place, that kindle ongoing hope and endeavor — along with the extraordinary poets she knows, some of whom gathered for the Blue Light Press Summer Writing Workshop. Klein's chapbook is *Bodies of Water, Bodies of Flesh*, and her new, full-length collection, *Where the Sky Opens, a Partial Cosmography*, is forthcoming in the Poeima Series from Cascade Books.

PHILIP KOBYLARZ is an itinerant teacher of the language arts and writer of fiction, poetry, book reviews, and essays. His first book of poems, *rues*, won the 2011 Blue Light Book Award. His new book of short stories, *now leaving nowheresville*, is also published by Blue Light Press.

KIRSTON KOTHS... Born in the Midwest, Kirston spent his first seven years in Wisconsin and Iowa, eagerly absorbing all of the experiences that make childhood an unforgettable time. While pursuing a liberal arts education at Amherst College, he became fascinated with music and dance. He has taught a traditional style of community dancing, known as Contra Dance, for 30 years. Along the way, a Ph.D. from Harvard in Molecular Biology opened the door to a career in biotechnology in California. For the past decade, Kirston has re-dedicated himself to his lifelong interest in the arts — from documentary filmmaking to writing poetry. His poems have appeared in *Common Ground Review*, *Plainsongs*, and *Askew Poetry Journal*. "Snow Reader" was previously published in *California Quarterly*.

JOHN KRUMBERGER's first full-length volume of poems, *The Language of Rain and Wind*, was published by Backwaters Press in 2008. He also has a chapbook, *In a Jar Somewhere*, (Black Dirt Press, 1999.) He works as a psychologist in St. Paul, Minnesota. He has been told that in his baby pictures, he strongly resembled Dwight Eisenhower.

LAURIE KUNTZ's bio is as elusive as her estrogen levels. Sometimes she remembers she is a poet and sometimes not. She has lived and worked as a writer and teacher in the Philippines, Thailand and Japan for thirty-five years, but is now in nomadic retirement mode. Her poetic themes are a result of working with Southeast Asian refugees, living as an expatriot, and being an empty nester. Three of her poems were nominated for a Pushcart Prize. Her chapbook, *Women at the Onsen*, was published by Blue Light Press. She enjoys long walks with her two dogs, Sage and Merlin, named for wisdom and magic.

MELODY LACINA grew up in Iowa and now makes her home in Berkeley, California. *Private Hunger*, her first collection, was published as part of the University of Akron Poetry Series. Her work also has appeared in numerous journals, including *Poetry East, Cimarron Review,* and *Rattle.* All of her poems in this anthology first appeared in *Private Hunger.*

DANIEL J. LANGTON lives and teaches in San Francisco. His *Querencia* won the Devins Award and the London Prize. His 7th collection, *During Our Walks,* was published in 2012 by Blue Light Press, and his new collection, *Personal Effects: New and Selected Poems,* was published in 2014 by Blue Light Press. "Popcorn" was first published in the *Atlantic Monthly.* "October Eighth" was previously published in the *Mississippi Valley Review.* "The Light by the Door" was previously published in the *Times Literary Supplement.*

CHARLIE LANGTON shares these poems from his book *Keep Silence, But Speak Out.* A graduate of the University of Iowa Writers Workshop, his poems have appeared in numerous magazines and in the anthology, *Voices on the Landscape.* He has been featured on *New Letters on the Air* and *Live at Prairie Lights.* He lives in the beautiful small river town of Decorah, Iowa.

RUSTIN LARSON's latest collections of poetry are *Bum Cantos, Winter Jazz, & The Collected Discography of Morning* (Blue Light Press, 2013), *The Wine-Dark House* (Blue Light Press, 2009) and *Crazy Star* (Loess Hills Books, 2005). His poems have appeared in *The New Yorker, North American Review, The Iowa Review, Poetry East* and other journals. He is the host of *Irving Toast, Poetry Ghost* on KRUU in Fairfield, Iowa and is a rostered artist with the Iowa Arts Council. A five-time Pushcart nominee, and graduate of the Vermont College MFA in Writing program, Larson was an Iowa Poet at The Des Moines National Poetry Festival in 2002 and 2004, a featured writer in the DMACC Celebration of the Literary Arts in 2007, 2008, and has been highlighted on the public radio programs *Live from Prairie Lights* and *Voices from the Prairie.*

DORIANNE LAUX is the author of three collections of poetry from BOA Editions: *Awake* (1990), introduced by Philip Levine; *What We*

Carry (1994), finalist for the National Book Critics Circle Award; and *Smoke* (2000). She is also co-author, with Kim Addonizio, of *The Poet's Companion: A Guide to the Pleasures of Writing Poetry* (W.W. Norton, 1997). Recent work has appeared in *The Best American Poetry, American Poetry Review, Shenandoah, Ploughshares, Barrow Street* and *Five Points*. Among her awards are a Pushcart Prize for poetry, two NEA fellowships, and a Guggenheim Fellowship. Laux is an Associate Professor in the University of Oregon's Creative Writing Program. "Girl in the Doorway" and "The Catch" are reprinted with the permission of Dorianne Laux. Her poems, "Aphasia," "The Lovers," and "The Thief," are from *What We Carry*. Copyright © 1994 by Dorianne Laux. "The Shipfitter's Wife" and "Trying to Raise the Dead" are from *Smoke*. All reprinted with the permission of The Permissions Company, Inc., on behalf of BOA Editions, Ltd., www.boaeditions.org.

DAWN LEAS' work has appeared in *Literary Mama, Southern Women's Review, Interstice, San Pedro River Review, Connecticut River Review, Pedestal Magazine* and elsewhere. Her chapbook, *I Know When to Keep Quiet*, was published by Finishing Line Press and is available in print and Kindle versions. Her poems can be found in *Everyday Escape Poems*, an anthology released by SwanDive Publishing. In past lives she was a copywriter, freelancer, admissions director and middle school English teacher. Currently, she is the associate director of the Wilkes University MA/MFA Creative Writing programs, and a contributing editor at *Poets' Quarterly* and *TheThePoetry*. She is also one of the poetry editors for *CityLitRag*.

Thirty years ago **LAUREN LIEBLING** left San Francisco for a holiday in Europe and stayed there. She lives in London, where she works as a body psychotherapist, so as well as following words across a page, she also follows energy through and across the body.

JUDY LIESE has been writing poetry since she first learned to make block letters in her red Big Chief writing tablet. Later, she became an RN who wrote poetry as a hobby. Going back to school in her forties turned her into poet who worked as an RN to support an addictive writing habit. She and her husband, Gary, live in Northern California with Miss Kitty, the cat, and Fargo, the wonder dog. Her greatest guilty pleasure, an ongoing, on-line poetry workshop with Diane Frank, led to the publication of her first book of poems, *I Was Albert Schweitzer's Secret Mistress*, published by Blue Light Press.

ROBIN LIM is a Guerrilla Midwife and was CNN Hero of the Year in 2011, awarded for her work as a midwife and healer in Bali. In her words, "I intensely advocate for the rights of mother and child to birth without violence. I am a grandmother, mom, wife, and my life shows me things which I must record as poems. I live with my huge family in a coconut, bamboo and grass house, in Bali, Indonesia." Lim has three poetry collections, *Stretch Marks*, *As a Child in the Religion of Gratitude*, and *The Geometry of Splitting Souls* (Blue Light Press), along with a novel, *Butterfly People*. Her books in the childbirth genre include *After the Baby's Birth* and *Eating for Two: Recipes for Pregnant and Breastfeeding Women*, both published by Celestial Arts, Berkeley, California. Her new book, *Placenta – The Forgotten Chakra*, is revolutionizing gentle childbirth.

Originally from Ohio, JEFF LUNDENBERGER lives in Asbury Park, New Jersey, with his husband. He does most of his writing on New Jersey Transit trains commuting to and from Manhattan, where he works in publishing. These are his first published poems.

ALISON LUTERMAN is the author of three books of poetry: *The Largest Possible Life*, *See How We Almost Fly*, and *Desire Zoo*. She is a frequent contributor to *The Sun*, and has also written numerous personal essays and plays. She teaches at The Writing Salon in Berkeley.

MATTHEW MACLEOD is a poet, songwriter and teacher who resides in northern Ontario, Canada. His poems have been published in *Ilya's Honey*, *Scrivener*, *Scribe*, *Lyrical Iowa* and *Arts Scene Iowa*. He was editor of *The Dryland Fish, An Anthology of Contemporary Iowa Poets*.

KEN MCCULLOUGH was born in Staten Island, but spent his formative years in Newfoundland. He lives in Winona, Minnesota with his wife and younger son. He recently completed his two year term as Poet Laureate of Winona. His most recent books are *Walking Backwards*, winner of the Blue Light Book Award in 2004, *Sicomoro Oropéndola* (Spanish translation), and *Broken Gates*. McCullough worked with Cambodian poet U Sam Oeur on a bilingual edition of *Sacred Vows*, as well as U's memoir, *Crossing Three Wildernesses*. Ken McCullough considers the mountains of Montana and Wyoming as his spiritual home. He was adopted into the Miniconjou band of the Lakota nation in 1993. Poems in this anthology were previously published in *No Exit, Old Crow, Nimrod, Rain City Review, River King Poetry Supplement*, and *Luna*.

SARAH McKINSTRY-BROWN... Winner of the 2010 Blue Light Book Award, the 2011 Nebraska Book Award for Poetry, and the Academy of American Poets Prize, Sarah McKinstry-Brown studied poetry at the University of New Mexico, the University of Sheffield, England, and received her MFA from the University of Nebraska. Published in numerous literary journals and poetry slam anthologies, she has taught performing and writing workshops in libraries, schools, and universities on the east and west coasts and everywhere in between. When she's not reading or teaching or writing, you can find Sarah in Omaha with her husband, the poet Matt Mason, and their two beautiful, feisty daughters.

NANCY LEE MELMON loves the taste of words. She lives with her husband, Ronny, and her westie, Maxwell, in Red Rock country, Sedona, Arizona. Nancy believes that writing poetry, arranging and rearranging words on the page, is an act of power. She also loves singing opera and jazz and playing the piano. She is a Feng Shui consultant, an Eden Energy Medicine practitioner, and a Reiki Master. She knows that life is meant to be an expression of Joy.

CONNIE LARSON-MILLER grew up in Iowa and returned to Ottumwa after living elsewhere for 20 years. Before retiring, she worked as a merchandiser for Recycled Cards and Leggs hosiery, and was a peer support counselor for the Iowa Coalition for Mental Health and Recovery. One of my favorite quotes from Connie: "Courage doesn't always roar. Sometimes courage is the quiet voice at the end of the day saying, I will try again tomorrow."

LouAnn Shepard Muhm is a poet and teacher from northern Minnesota. Her poems have appeared in *qartsilluni*, *North Coast Review*, *Alba*, *Red River Review*, *Eclectica*, *Poems Niederngasse*, and *Calyx*, and she was a finalist for the Creekwalker Poetry Prize and the Late Blooms Postcard Series. Muhm is a recipient of Minnesota State Arts Board Artist Initiative Grants in Poetry in 2006 and 2012, and has been featured twice in the "What Light" poetry sponsored by the McKnight Foundation and the Walker Art Museum. Her full-length poetry collection, *Breaking the Glass* (Loonfeather Press, 2008), was a finalist for the Midwest Book Award in Poetry.

Sharon Lask Munson was born in the motor city, Detroit, Michigan. She learned to drive in her father's pink and gray four-door Dodge, and many of her poems mention automobiles. She graduated college with an elementary teaching degree, and immediately went overseas for five years and taught in Department of Defense schools for American children of servicemen. In those years she drove an ancient steel-gray, right hand drive, Morris Minor. After returning home, she headed north to Anchorage, Alaska in a second-hand blue Oldsmobile. There she met her husband, married, and taught in public schools for the next twenty years. She now lives in Eugene, Oregon, where she spends her time reading, writing poetry, riding her bicycle, gardening, and taking long and interesting road trips. She is the author of three books, *Stillness Settles Down the Lane* (Uttered Chaos Press, 2010), *That Certain Blue* (Blue Light Press, 2011), and *Braiding Lives*, (Poetica, 2014).

Kambiz Naficy is a Persian poet and well loved by many of the writers in this anthology. He lives in Iran, where he serves as a poet, meditation master, and spiritual healer who is committed to helping individuals reach their full life potential through inner development and growth. Kambiz recalls his own personal deep connection with the wisdom of the Persian poets, like Rumi and Hafiz, as recited to him by his father when he was a just a boy with a philosophical nature. His writing reflects the joy of life, revealed from a deep place in his soul.

TAMMY NUZZO-MORGAN is the first woman to be appointed Suffolk County Poet Laureate (2009-2011). She is the founder and president of The North Sea Poetry Scene, Inc., publisher of The North Sea Poetry Scene Press, and editor of the *Long Island Sounds Anthology*. She has been honored with a Long Island Writers Group Community Service Award and the *Mobius* Editor-In-Chief's Choice Award. She completed an MFA from Stony Brook University-Southampton, and is now enrolled in a Ph.D. program for Interdisciplinary Studies in Humanities & Culture. She teaches at Briarcliffe College and maintains an active schedule of workshops and performances. She is also the founder and director of an archival arts center for Long Island Poetry, which serves as a literary research center and gathering place for poets.

KIM NIYOGI was born and raised in New York State. She left her social work career to pursue tarot and symbology studies. She returned to her childhood love of poetry writing at age 41, after the birth of her daughter. Her poems have appeared in *Bottle Rockets, Chantarelle's Notebook* and *Drown in My Own Fears*. She now lives and writes in Easton, Pennsylvania.

GRACE C. OCASIO is a 2014 North Carolina Arts Council Regional Artist Project Grant recipient. She won honorable mention in the 2012 James Applewhite Poetry Prize, the 2011 Sonia Sanchez and Amiri Baraka Poetry Prize, and was a 2011 Napa Valley Writers' Conference scholarship recipient. Her first full-length collection, *The Speed of Our Lives*, was published by BlazeVOX Books (2014). Her chapbook, *Hollerin from This Shack*, was published by Ahadada Books in 2009. She received her MFA in Poetry from Sarah Lawrence College and her MA in English from the University of North Carolina at Charlotte.

NYNKE PASSI was born in the Netherlands and received her MA in Creative Writing from San Francisco State University. She is director of The Luminous Writer Literary Center. Her writing has been published in *The Gulf Coast Review*, *The Anthology of New England Writers*, *The Dryland Fish*, *This Enduring Gift*, and the *Brook Road Literary Anthology*. With Rustin Larson and Christine Schrum, she edited the poetry anthology *Leaves by Night, Flowers by Day*. Her story "The Kiss" was nominated for a Pushcart Prize, and her essay "Oom Ealse and the Swan" was a finalist in the 2014 Jeffrey E. Smith Editor's Prize of *The Missouri Review*. "Bones" was first published in *The Dryland Fish*.

DIANE PORTER is a naturalist, teacher, writer, and nature photographer. She has a passionate interest in wild birds and is a contributing editor for *Bird Watcher's Digest*. She speaks at birding festivals on how to become the world expert on the birds in your own backyard, the intelligence of birds, and other birding topics. You can check out her website at www.birdwatching.com. She lives with her husband Michael in southeast Iowa on a beautiful piece of forested land, their homestead, which they call Aranyani.

DEBORAH RAMOS is an artist, poet, teacher, lover, mother, grandmother, tree-hugger and recycler. She grew up in Ocean Beach, a small beach community in San Diego, California, and studied art, textiles and costume design at San Diego State University. She's worked in costume shops, print shops, and flea markets, but art and writing have always been her passion. When Deborah is not writing or painting, she works as a Special Education Para-professional with special needs high school students. Her collection of poetry, *Road Warriors*, was named the Best Unpublished Poetry Chapbook 2010, by the San Diego Book Awards Association.

STEFANIE RENARD began writing poems on her canopy bed at the age of five. Her writing explores the capacity for language to transform personal experience into something transcendent. Stefanie is inspired by wild places, music and the images of daily life. She lives in the San Francisco Bay Area, where she teaches yoga, hikes often and listens to *Kind of Blue* as much as she can.

CLAUDIA M. REDER, author of *Uncertain Earth* (Finishing Line Press) and *My Father & Miro* (Bright Hill Press), is thrilled to have her poems included in this anthology. She teaches at California State University, Channel Islands.

ALICE ELIZABETH ROGOFF grew up in New York State. She has an MA in Creative Writing from San Francisco State University and a Certificate in Labor Studies from City College, San Francisco. Her poetry book *Mural* received the 2004 Blue Light Book Award and her book *Barge Wood* was published by CC. Marimbo. In 2012, she won an Individual Literary Cultural Equity grant from the San Francisco Arts Commission. She is a Co-Editor of the *Haight Ashbury Literary Journal*. She enjoys singing and playing classical guitar.

MARY KAY RUMMEL is Poet Laureate of Ventura County, California. Her seventh book of poetry, *The Lifeline Trembles*, was published by Blue Light Press as a winner of the 2014 Blue Light Book Award. She is a long time participant in the inspiring Blue Light Press Online Poetry Workshop with Diane Frank, and many poems from this book came out of that workshop. Her poetry book, *What's Left is the Singing*, was published by Blue Light Press in 2010. Mary Kay has been a featured reader in the U.S., in London, and at several poetry festivals including Ojai and San Luis Obispo, California, often performing poetry with musicians. She is retired from the University of Minnesota and teaches part time at California State University, Channel Islands.

BECKY DENNISON SAKELLARIOU was born and raised in New England and has lived most of her adult life in Greece. Her poems have appeared in a wide variety of journals, and she has been nominated twice for the Pushcart Prize. She has published four books: *The Importance of Bone* (Blue Light Press, 2005), *Earth Listening* (Hobblebush Books, 2010), *What Shall I Cry?* (Finishing Line Press, 2013) and *The Possibility of Red* (bilingual, Greek and English, Hobblebush Books, 2014). Becky can be found either in Peterborough, New Hampshire, where she is endlessly amazed at the clouds, the snow and the trees, and the power of memory, or in Euboia, Greece, where she lives amongst the olive, fig, almond, pomegranate, lemon, apricot and eucalyptus trees, drawn by the senses and the mystery of place. "Breathing" was previously published in *Kindled Terraces: American Poets in Greece*; "Shards" in *The Importance of Bone*; and "Praise Song for Winter" in the *Northern New England Review*.

BARBARA SAXTON graduated from the University of California, Santa Barbara with a degree in Asian Studies. She has worked as a translator, a financial services consultant, and a middle and high school English teacher. Other life pursuits include performing classical and folk music, Eastern European folk dance, and writing poetry. Recent retirement has allowed her more time to create and polish more of her writing. Her chapbook, *Dual Exposure*, was published in 2015 by Blue Light Press.

TERESA SAYRE is a sailor and photographer of creatures above and below the ocean. She lives with her First Mate and five cats on a hill overlooking the Caribbean Sea in the Virgin Islands. Her house is always open to warm trade winds, geckos, friends and family.

STEVEN P. SCHNEIDER is Professor of English at the University of Texas-Pan American. He is the co-creator with his artist wife, Reefka, of the traveling exhibit and book *Borderlines: Drawing Border Lives, Fronteras: Dibujando las Vidas Fronterizas*. He is the author of two other books of poetry, *Prairie Air Show* and *Unexpected Guests*; a scholarly book entitled *A.R. Ammons and the Poetics of Widening Scope*; and editor of *Complexities of Motion: New Essays on A.R. Ammons's Long Poems*; and *The Contemporary Narrative Poem: Critical Crosscurrents*. His awards include a Wurlitzer Foundation residency, the Anna Davidson Rosenberg Award for Poetry, a Nebraska Arts Council Fellowship, along with three grants from the National Endowment for the Arts.

CHRISTINE SCHRUM is an essayist and poet living on Vancouver Island. Her work has appeared in *The Atlantic*, *McSweeney's Internet Tendency*, *The Writer*, *A Verse Map of Vancouver*, *Quills Canadian Poetry*, and *Sulphur III*. Her poem "Rebirth" won first prize in the

17th Northern Ontario Poetry Competition (2012), and her poem "Treading Water" claimed third place in the 12th annual Popsicles and Kisses Poetry Contest. She has an M.A. in Professional Writing and co-edited the poetry anthology *Leaves by Night, Flowers by Day* (2007) with Rustin Larson and Nynke Passi.

ROBERT SCOTELLARO is a poet and short fiction writer who, in the early seventies, journeyed from Manhattan to California in a fifties school bus lined with mattresses and a few close friends. He is the author of seven literary chapbooks, including *Rhapsody of Fallen Objects* (Flutter Press, 2010), and *The Night Sings A Cappella* (Big Table Publishing, 2011), a full length collection of flash fiction, *Measuring the Distance* (Blue Light Press, 2012), and a new book of prose poetry: *What We Know So Far* (Blue Light Press, 2015). His story "Fun House" is included in the anthology *Flash Fiction International* (W.W. Norton, 2015). He was the recipient of *Zone 3's* Rainmaker Award in Poetry. With Dale Wisely, he co-edits the journal, *One Sentence Poems*. Raised in Manhattan, he currently lives with his wife in San Francisco.

CAMERON SCOTT received an MFA in Poetry from the University of Arizona. His work has most recently appeared in *Silk Road, Borderlands: Texas Poetry Review, Clerestory*, and *The Fly Fish Journal*. He has been a Writer-in-Residence/teacher for Fishtrap and Chiloquin Visions in Progress and writes a monthly column for *La Grande Observer* called "Steelhead Nation." He currently spends his summers as a fly fishing guide in Colorado and teaches digital storytelling for Fishtrap Story Lab in the winter. *The Book of Ocho*, his first collection of poetry, was published by AGS Press. If you have leftovers, he will eat them.

CHRISTOPHER SEID's most recent book of poems, *Age of Exploration*, is the winner of the 2015 Blue Light Book Award. His first book of poems, *Prayers to the Other Life*, won the Marianne Moore Poetry Prize. Born and raised in Iowa, he has lived in Brooklyn, Boston, California, and many points in between. For the past 12 years, he's made his home in Yarmouth, Maine, with his two children. He works as a freelance writer and serves on the board of The Telling

Room, a nonprofit writing center for children and young adults in Portland, Maine. He spends as much time as he can outdoors with his children and an imaginary dog.

PRARTHO SERENO's poetry books include *Call from Paris* (winner of the 2007 Word Works Washington Prize); *Causing a Stir: The Secret Lives and Loves of Kitchen Utensils* (winner of a 2008 IPPY); and *Elephant Raga*, winner of the 2014 Blue Lynx Prize, (Lynx House Press, 2015.) All poems in this anthology were previously published in *Elephant Raga*. Prartho's poems have appeared in *Atlanta Review, Memoir, Main Street Rag, Rattle, Chautauqua Review*, and many anthologies. She is Poet Laureate of Marin County, California; a California Poet in the Schools, and has an MFA from Syracuse University. "Frogs, Deer, Kitchen Window" originally appeared in the *Marin Poetry Center Anthology 2008*. "Heart Sutra" originally appeared in *Main Street Rag*.

BETSY SNIDER is a retired attorney who lives on a lake in rural New Hampshire with her black cat Sophie and the ghosts of her many dogs. When she is not hiking or swimming, she writes poetry and volunteers as a CASA Guardian ad Litem for abused and neglected children. Her poetry has been published in a variety of journals and anthologies, most recently in *Love Over 60: An Anthology of Women Poets*. Like Kay Ryan, Betsy grew up wanting to be a stand-up comic or a folk singer, but she still can't remember punch lines or stay on key. Her new book of poems, *Hope is a Muscle*, is forthcoming from Blue Light Press.

JOHN STIMSON was born in Philadelphia in 1958; formative years were on Cape Cod, where the lessons of divine desolation (in sand dunes and salt marshes) imprinted themselves. Attended Maharishi International University in Fairfield, Iowa, then moved his printing press and antique books there in 1983. Living as a freelance graphic artist and folk dancer/musician/singer. "Haiku for a Bachelor" no longer applies: happily enjoying family life with fiancée and daughter.

PAUL JOHAN STOKSTAD is author of *Butterfly Tattoo*, published by Blue Light Press. He has a varied life that includes tennis and disco balls, web design, class syllabi, contact improv, a ten-year-old child, a mystic healer wife, and a Netflix habit. Running parallel to that is a life in poetry that has had as its milestones a mother poet with a quiet, poignant, spare oeuvre of a few unforgettable poems, a father who, in thousands of attempts, wrote one memorable poem (now lost), a fondness for Bly, cummings, haiku, and the just discovered world of magical realism, and littered along the path, many, many poems, now collected and languishing in a shoebox, waiting to be free.

MICHAEL ANGELO TATA's *Andy Warhol: Sublime Superficiality* received international critical acclaim from Intertheory Press in 2010. His lyrical essays on poetics, psychoanalysis and philosophy appeared in *Psychoanalysis in Context*, *The Salt Companion to Charles Bernstein* and *Neurology and Modernity: A Cultural History of Nervous Systems, 1800-1950*, the British journal *Parallax*, Italy's *Rivista di* Estetica, and the American ezine *The Qouch*. His poetry and graffiti are featured in *Rattle* and *Xanadu*. He also writes reviews of contemporary aesthetics titles for Temple University's and Mount Holyoke College's *Journal of Aesthetics and Art Criticism*. He sits on the editorial boards for *Kritikos* and *rhizomes*. His chapbook, *The Multiplication of Joy into Integers*, won the Blue Light Poetry Prize and was published by Blue Light Press.

JANET THOMAS grew up in Australia in a family enchanted with words. When she moved to Iowa in 1987, she delighted in the opportunity to share her love of language with so many gifted and talented students. After twenty years in the USA, she is currently home on the exquisite Gold Coast in Queensland, Australia. She continues to write, along with teaching workshops for gifted and talented students in Queensland. Her poems have previously been published in *This Enduring Gift, Lyrical Iowa*; and *Leaves by Day, Flowers by Night*; and received the 2006 Helen Vaughn Memorial Haiku Award.

VIKTOR TICHY grew up in Czechoslovakia and now lives in Fairfield, Iowa. When he was 17 years old, he tried to stop the Russian tanks by reading poetry from the top of the national monument. Then he spent a night in jail for trying to crash the iron curtain but was too young to make it a home. Architect, engineer, and artist by education, he designed exhibits in Prague, condominiums in Vienna, and bridges in Boston. In Iowa, he developed real estate, worked with graphic design, and taught art. Father of four and a one-time daycare operator, he is finishing a book called *Genius in Diapers* about nurturing the talents all babies are born with. He began to write poetry in English in Diane Frank's workshop 20 years ago, and has won prizes and publications in over 120 international, national, and state poetry contests. His forthcoming book, *Architecture of Light*, won the 2010 Blue Light Book Award.

JR TUREK collects inspirations (a-poem-a-day ritual), collects shoes (more than a-pair-a-day habit), and collects a salary as a bookkeeper (5-day-a-week sentence). An active member of the Long Island poetry community, she is an editor, poet, proser; author of *They Come and They Go*; and serves as moderator of the Farmingdale Creative Writing Group. She resides in East Meadow, Long Island with her soulmate husband, their four dogs, and the spirits of poems to come.

JOYCE UHLIR (1935–2011) is author of *Mysterious Light*, published by Blue Light Press. She received her BA in Art Education from Dominican College of Racine, Wisconsin at age thirty-five. Teaching for several years in an elementary setting, she saw a need for children to express themselves through non-threatening media, like paint, clay and natural materials. Moving on, she worked two years at Norris Adolescent Center for adjudicated youth in Racine County near her home in Union Grove, Wisconsin. She later transferred to a treatment center in Milwaukee, working as an Art Therapist with exceptional education students. She earned her graduate degree (Masters in Emotional Behavior Disorders) from the University of Wisconsin.

LORETTA DIANE WALKER knew from her earliest days growing up in Odessa, Texas that she would spend her life writing. With a BA in Music Education and an MA in Elementary Education, she is in her thirty-second year teaching music to children in Odessa, Texas. She is a member of the Poetry Society of Texas, The Pennsylvania Poetry Society, and The National Federation of Poetry Societies. Her first book of poems, *Word Ghetto*, won the 2011 Blue Light Book Award and was published by Blue Light Press.

GEORGE WALLACE... As Writer In Residence at the Walt Whitman Birthplace, George Wallace has broadened the base of his poetry from his roots in French Surrealism and Beat Era bop prosody to the visionary and ecstatic tradition of 19th century American Transcendentalism. Long known as a purveyor of poetry that is at once smart and entertaining, this New York performance poet — author of 20 chapbooks of poetry — reaches to new levels of literary sophistication in his most recent work.

GLENN WATT is a 63-year-old husband, father and grandfather. Originally from the Wind River Valley of Wyoming, he has made his home between the Skunk and Des Moines Rivers in southeastern Iowa for the last thirty-five years. An avid birdwatcher and naturalist, as well as a poet, he loves to walk the remnant hardwood forests and tallgrass prairies while working out the sounds and rhythms of his poems. "On Hope" was originally published in *The MacGuffin*, "The Wound" in *Passages North*, and "Interstate Round" in *The Contemporary Review*.

ANTHONY WRIGHT is a piano technician, harper, Western astrologer, and radio producer. He wrote his dissertation on Chinese philosophy and complexity science. Originally from Minneapolis, he now lives in West Marin County, California.

ABOUT THE ART

I seek to express realms beyond surface perception, to provide a bridge between what is seen and unseen. –Melanie Gendron

The art in this anthology, created by Melanie Gendron, mainly consists of original color paintings displayed in grayscale, line drawings and digitally mastered art in Photoshop. Reproductions are available at MelanieGendron.com.

In Order of Appearance

ii. INSIDE THE TREE, acrylic on canvas, 12"x24," 2009.

xvi. NURTURING FOREST SOUTH, serigraph, 35"x36," 1976.

xviii. INNER GLANCE, drawing, 7" diameter, 1985, published in *The Goddess Remembered, A Spiritual Journal*, 1990, Crossing Press; and *A Goddess Journal*, Annie Elizabeth and Melanie Gendron, 2015, River Sanctuary Publishing.

7. DRAGONFLY MANDALA, drawing, 5" diameter, published in *Entering the Word Temple*, Diane Frank, 2005, Blue Light Press.

16. WE THE PEOPLE, acrylic on canvas, 45"x45," 1990, private collection.

36. II OF WANDS, digitally mastered in Photoshop, published in *The Gendron Tarot*, 1997, U.S. Games Systems, Inc.; and *Oracles for Night-Blooming Eccentrics*, Nancy Berg, 2007, Blue Light Press.

39-40. BEES, digitally mastered photo, 2014.

42. FLOWER & BUTTERFLY, drawing, 5" diameter, published in *Swan Light*, Diane Frank, 2013, Blue Light Press.

54. FLOWER & HUMMINGBIRD, drawing, 5" diameter, published in *Swan Light*, Diane Frank, 2013, Blue Light Press.

86. BLACK SWAN, digitally mastered photo, 3"x4," 2013.

88. DRAGONFLY, digitally mastered photo, 3"x4," 2013.

91. BLUE PEARL, acrylic on canvas, 45"x45," 1986, private collection.

106. THE CHANGELING, acrylic on canvas, 24" diameter, 1979, private collection.

108. NEPTHYS, drawing, 8"x10," 1990, published in *A Goddess Journal*, Annie Elizabeth and Melanie Gendron, 2015, River Sanctuary Publishing.

115. CREATION OF LOVERS, acrylic on canvas, 27"x36," 1985, private collection.

117. ART DECO WOMAN 3, drawing, 4"x6," published in *The Goddess Remembered, A Spiritual Journal*, 1990, Crossing Press; and *A Goddess Journal*, Annie Elizabeth and Melanie Gendron, 2015, River Sanctuary Publishing.

125. Sunfire, drawing, 3"x3," published in *Rhododendron Shedding Its Skin*, Diane Frank, 2001, Blue Light Press.

129. CEDAR, drawing, 5"x7," published in *Cedar Crossings*, Alixa Doom, 2010, Blue Light Press.

130. CREATION, acrylic on canvas, 24" diameter, 2011.

143. OF BYZANTIUM, acrylic on canvas, 24"x24," 1990, private collection.

162. EMERGENCE, acrylic on canvas, 20"x20," 2012.

165. AIR, color drawing, 7" diameter, 1996.

168. THREE BIRD MANDALA, drawing, 5" diameter, published in *Entering the Word Temple*, Diane Frank, 2005, Blue Light Press.

174. FLYING INTO NIGHT, drawing, 3"x3," published in *Rhododendron Shedding Its Skin*, Diane Frank, 2001, Blue Light Press.

179: SIX BIRD MANDALA, drawing, 5" diameter, published in *Entering the Word Temple*, Diane Frank, 2005, Blue Light Press.

185. ROSE ANGEL, drawing, 6"x9," published in *The Goddess Remembered, A Spiritual Journal*, 1990, Crossing Press; and *Rhododendron Shedding Its Skin*, Diane Frank, 2001, Blue Light Press; and *A Goddess Journal*, Annie Elizabeth and Melanie Gendron, 2015, River Sanctuary Publishing.

186. NEST MANDALA, drawing, 5" diameter, published in *Entering the Word Temple*, Diane Frank, 2005, Blue Light Press.

191. BABY, drawing, 8"x8," 1990.

193. MOON 1, drawing, 3"x3," published in *Rhododendron Shedding Its Skin*, Diane Frank, 2001, Blue Light Press.

197. DIANA, drawing, 8"x10," published in *The Goddess Remembered, A Spiritual Journal*, 1990, Crossing Press; and *A Goddess Journal*, Annie Elizabeth and Melanie Gendron, 2015, River Sanctuary Publishing.

201. ONLY AN EGG, AMERICA (detail), acrylic on canvas, 24"x48," 1975.

214. KISSING SWANS, digitally mastered photo, 3"x5," 2013.

219. SANDI IN THE TREE, sun photo print & gouache, 11"x14," 1987, 2011.

226. BRIGITTE, acrylic & color drawing, 11"x14," 1983.

227. FLYING FISH, drawing, 2"x4," 2014, published in *The Lifeline Trembles*, Mary Rummel, 2005, Blue Light Press.

229. TREE NYMPH, drawing, 8"x10," published in *The Goddess Remembered, A Spiritual Journal*, 1990, Crossing Press; and *A Goddess Journal*, Annie Elizabeth and Melanie Gendron, 2015, River Sanctuary Publishing.

246. CROW, drawing, 2"x4," 2014.

249. SNAKE, drawing, 3"x3," published in *Rhododendron Shedding Its Skin*, Diane Frank, 2001, Blue Light Press.

255. BUXOM ANGEL, drawing, 8"x10," published in *The Goddess Remembered, A Spiritual Journal*, 1990, Crossing Press; and *A Goddess Journal*, Annie Elizabeth and Melanie Gendron, 2015, River Sanctuary Publishing.

257. BIRDS FLYING INTO NIGHT, drawing, 5" diameter, published in *Entering the Word Temple*, Diane Frank, 2005, Blue Light Press.

259. ANGELIC WOMAN, drawing, 8"x10," published in *The Goddess Remembered, A Spiritual Journal*, 1990, Crossing Press.

264. BLACK CAT DAY, digitally mastered in Photoshop, 8"x8," 2000.

269. NOAH'S ARK, acrylic on canvas, 30"x30," 1975.

281. SELF AS BRYCE DESERT, acrylic on canvas, 24"x48," 1975, published in *This Moment's Daughter*, June Rachuy Brindel, 2012, Blue Light Press.

304. BIRDS THREE, drawing, 3"x5," published in *Aurora*, Devorah Rubin, 2013, Blue Light Press.

313. THE KISS, watercolor, 20" diameter, 1986, private collection.

318. SNOWFLAKE, drawing, 3"x3," 2013.

322. AURORA, drawing, 8"x10," published in *The Goddess Remembered, A Spiritual Journal*, 1990, Crossing Press; and *A Goddess Journal*, Annie Elizabeth and Melanie Gendron, 2015, River Sanctuary Publishing.

325. BUTTERFLY WOMAN, acrylic on canvas, 27"x36," 1987, published in *We'Moon 2015*, Mother Tongue Ink, private collection.

328. PARROT FISH, acrylic on wood panel, 20"x20," 1983.

337. FLOWER MANDALA, drawing, 8"x10," 1990.

342. ISIS, drawing, 8"x10," 1993.

348. DAKINI 2, drawing, 8"x10," published in *The Goddess Remembered, A Spiritual Journal*, 1990, Crossing Press; and *A Goddess Journal*, Annie Elizabeth and Melanie Gendron, 2015, River Sanctuary Publishing.

359. GULL 3, drawing, 3"x3," published in *Rumors of Shore*, Paul Fisher, 2009, Blue Light Press.

361. GULL 2, drawing, 3"x3," published in *Rumors of Shore*, Paul Fisher, 2009, Blue Light Press.

362. GULL 4, drawing, 3"x3," published in *Rumors of Shore*, Paul Fisher, 2009, Blue Light Press.

373. IRIS, drawing, 4"x6," published in *Oracles For Night Blooming Eccentrics*, Nancy Berg, 2007, Blue Light Press.

374. ANEMONE, digitally mastered photo, 4"x6," 2001.

383. A LOOK WITHIN SPRING, color drawing, 8" diameter, 1996.

387. PRINCESS OF SWORDS, digitally mastered in Photoshop, published in *The Gendron Tarot* deck and book, 1997 & 2004, U.S. Games Systems Inc.

395. MOON RAVEN, drawing, 8" diameter, 1993.

401. VENUS, drawing, 8"x10," published in *The Goddess Remembered, A Spiritual Journal*, 1990, Crossing Press; and *A Goddess Journal*, Annie Elizabeth and Melanie Gendron, 2015, River Sanctuary Publishing.

404. BUTTERFLY MANDALA, drawing, 5" diameter, published in *Entering the Word Temple*, Diane Frank, 2005, Blue Light Press.

413. PANTHER SHIELD, color drawing, 10" diameter, 1996.

439. CHAGAL INSPIRED, drawing, 5" diameter, published in *Entering the Word Temple*, Diane Frank, 2005, Blue Light Press.

444. CAT, drawing, 5"x7," published in *A Journal for Cat Lovers*, 1990, Crossing Press.

466. BUTTERFLY FAIRY, drawing, 8"x10," published in *The Goddess Remembered, A Spiritual Journal*, 1990, Crossing Press.

469. BINDI, drawing, 4"x5," published in *The Goddess Remembered, A Spiritual Journal*, 1990, Crossing Press; and *A Goddess Journal*, Annie Elizabeth and Melanie Gendron, 2015, River Sanctuary Publishing.

489. MELOS APHRODITE, drawing, 8"x10," published in *The Goddess Remembered, A Spiritual Journal*, 1990, Crossing Press; and *A Goddess Journal*, Annie Elizabeth and Melanie Gendron, 2015, River Sanctuary Publishing

503. THREE GRACES, drawing, 8"x10," published in *The Goddess Remembered, A Spiritual Journal*, 1990, Crossing Press; and *A Goddess Journal*, Annie Elizabeth and Melanie Gendron, 2015, River Sanctuary Publishing.

508. MEDICINE WAY SHIELD, drawing, 8"x10," 1990.

510. DAKINI 1, drawing, 5"x7," published in *The Goddess Remembered, A Spiritual Journal,* 1990, Crossing Press; and A *Goddess Journal,* Annie Elizabeth and Melanie Gendron, 2015, River Sanctuary Publishing.

526. ONLY AN EGG AMERICA, acrylic on canvas, 24"x48," 1975, published in *Blood Rivers,* Lisha Adela Garcia, 2009, Blue Light Press.

561. RING OF FIRE, drawing, 5" diameter, published in *Swan Light,* Diane Frank, 2005, Blue Light Press.

Printed in the United States of America

CPSIA information can be obtained
at www.ICGtesting.com
Printed in the USA
FSOW01n0342160616
21622FS